Sandra Burman, a Research Officer at the
Centre for Socio-Legal Studies, Wolfson
College, Oxford, has introduced and edited this
volume of original research on women's work
and the domestic ideal, viewed from the
different perspectives of several social sciences.
Work in social history by Catherine Hall, Anne
Summers, Leonore Davidoff and Jill Liddington
is followed by contributions from a lawyer,
Katherine O'Donovan, an economist, Maureen
Mackintosh, and two sociologists, Kate Purcell
and Mary McIntosh.

FIT WORK FOR WOMEN

FIT WORK FOR WOMEN

EDITED BY SANDRA BURMAN

ST. MARTIN'S PRESS   NEW YORK

Copyright © 1979 Sandra Burman, Catherine Hall, Anne Summers,
Jill Liddington, Leonore Davidoff, Kate Purcell, Katherine O'Donovan,
Mary McIntosh, Maureen M. Mackintosh

All rights reserved. For information write:
St. Martin's Press Inc., 175 Fifth Avenue, New York, N.Y. 10010
Printed in Great Britain
ISBN 0—312—29417—4
First published in the United States of America in 1979

Library of Congress Cataloging in Publication Data

Main entry under title:

Fit work for women.

    Papers presented at a series of interdisciplinary
seminars organized by the Women's Studies Committee and
held at Oxford University during the 2d term, 1977/78.
    Includes index.
    1. Women — Employment — Great Britain — History —
Congresses. I. Burman, Sandra. II. Oxford. University.
Women's Studies Committee.
HD6135.F57 1979   331.4'0941   78—25895
ISBN 0—312—29417—4

Printed and Bound in Great Britain

CONTENTS

Preface   7

Introduction *Sandra Burman*   9

1. The Early Formation of Victorian Domestic Ideology
   Catherine Hall   15

2. A Home from Home — Women's Philanthropic Work in
   the Nineteenth Century
   Anne Summers   33

3. The Separation of Home and Work? Landladies and
   Lodgers in Nineteenth- and Twentieth-Century England
   Leonore Davidoff   64

4. Women Cotton Workers and the Suffrage Campaign:
   The Radical Suffragists in Lancashire, 1893–1914
   Jill Liddington   98

5. Militancy and Acquiescence Amongst Women Workers
   Kate Purcell   112

6. The Male Appendage — Legal Definitions of Women
   Katherine O'Donovan   134

7. The Welfare State and the Needs of the Dependent Family
   Mary McIntosh   153

8. Domestic Labour and the Household
   Maureen M. Mackintosh   173

Name Index *Compiled by Carol Bundy*   192

Subject Index *Compiled by Carol Bundy*   196

PREFACE

This book is the second in a series resulting from a new programme of interdisciplinary seminars organised at Oxford University throughout the academic year of 1977-78. Until then, no official interdisciplinary programme of Women's Studies existed within the University, although a considerable amount of work in the field was going on. For instance, an informal weekly seminar of women social anthropologists had been taking place since 1973, and its participants had published a number of their papers in various issues of the *Journal of the Anthropological Society of Oxford* and in *Perceiving Women*, edited by Shirley Ardener in 1975. In the autumn of 1976, however, a small University fund became available through the generosity of Keith Hope, which was allocated, at his suggestion, to Women's Studies. This enabled the Women's Studies Committee, which was then formed, to organise seminars for the next academic year. The papers were grouped round three themes. Those of the first term, on 'Women: Some Biological and Cultural Perspectives', were published in late 1978 in a volume entitled *Defining Females: The Nature of Women in Society* (ed Shirley Ardener). The Committee felt that studies of women in a number of very different societies might highlight many important aspects of women in our own, the significance of which were overlooked because of their familiarity — an expectation which was fully realised. In the second term we turned to more ethnocentrically based material, although even here at least one theoretical problem gained greatly from a discussion of comparative African material, and two other papers drew on Third World examples to illustrate points they were making. The term's theme was 'Woman's Work: Social, Legal and Political Perspectives' and these papers form the basis of the present book. The discussions in the third term were on 'Women and Literature' (forthcoming in 1979 under the title of *Women Writing and Writing about Women*, ed. Mary Jacobus). As the seminars were all attended by large audiences, it is hoped to be able to continue the series (with help from the royalties from these volumes) to encourage further Women's Studies in the University. A fuller account of the Committee's other projects can be found in the first volume of this series.

Our seminar audience included specialists in the range of disciplines covered, undergraduates and those with personal rather than academic

7

interest in the subjects. Contributors were therefore asked to attempt the difficult task of writing both for the specialist and the interested layman. We hope that readers will understand that we are addressing ourselves to a wide audience and will make due allowance for this in their assessment of our efforts.

The contributors (a number of whom studied at Oxford) are now scattered in various centres. Leonore Davidoff, Mary McIntosh and Catherine Hall work in the Sociology Department of the University of Essex. Katherine O'Donovan teaches law at the University of Kent, Maureen Mackintosh lectures in economics at the Polytechnic of North London, and Jill Liddington and Kate Purcell are based at the Manchester Polytechnic. Anne Summers works in community education in Oxford and is an editor of *History Workshop Journal*.

The Women's Studies Committee would like to thank Keith Hope for his generosity in making these seminars possible and for his continuing interest and support. Our thanks too to the authors of the papers presented here for giving their time and skills, and to Queen Elizabeth House for providing the venue for our seminars. I must add my own thanks for their invaluable assistance to Shirley Ardener, Carol Bundy, John Eekelaar, Alan Hartford, Keith Hope, Ursula Owen, Anne Summers, Gavin Williams and Gillian Williams.

Sandra Burman

INTRODUCTION

Sandra Burman

Debates on women's work today tend to centre on such questions as equal pay, the pros and cons of positive discrimination in favour of women, or whether mothers of young children should go out to work. Yet underlying all such discussions are many basic assumptions about women's roles that people make but which they do not explicitly verbalise. One set of assumptions that became all-pervasive in British society in the recent past, and which is likely to persist for many years to come, embraces the ideas that a woman's primary duties are as wife and mother and that her proper place is therefore in the home. Any work she does outside it must be subordinated to her domestic obligations and should not interfere with men's rightful priority in paid work. Another assumption is that although her main activity should be unpaid domestic work, such work is not 'real' work. This book contains several papers that discuss this theme and other activities usually undertaken by women but either not defined as work or accorded an ambiguous status.

Further, as Shirley Ardener points out in *Defining Females*, there is a close correlation between what is thought *fitting* for people to do and what they are thought *capable* of doing. Assumptions that women's main activities are not 'real' work have a detrimental effect on what women are thought to be able to achieve. A belief that women should not do certain skilled, professional or political work is often bolstered by the 'proof' of their inability to do it. The low pay earned for, or inferior status of, the wage work done by the vast majority of women wage earners is taken as proof of their inability to do any other. Yet, as both Kate Purcell and Jill Liddington demonstrate, women undertake poorly paid work of inferior status, or fail to participate effectively in other activities, largely because they are hamstrung by the ideology of domesticity. As a result, an examination of the effect of the domestic ideal on any aspect of woman's wage work is of prime importance, not only for a clearer perception of social attitudes to the occupation itself or of the group of workers being studied, but for an understanding of women's position in modern British society. The papers in this book therefore attempt to provide insights into the nature of women's roles today by examining the changing nature of and attitudes to woman's

9

work and the domestic ideal.

The book begins with a discussion of how woman's work came to be defined as primarily domestic. Catherine Hall traces the rise of capitalist production in which workers sold their labour power in exchange for money. With the rise of the industrial bourgeoisie, productive work moved from the home to the factory, with the consequent separation of the spheres of home and work-place. Hall discusses the mediating role of the Evangelicals in a rapidly industrialising Britain and why their political and religious aims resulted in a redefinition of the position of women. Their emphasis on the non-commercial and private nature of the home and family life resulted in the formation of the ideology of domesticity, which was subsequently moulded to other purposes by economic forces.

Within this ideology, the one public arena considered suitable for women's work was philanthropy, and the widespread practice of voluntary women workers visiting the poor is the subject of Anne Summers' paper. With 'work' increasingly defined as labour power that could be sold for a wage, work done without payment came to be regarded as not proper work, and visiting the poor, together with domestic labour, fell within this category. As Summers points out, one of the tasks of feminist history is 'to rescue women's work from oblivion and ridicule, and to demonstrate the effort, motivation and skills which a male-dominated society exploits and takes for granted'. She examines these aspects of 'visiting' in relation to its immediate political import-ance in both town and countryside and its more long-term effects. It increased the influence of middle-class women in the community and on official policies towards the poor in a variety of ways, and it also determined the form in which state social work was first – and, it might be argued, still is – undertaken. Yet, while 'visiting' was promoting middle-class women's greater freedom from domesticity, Summers points out that it was spreading that very ideology among the working class and thereby making the life of working-class women more difficult. The paper highlights how the domestic ideal had (and still has) very different effects on different sections of society, depending on such factors as the diverse practical circumstances in each class and also on middle-class attitudes to working-class homes.

This point also emerges from the next paper. In contrast to the activities of unpaid women workers who ventured beyond their domestic circle, Leonore Davidoff's study examines the work of a large and varied section of the female population that took place within the home and for which they received pay – that of landladies. Davidoff discusses the way in which the ideology of domesticity, with its stress on the sanctity and non-commercial nature of the home, affected attitudes to the practice of taking lodgers and of inspecting lodgings. She also demonstrates its effect on attitudes to goods and services expected and received, and to the image and status of the landlady. In addition, her work has interesting implications for theories of women's autonomy and for the domestic labour debate.

Another group of working women who have received very little academic attention is examined by Jill Liddington, who writes on the women cotton workers who ran a grass-roots, working-class campaign for the vote in the Lancashire cotton towns at the turn of the century. Since they left few records, their role in the suffrage campaign has been virtually ignored, yet their problems with the Labour Party are part of a continuing debate – dealt with in Mary McIntosh's paper, for example – on whether feminist movements subvert radical class campaigns for social and political reform. In addition, these women and the land-ladies discussed by Davidoff are of particular interest today, in view of the modern increase in the numbers of wage-earning women and expect-ations of the liberating effect this should have. In the case of the radical suffragists, their story illustrates how the domestic ideal handicapped working-class women even where they operated in one of the few areas of England where it was commonplace for women to go out to work before and after marriage, to earn wages comparable to men, and to join a trade union.

These last three papers are all indicative of increasing attempts by feminist historians to investigate what many types of women's work in the past – often till now unrecognised as such – were really like, and how women saw their own lives and labour. For the historian, the means of discovering what various sections of the female, rather than male, population thought are relatively few and some of these sources reflect more men's views of what women thought or even ought to think. It is therefore particularly useful to have oral history recorded, as in Liddington's paper, from groups of women still available to share their experiences.

The effect of the domestic ideal on women wage workers is further examined, this time in contemporary British society, by Kate Purcell, who also actually asked women for their own reactions. She investigates militancy and acquiescence amongst women workers and questions the stereotype of women wage workers as less interested in conditions of work and pay because of domestic commitments. Her paper demon-strates how the domestic role ascribed to women tends to handicap them both in employment and in trade union activities, but argues that, in the light of empirical evidence and the social framework in which women operate, the widespread existence of the passive woman worker is a myth.

Katherine O'Donovan deals with the effect of the domestic ideal in a different context. She discusses how the legal system (in the broad sense of all legal rules by which the state will intervene in citizen's lives) reinforces activity specialisation according to gender by means of gender role allocation and by the treatment of the married couple as a single unit. O'Donovan outlines how the requirements of capitalism led to this situation and points out the ways in which the legal system penalises those who do not undertake the tasks it assigns to them. She stresses that there is built into much current legislation the assumption that the roles of houseworker and child-rearer are both naturally and indivisibly performed by the female of any couple, despite the fact that it is possible for different people, none of whom need be female, to under-take these tasks, and that a variety of dubious results flow from this assumption. While recognising that many of the problems facing women are rooted in economic circumstances that require radical social change, O'Donovan advocates neutralising sex-based legal roles as a necessary condition for true equality between the sexes.

Mary McIntosh takes the analysis further by discussing how the in-stitution of the dependent family, supported by a male breadwinner and free domestic labour from women, is at present the basis of capitalist reproduction. She then points out the inadequacies of the wage system in recognising the needs of unwaged individuals of the working class, and considers the types of provision with which the welfare state seeks to deal with these inadequacies in order to bolster the family system. Her paper ends with a discussion of why such provision has been insufficient to supplement the needs of dependants and what measures should be taken by women to rectify the situation.

The last paper further develops the analysis of the relationship between wage and domestic labour, and brings us to the crucial question of the nature of domestic work in our society. Maureen Mackintosh outlines the cul-de-sac into which the domestic labour debate has argued itself and suggests a new approach to the problem. She adopts the novel perspective provided by the situation in a society, Senegal, as yet incompletely dominated by the law of value, where much of the work done in Britain outside the home is in that society still household-based. This enables her to illustrate how the use of data taken only from the capitalist West has led to certain distinct phenomena being conflated and, as a result, to the begging of a vital question not usually perceived to be at the root of this debate — that of how the marriage relation operates to constitute the economic institution of the household in our society. She ends by suggesting an answer to this question and the implications it has for a theory of domestic labour.

Mackintosh's conclusions, combined with the earlier papers, bring us to the question of the role of the domestic ideology in women's oppression. McIntosh and O'Donovan argue that unpaid domestic work by women has been essential for the development of the capitalist wage system and that this pattern of free female labour was therefore reinforced by the legal system and the welfare state. The ideology of domesticity, which tied the wife to the home and unpaid labour, was not, as Hall shows, developed to subordinate women to the needs of the capitalist state, but subsequently became subverted to this purpose, since it fitted these requirements so well. However, Mackintosh argues that the basic reason for women's oppression is that our society needed to control the process and result of human reproduction. Marriage was therefore a subordinating relationship for the woman and domestic labour the economic content of her subordination. The marriage relationship, however, was a sufficient but not a necessary condition for the performance of domestic labour. Women's oppression therefore predates the capitalist state — as the historical facts would indeed seem to indicate. In other words, even if all women were freed from doing unpaid domestic work and able to earn a good income — both of which are at present infrequent events due to the requirements of capitalism — that would not necessarily remove the primary cause of their disadvantaged situation in society, despite greatly increased legal equality.

This is not to argue that domestic labour does not disadvantage women. On the contrary, as these papers show, it constitutes a major disadvantage for female wage earning, and the domestic ideal has resulted in a variety of handicaps for women. But the argument is that, much as it reinforced female subordination, it was not the original root cause of the problem. If this is so, it is very possible that not all the modern social and psychological consequences for women of their oppression are a direct result of the domestic ideal, or that its removal would lead to their disappearance. To what extent our society still has an underlying necessity to place the control of the process and result of human reproduction under male domination is a separate question that requires investigation. Certainly such control is still a strong underlying preoccupation of many societies, both in Europe and in other parts of the world, as *Defining Females* showed. As it also showed, a wide variety of means that achieve this end have developed, of which housework is one (Hirschon and Humphrey in *Defining Females*, 1978), but only one of several. Further research on this question may help us to understand better women's role in modern British society.

1 THE EARLY FORMATION OF VICTORIAN DOMESTIC IDEOLOGY

Catherine Hall

The Victorian middle-class ideal of womanhood is one that is well documented — the 'angel in the house', the 'relative creature' who maintained the home as a haven, is familiar from novels, manuals and even government reports. There is plenty of evidence to suggest that by the 1830s and 1840s the definition of women as primarily relating to home and family was well established. But what were the origins of this ideal? 1780-1830 has been called the period of the making of the industrial bourgeoisie. That class defined itself not only in opposition to the new proletariat, but also to the classes of landed capitalism — the gentry and the aristocracy. Their class definition was built not only at the level of the political and the economic — the historic confrontations of 1832 and 1846 — but also at the level of culture and ideology. The new bourgeois way of life involved a recodification of ideas about women. Central to those new ideas was an emphasis on women as domestic beings, as primarily wives and mothers. Evangelicalism provided one crucial influence on this definition of home and family. Between 1780 and 1820, in the Evangelical struggle over anti-slavery and over the reform of manners and morals, a new view of the nation, of political power and of family life was forged. This view was to become a dominant one in the 1830s and 1840s. The Evangelical emphasis on the creation of a new life-style, a new ethic, provided the framework for the emergence of the Victorian bourgeoisie.

It has been argued that Evangelical morality was probably the single most widespread influence in Victorian England.[1] Evangelicals were staunch members of the Church of England who believed in reform from within rather than in following the example of John Wesley, who in the 1780s had in effect seceded from the established Church to form the Methodist sect. The crucially important position of the Clapham Sect, as leaders of the Evangelicals, and their influence on nineteenth-century England has long been recognised. They occupy a position of distinction in Whig history, but have been less revered by radicals.[2] The Whig interpretation sees the sect as having played a vital role, not only in establishing the great nineteenth-century tradition of extra-Parliamentary agitation, but also as a group marked by moral superiority and freedom from self-interest. The origins of the group lay in Henry Thornton's house at Clapham and the focus which that provided for a number of prominent Evangelicals at the end of the eighteenth century. The Thornton family were prosperous bankers and John Thornton, Henry's father, was an influential Evangelical. Clapham became a centre for a number of families who were united in their interests and interconnected by marriage. The major figures were Henry Thornton, William Wilberforce, Zachary Macaulay (who was editor of the Evangelical *Christian Observer* and did much of the research and writing on the slavery issue), James Stephen (a barrister) and Lord Teignmouth (who was Governor General of India for five years). All of them lived in Clapham for long periods, where an Evangelical, John Venn, held the living. In addition, there were other people who were very closely associated and paid frequent visits – Thomas Gisborne, for example, a country gentleman, cleric and author; Hannah More, the celebrated author; and Charles Simeon, who was the Evangelical leader in Cambridge. The sect's work was primarily devoted to the furtherance of Evangelical principles in various political and social fields. They are best known for their contributory effort to the abolition of the slave trade and of slavery, their missionary activities both within and beyond England, and their influence on the foundation of Sunday schools and many other philanthropic and reforming institutions. In a much quoted entry in his diary in 1787, Wilberforce wrote that his mission was to abolish the slave trade and reform the manners and morals of the nation; virtually all the activities of the Clapham Sect sprang from these two commitments.

The Reform of Manners and Morals

The Sect's second campaign—the attempt to transform national morality – had less clear legislative goals than the anti-slavery movement. Its concern was to redefine the available cultural norms and to encourage a new seriousness and respectability in life. The Clapham Sect aimed to provide a new model that would displace the licentiousness and immorality which they saw around them. This *modus vivendi* would be widely propagated by means of pamphlets, manuals, sermons and as many other media as could be utilised. At the same time it would be reinforced institutionally by getting legislation passed on such issues as public amusements, sabbatarianism and obscene publications. The onslaught on morality was a highly organised campaign, and although it did not fire the national imagination in the same way that the anti-slavery issue had, it nevertheless had an important impact on manners at the beginning of the nineteenth century.[3]

The Evangelical concern with national morality had, as its premise, their belief that religion should be a daily rule of life rather than a question of doctrinal purity. Like the Methodists, they emphasised the importance of a well-ordered daily routine. Their overwhelming sense of sin necessitated the formulation of rules for daily life, in an attempt to reduce the possibilities of collapse into the natural condition. Hannah More and Wilberforce wrote journals which give us considerable insight into the practices of Evangelical living. Both of them see self-examination as absolutely central in their attempt to live according to God. Passivity and obedience were demanded in relation to God's word. A vital distinction was made between nominal and real Christianity: the nominal Christian accepts only the forms. The eighteenth-century religious revival was concerned with an attempt to get beneath the forms, to transform the meaning of religion *from within*. The Evangelical decision to stay inside the established Church meant that pressure for internal reconstruction was perhaps even stronger on them than on the Methodists — since the latter were creating new external forms of religious organisation as well. Wilberforce's immensely influential *Practical Christianity* gives us one of the clearest statements of Evangelical views. He insisted on the distinction between real and nominal belief. Christianity, he argued, 'is a state into which we are not born, but into which we must be translated; a nature which we do not inherit, but into which we are to be created anew. . . . This is a matter of labour and difficulty, requiring continual watchfulness, and unceasing effort, and unwearied patience'.[4] Life is a journey towards salvation and the image of the pilgrim is constantly there. Wilberforce and Hannah More both experienced conversion in adulthood and, as a result, reconstructed their lives. Wilberforce aimed to live by rule and to subject his life to constant scrutiny in an attempt to be of the greatest productive use to others. He believed that an individual's only strength sprang from a deep and abiding sense of his own weakness and inadequacy — hence the constant need for self-criticism and self-examination. Criticism, moreover, should be not just an individual practice but a mutual practice amongst the believers. Self-discipline was therefore a *sine qua non* in the Evangelicals' philosophy. Their letters and diaries bear constant witness to the difficulties of achieving it. It is important not to read back into this early phase of Evangelicalism the critique of its aspects in Victorian England with which we are familiar from Dickens, Thackeray or Butler. Between 1790 and 1820 the movement was in struggle, constantly on the attack against the evils it saw surrounding it, and attempting to transform English life. After 1820 Evangelicalism increasingly established itself as a part of the dominant culture. It lost its early purity and could justly be accused of priggishness, conventionality, hypocrisy and conservatism. But the first generation of the Clapham Sect were unceasingly diligent in their efforts to behave properly, to live as *real* Christians should, and to change their way of life.

In the 1780s the Evangelicals were convinced of the necessity for a national reform of manners. They wanted to attack the aristocracy's laxness and impose a new rule of life. In current political weakness they saw a reflection of moral depravity. It seemed clear that moral reform was impossible without the support of the ruling class and the established Church – and those were their initial constituencies. If – as they believed – Wesley's attempt at it had been doomed from the start by his reliance on preaching the word, then they instead would exploit any political channels open to them. Society was seen to be in need of effective leadership and guidance. The growth of the middle class made this particularly urgent because it was in danger of adopting the lax principles of those of higher rank; furthermore, the commercial spirit did not appear naturally favourable to the maintenance of religious principles.

The attack on manners and morals was initially organised mainly around producing propaganda aimed at the upper classes.[5] It took the French Revolution to transform a modest campaign into a major national force. In the dangerous years of the 1790s a simple, repressive policy was not enough; an active regeneration was also necessary in support of England. As Lady Shelley wrote in her diary, 'The awakening of the labouring classes after the first shocks of the French Revolution, made the upper classes tremble. Every man felt the necessity for putting his house in order.' E.P. Thompson has added to this – 'To be more accurate, most men and women of property felt the necessity for putting the houses of the poor in order.'[6] But to put the houses of the poor in order was only one part of the Evangelical campaign. They believed in self-regeneration as well as the proper instruction of the poor, and it was this duality which gave their movement such power. Their position cannot be equated with Toryism – they were subject to vitriolic attacks from sections of the ruling class as well as from radicals. The Evangelicals only ever had a limited amount of support from aristocratic and landed circles. Their major support, despite the intentions of the Clapham Sect, came from the middle ranks.

Between 1780 and 1832 England was in a period of transition – from an aristocratic and mercantile capitalist society, where land was still the major source of power, to an industrial capitalist society with a large and influential bourgeoisie. The Evangelicals were able to play a mediating role in this transition. They neither unquestioningly supported the old society nor uncritically welcomed the new. Their religious position drew on some of the same criticisms of established religious forms as had the Methodists, yet they remained staunch Anglicans; and unlike the Methodists, they never developed a popular base amongst the labouring classes. They insisted on the possibility of reform from within rather than by creating new structures. Similarly, in political terms, they advocated transformation from within, rather than a direct change in the distribution of political power. They believed in the traditional power of the aristocracy and appealed to the old ruling groups, yet their desire for particular kinds of change drove them to seek support from the expanding middle class. In order to achieve the abolition of the slave trade and of slavery, for example, they needed pressure group organisation on a massive scale — yet they still believed in the absolute power of an unreformed House of Commons to make legislative decisions. The success of the anti-slavery campaign marked an important transitional moment on the way to a full demand for recognition of middle-class power.[7]

The religious base of the Evangelicals allowed them to insist that the issues they took up were moral, not political. Anti-slavery came to be seen as 'above politics'. Their solution to the political problems facing England in the wake of the French Revolution was declared to be a religious solution — not a political one. It was the religious consciousness of England, they argued, which determined her political condition.

> To the decline of Religion and morality our national difficulties must both indirectly and directly be chiefly ascribed ... My only solid hopes for the well-being of my country depend not so much on her fleets and armies, not so much on the wisdom of her rulers, or the spirit of her people, as on the persuasion that she still contains many, who in a degenerate age, love and obey the Gospel of Christ; on the humble trust that the intercession of these may still be prevalent, that for the sake of these Heaven may still look upon us with an eye of favour.[8]

Real Christianity must be cultivated to arrest the progress of political decay.

The Clapham Sect members were neither old style aristocrats nor new style manufacturers. Yet they came to be seen as representing the interests of England and of sections of the middle classes. The major interests of the Sect were in financial and mercantile capital. The Wilberforce family money came from the Baltic trade and by the 1770s had been partly invested in land. The Thorntons were well-established bankers. Macaulay's money derived from African trade. There were remarkably few manufacturers involved. The Evangelicals always looked for wealthy and aristocratic support; they believed in the importance of influencing the great, and rejoiced in titled and royal backing. Wilberforce was one of Pitt's closest friends and mixed regularly with the governing elite. Nevertheless, this group was associated from its early days with the new middle-class culture of industrial England. The Clapham Sect came to articulate and represent the needs and changing consciousness of a new society. Their own links with the old mercantile bourgeoisie and the landed aristocracy enabled them to form a bridge between the old ruling groups and the aspirant middle classes. Organisations like the anti-slavery movement created a forum where these different class fractions could meet and co-operate. The Evangelicals were able to bridge class divisions because they had a strikingly new view of desirable life-styles and political responsibilities. Their great influence lay not only in their own power, but also in having the ear of others in authority. An important geographical factor was also involved in their potential to form a link between classes: London was the capital and the centre of political life, and the Sect was effectively based there. London was also a major centre of middle-class life. It was, however, not an expanding area for the factory system — and it remained the heartland of financial and commercial capitalism where the Evangelicals were so well represented. When manufacturers and industrialists came to London, they did so partly to enjoy metropolitan life and to engage in London politics. Consequently it was possible for the Sect to bridge the gap in London more easily than in Manchester or Rochdale, where the balance of class forces was different.

It is important to take account of the hostility of sections of the ruling class to Evangelicalism and the attempted reforms. Once the first fury of the French Revolution was over, with its initial effect of binding all property owners together, the High Church began to attack the Evangelicals. In the Evangelical campaign, 1797 had been a crucial year — a year of moral panic in England.[9] There were mutinies in the fleet, fears of a French invasion and of rebellion in Ireland, and a widespread belief in a conspiracy to undermine religion and morality. The fears about internal conditions had been manageable until there was also a serious threat from outside. Then the combination of the threat both from without and within England provoked a grave crisis of confidence; it was in this context that Wilberforce published *Practical Christianity,* with such immediate success. Moral and sexual subversion seemed to many to be the greatest dangers facing the country. But a High Church/Evangelical alliance over the moral dangers confronting the nation was not to last. High Churchmen associated immorality with French influence and mismanagement. The Evangelicals saw it as the result of the lack of true religion and the sinful heart of man. This marked a fundamental disagreement and the High Church inaugurated a campaign against the attempted Evangelical infiltration of the seats of power.[10] This was a struggle within sections of the ruling class and the Evangelicals were increasingly forced to look for support to the middle ranks.

In the wake of the French Revolution England was split politically. Evangelicalism provided a rallying point against Jacobinism. The beliefs and values of the truly religious were totally opposed to those of Godwin and the Jacobin circles. Because they regarded themselves as a campaigning movement engaged in struggle, the Evangelicals built a network and an organisation across the country which permeated English life. By means of the anti-slavery associations, the Cheap Repository Tracts, the sunday schools and many other societies, they penetrated aspects of daily life and provided a politics and morality that recognised the power of the French and industrial revolutions and responded to that challenge. That response was in open conflict with both new working-class organisation and consciousness, and with Old Corruption. It is not that the Clapham Sect simply represented and reflected the interests of the new capitalist class: at a particular historical moment a particular class fraction or group can represent the interests of other factions or classes and can embody ideas and practices which have repercussions far beyond them. It is in this sense that the Clapham Sect spoke for others and, therefore, came to be seen as something other than what it was. It was understood selectively and taken up in part.

Women, the Family and the Religious Household

Central to the Evangelicals' attempt to reconstruct daily life and create a new morality with liberal and humanist parameters on the one hand (the attack on slavery), yet buttressed by social conservatism on the other (the reform of manners and morals), was the redefinition of the position of the woman in the family. The Evangelical attempt to transform daily life was based on the belief in the universality of sin and the need for constant struggle against it. A primary arena of this struggle must be the home and family. The Evangelical ideal of the family and the woman at home was developed well before the French Revolution. Cowper, for example, 'the poet of domesticity', was writing in the 1780s. But it was the debate about the nature and the role of women, produced by the Revolution, which opened the floodgates of manuals from Evangelical pens. Mary Wollstonecraft's *Vindication of the Rights of Women* was first published in 1792 − before the tide had really been turned in England by the Terror. Hannah More was appalled by the book and she became the major protagonist of an alternative stance.

The Vindication is basically a plea for equality with bourgeois men − educational, legal and political equality. It is also an attack on the idea of femininity. Wollstonecraft was fired by the example of the Revolution to demand an extension of the rights of men to women. She saw women's inferior status as resulting from their environment − not from a lack of natural abilities. She argued for better education for women, to equip them for the world.[11] The Evangelicals started from a fundamentally different position: men and women are not equal; the sexes are naturally distinct; women should be better educated, but only to make them better wives and mothers. The 1790s saw a flood of writing defining, arguing and extending this position. The feminist belief in the equality of the sexes was absolutely rejected. Paine was dangerous in that he proposed equality between men, but if that argument were to be extended to women the whole social fabric would be under attack. At least it could be demonstrated that there was a *natural* division between the sexes. Arguments about social hierarchies also began with assumptions about nature, but less easily gained acceptance: the ideological underpinning of the 'natural constitution' was more apparent than in beliefs in the inevitable concomitants of the sexual division. The debate on women, the family and the sexual division of labour was thus an integral part of the 1790s discussions about the organisation of society. The Evangelical beliefs in the special and important duties of women in the home again played a mediating role between radicals and Old Corruption. It is dependence which binds people together, argues More, both in the family and in the social hierarchy.

Now it is pretty clear, in spite of modern theories, that the very frame and being of societies, whether great or small, public or private, is jointed and glued together by dependence. Those attachments which arise from, and are compacted by, a sense of mutual wants, mutual affection, mutual benefit, and mutual obligation, are the cement which secures the union of the family as well as of the State.[12]

The Evangelicals pilloried aristocratic ideals of women – they attacked as inadequate the way in which women were educated and the refusal to take them seriously. They denounced the double standard and championed the value of a good marriage. They drew on the eighteenth-century debate about women – they admired Richardson and agreed with the early Cobbett about, for example, the unfortunate apeing of their betters by aspirant farmers' wives. They were responding again to the major social transformation which was taking place in England as a result of the development of capitalism. They were concerned with the problem of defining for the middle ranks a way of life best suited to their affluence and leisure. By the 1780s, existing material conditions enabled many more women to forego employment – and a 'lady of leisure' enjoyed the hallmark of gentility. As Pinchbeck has demonstrated, the number of well-to-do women in mercantile and commercial ventures was dropping.[13] How were these women, with their new-found wealth and time, to behave? And who was to provide the model? Hannah More, Gisborne, Wilberforce, Mrs West, Mrs Sherwood and many others were adept and successful in assuming the role of mentors.

Evangelicalism has been described as 'the religion of the household' and it is clear that the notion of home and family was central to their religious views. Cowper refers to

Domestic happiness, thou only bliss
Of paradise that has survived the Fall.[14]

Home was one place where attempts could be made to curb sin – in the world outside it was obviously far more difficult. The household was seen as the basis for a proper religious life – morality began at home. The Clapham Sect were champions of family life themselves and in many ways lived like a large extended family. They lived with each other (often for long periods), they intermarried, they went on holiday together, and the men worked together. The values of domestic life were highly prized. Stephen, in his essay on the Sect, takes the unusual step of including domestic portraits of the key members as well as a discussion of their public contributions. He sees Wilberforce as at his best in the home and argues that the example of his household was a wonderful incentive to the practice of religion. 'There is something peculiar in Wilberforce's character and situation,' he writes, 'that seems to point it out as the design of Providence, that he should serve his Master in this high and special walk, and should have, so to speak, a kind of *domestic publicity* — that he should be at home a candle set on a candlestick as well as abroad a city built upon a hill.'[15]

Hannah More, in her novel *Coelebs,* offers the ideal example of the religious home. Set in their country house, the Stanley family are presented as the epitome of a religious household, living out their Evangelical and Utilitarian practice on a daily basis.[16] The country ambience is important. More, like Gisborne and other Evangelicals, believed that the ideal of a new-style benevolent paternalism was more viable in a rural than in an urban environment. Religious and domestic virtues were linked in the concept of a religious household. Sunday abstinence, for example, acquired significance when Sunday was defined as a family day. This linking of the religious with the domestic was extended to the division between the public and the private sphere, and was crucial to Evangelical thinking about the home. The basic split was between the world as hostile and the home as loving — a split that became commonplace in Victorian England.

The Evangelical movement was both intensely public and intensely private. The emphasis on the individual religious life came from a view of the world as immoral and distracting. But once people had been converted, they were needed in that world as moral missionaries. They were fired by the most private of passions — for sincerity and terrible truthfulness, with great emotional warmth on moral issues — and they had to carry all this with them into a public sphere which might be indifferent, cynical or hostile. 'They' were all men (except in philanthropy, where women were allowed a supporting role); consequently, the split between the private and the public spheres became a split between the sexes of a peculiarly exaggerated kind. Home became the sphere of women and the family; the world outside became the sphere of men. Wilberforce's letters abound with the imagery of conflict and trouble in the world, peace and calm at home. When away from his family on business, he wrote to his wife very regularly. 'Pray for me,' he wrote just before Parliament reassembled, 'that I may be enlightened and strengthened for the duties of this important and critical session. Hitherto God has wonderfully supported and blessed me; oh how much beyond my deserts! It will be a comfort to me to know that you all who are, as it were, on the top of the mountain, withdrawn from and above the storm, are thus interceding for me who am scuffling in the vale below.'[17] This idealised view of the home was common to the Clapham Sect. Family prayers became a symbol of the togetherness.

Cowper evokes the warmth and cosiness of an Evangelical family evening:

> Now stir the fire and close the shutters fast,
> Let fall the curtains, wheel the sofa round,
> And, while the bubbling and loud hissing urn
> Throws up a steaming column, and the cups
> That cheer but not inebriate, wait on each
> So let us welcome peaceful evenings in.[18]

Within the household it was quite clearly established that men and women had their separate spheres. Hannah More defined certain qualities and dispositions as 'peculiarly feminine'. Cultural differences were seen as natural. Women were naturally more delicate, more fragile, morally weaker, and all this demanded a greater degree of caution, retirement and reserve. 'Men, on the contrary, are formed for the more public exhibition on the great theatre of human life';[19] men had grandeur, dignity and force; women had ease, simplicity and purity. This absolute distinction between men and women is repeated time and again in Evangelical writing.

Evangelicals expected women to sustain and even to improve the moral qualities of the opposite sex. It is at this level that the Evangelicals offered women an area of importance which, therefore, holds within itself considerable contradictions. Women, it was believed, could act as the moral regenerators of the nation. They occupied a key position in the struggle to reform and revive the nation. Women in the home could provide, as it were, a revolutionary base from which their influence could shine forth: 'If our women lose their domestic virtues, all the charities will be dissolved, for which our country is a name so dear. The men will be profligate, the public will be betrayed, and whatever has blessed or distinguished the English nation on the Continent will disappear' wrote a friend to More, congratulating her on her book on female education.[20] That book, published in 1799 in the wake of the moral panic, exhorted women to play their part in the struggle for national survival. They were being offered a field where they could be allowed to wield some power and influence within the moral sphere. They could play an important part in the reform of manners and morals. Wilberforce made a similar plea for women's support in *Practical Christianity*. He argued that women were especially disposed to religion; this was partly because their education was limited and they were not exposed to the moral dangers of the classics. The woman, therefore, had the particular duty of encouraging her husband's religious sensibilities: 'when the husband should return to his family, worn and harassed by worldly cares or professional labours, the wife, habitually preserving a warmer and more unimpaired spirit of devotion, than is perhaps consistent with being immersed in the bustle of life, might revive his languid piety.' Women had open to them a most noble office: 'we would make them as it were the medium of our intercourse with the heavenly world, the faithful repositories of the religious principle, for the benefit both of the present and the rising generation.'[21] Because the major problem in England was seen by the Evangelicals as being the prevalent state of religious and moral decadence, this emphasis on the religious power of the woman considerably modified their emphasis elsewhere on subordination. In a later period, Victorian feminists like Mrs Jamieson were to build on this contradiction.

The good Evangelical woman had recognisable characteristics: she was modest, unassuming, unaffected and rational. ('Rational' was used as the opposite to 'sentimental' or 'subject to violent feeling'.) Babington, a prominent figure in the Clapham Sect, wrote to Macaulay on the eve of his marriage in 1799, detailing the distinction between the male and female spheres.

> You have been a grave and active African governor, surrounded by business and difficulties and dangers, and enjoying little affectionate and no female society. Selina has been entirely with females, and her companions have been her near relations and friends. Under these circumstances you meet as man and wife, with habits of domestic life more different than those of men and women, who act on the same principle, generally are. She must endeavour to assimilate herself to you, and you to her, without either of you departing from your proper sphere. . . . Hours of relaxation are among the most useful, as well as most pleasant seasons of matrimonial life, if they do not recur too frequently, and if the source of enjoyment be pure and hallowed. . . . In general you should lead her through cheerful cornfields, and pastures, and when opportunity offers go out of your way a little to show a flowery meadow or a winding stream.[22]

The implication is clear that the man is wiser and will guide the woman into the area appropriate to her, occasionally introducing her to new ideas.

The right choice in marriage was seen as vital to a good Evangelical life. Since the religious household was the basis of Christian practice, it

was essential to find the right partner in marriage. *Coelebs* is structured
around the hero's search for a wife:

> In such a companion I do not want a Helen, a Saint Cecilia, or a
> Madame Dacier; yet she must be elegant or I should not love her;
> sensible, or I should not respect her; prudent, or I should not confide
> in her; well-informed, or she could not educate my children; well-
> bred, or she could not entertain my friends; consistent, or I should
> offend the shade of my mother; pious, or I should not be happy
> with her.[23]

The striking feature of this passage is that the woman is seen only in
relation to the man. She is, in Mrs Ellis's later phrase, a 'relative
creature'. Hannah More, although herself an independent and unmarried
woman, consistently relegated women to a dependent role. There can
be no higher praise for a woman than that she is worthy of her husband,
whose happiness she creates. As Coelebs puts it, 'It appears to me that
three of the great inducements in the choice of a wife are, that a man
may have a directress for his family, a preceptress for his children, and
a companion for himself.'[24] There is no suggestion of what the woman
might want for *herself*. The letters and diaries of the Clapham Sect
demonstrate the degree to which these views were lived through—they
were not simply presented in manuals for others. Women were both
central to and absent from the Clapham Sect. They were central in that
the definition of their position constituted a major area of Evangelical
thought and writing. They were absent in that the absolute assumption
of their subordination meant that their activities were hidden. Apart
from Hannah More, the majority of writing about the Sect was by men.
This was no doubt partly because the women's letters were not seen as
worth keeping. Halévy describes More as 'one of the great men of the
party'[25] — since she does not fit the stereotypes of what an Evangelical
woman, or indeed any woman, should be, she is presented as exceptional.
When Stephen described the domestic lives of the Sect, the wives were
there as supportive backcloth, help-meets to their husbands. Wilberforce
frequently gave an account of family parties and documented all those
present, except his wife. It is tempting to assume that this was because
she was so taken for granted that she did not have to be mentioned.
The woman, after all, was private property. Gisborne saw the duties of
the woman as three-fold: first, to look after husbands, parents, children,
relatives and friends; second, to set a good example to men and improve
manners by that example; third, to care for children.[26] The whole

notion of duty was, of course, central to Evangelicalism.

The unmarried woman had to do what she could; basically, Evangelical writing on women assumed marriage and the family. Within marriage it was quite clear that the wife was subordinate to her husband — it was not a question open to 'speculative arguments'. Faithful and willing obedience on the part of the wife was essential, even in cases of domestic management. The first set of duties — looking after the home and family — was, in St Paul's terms, 'guiding the house'. The superintendence of domestic management is clearly demarcated from doing the work itself; there was an absolute assumption that servants would be available. Domestic management required regularity of accounts and the proper care of money. Home should be seen as the wife's centre. There she could influence to the good her children, her servants and her neighbours. It is in the home that 'the general character, the acknowledged property, and the established connections of her husband, will contribute with more force than they can possess elsewhere, to give weight and impressiveness to all her proceedings'.[27] Women were consequently advised not to leave home too much — it was only there that they could achieve moral excellence.

A great deal of emphasis was placed by the Evangelicals on the power of women to demonstrate by example. Daily practice in the home must be an attempt to live out principles. The letters and journals of the Clapham Sect would suggest that their daughters and wives did try to do this. But there was also one public arena open to them and that was philanthropy. The activities of women in charitable organisations between 1790 and 1830 gives us the most concrete evidence so far available of the power of the Evangelical example on women's lives.[28] Charity was seen as the proper activity of a lady. 'I have often heard it regretted,' says Mrs Stanley in *Coelebs*, 'that ladies have no stated employment, no profession. It is a mistake. Charity is the calling of a lady; the care of the poor is her profession.'[29] More argued that women were peculiarly suited to philanthropic activities — they had leisure, an acquaintance with domestic wants and more sympathy with female complaints. Charity should become a part of daily life. Being philanthropic was, of course, both a reflection of virtue and a relief from a life bounded by the home.

If women were to be able to exercise a proper moral influence, they must be well educated. A clear distinction was made between the education of the daughters of the poor and those of the upper and middle classes. The daughters of the poor should be trained as servants or as good wives; the emphasis in their schooling should be on industry, frugality, diligence and good management. The daughters of the well-to-do, on the other hand, should be educated for moral excellence, and that meant that the traditional girls' training which they had been receiving was quite inadequate. To be able to dress well, to dance and play the piano, was not enough. 'The profession of ladies,' wrote More, 'is that of daughters, wives, mothers and mistresses of families.'[30] They should, therefore, be trained for that. Given these considerations, there was much to be said for educating girls at home. A mother was the best person to train her daughter. The purpose of that training was not to enable women to compete with men, but to prepare them in the best possible way for their relative sphere. Mothers were responsible for the children of both sexes in infancy, for their daughters until they left home. The Evangelicals stressed the importance of parental responsibility and the religious implications of good motherhood. The fathers took especial responsibility for their sons, but often had very close domestic ties with their daughters as well.

The Evangelical ideology of domesticity, it has been argued here, was not an ideal constructed for others, but an attempt to reconstruct family life and the relations between the sexes on the basis of 'real' Christianity. The Puritans had developed many similar views on marriage in an earlier period. The two groups shared the experience of living through a period of very rapid social, political and economic change; the articulation of their response was in religious terms, but it cannot be understood outside the particular historical conjuncture. Changing ideas about women and the family must be seen in relation to changes in the mode of production and in the social relations of production and reproduction. The Puritans and the Evangelicals shared a need to build a protected space in a hostile world, from which the great campaign of evangelisation could be securely launched. The home was an area which could be controlled and which was relatively independent of what went on outside. The home did provide a haven. The expansion of capitalist relations of production in the late eighteenth century meant that homes were increasingly separated from work places, although this was a lengthy process and, in some trades, family workshops survived for a very long time. It has also been suggested that domestic demand for such items of household utility as china provided one of the main factors in the industrial 'take-off' at the end of the eighteenth century.[31] In other words, the emergence of a particular kind of home was directly related to the expansion of productive forces. But the way that home was realised, lived in and experienced within the middle ranks was crucially mediated by Evangelicalism.

Conclusion

The Clapham Sect set some of the boundaries for public and domestic life in Victorian England. Their ideas were not, however, always understood in the way that they would have wished. They were benevolent paternalists but they were understood as the precursors of Utilitarianism and the power of the bourgeoisie. They were mercantile princes and clerics but they ushered in the machine age. They were a group with aristocratic connections, some of them belonging to the governing elite of England, yet they paved the way for the alliance between that old ruling class and the manufacturers. Their importance lies in the mediating role which they were able to play, by virtue of their class position, in the transitional period between the era of mercantile capitalism and the recognised dominance of industrial capitalism. They belonged to neither side and so were able to speak to both.

The campaign on slavery gave the Sect national status; it established the claim to represent the middle classes and articulate their demands. The campaign in itself was massively influential in shaping those demands — steering the 'middling ranks' towards liberalism and a national consensus rather than towards a more radical perspective and an alliance with the new industrial proletariat. The campaign on manners and morals would undoubtedly have been far less effective if the anti-slavery movement had not been such a success. The religious principles of the Evangelicals drove them from within. They became moral entrepreneurs committed to struggling for widescale conversion to their views. Their evangelising campaign gained massive support, but only up to a certain point. Anti-slavery became identified as the British way. England claimed moral superiority in her style of colonisation. Respectability and decorum ruled, but the double standard reigned supreme in Victorian England. The split between the public and the private sphere, the subordination of the woman in the family, and the protection of private property were key features of nineteenth-century England; but the truly religious households remained a minority phenomenon. The forms, shaped by the Evangelicals for one purpose, were moulded to another. Just as the Puritan notion of the family was partly a response to the development of productive forces and partly an ideological form that must be understood in terms of its own logic, so was the Evangelical. But the Evangelical capacity to respond to the changing social relations of industrial capitalism and redefine the family form ensured that notions of home and domesticity in the nineteenth century would be heavily influenced by the Mores, Gisbornes, and Thorntons of this world.

Inside that dynamic, the bourgeois ideal of the family became a part of the dominant culture and, by the 1830s and 1840s, was being promoted through propaganda as the only proper way to live.[32] In the government reports of that period working wives and mothers are presented as something unnatural and immoral. Working-class women were castigated for being poor housewives and inadequate mothers. If married women were to enter paid employment, they should not be seen; they should work at home. They should not flaunt their independence as the mill girls did. It is worth noting that the early campaigns to improve the working conditions of women focused on the factory system and the mines and did not come to grips with more hidden areas, such as the sweated trades. The bourgeois family was seen as the proper family, and that meant that married women should not work. The ideology of the family thus obscured class relations, for it came to appear above class. That ideology also obscured the cultural definition of the sexual division of labour, since the split between men and women came to be seen as naturally ordained. Nature decreed all women were first and foremost wives and mothers.

Notes

1. E.g. N. Annan, *Leslie Stephen* (London, Macgibbon and Kee, 1951).

2. Cf. G.O. Trevelyan, *The Life and Letters of Lord Macaulay* (London, Longman, Green and Co., 1876). A more recent version is E.M. Howse, *Saints in Politics* (London, George Allen and Unwin, 1953). For a contemporary radical critique see W. Cobbett, *Political Register,* 3 October 1818.

3. The most helpful secondary source on this is M. Quinlan, *Victorian Prelude: A History of English Manners 1700-1830* (New York, Columbia University Press, 1941).

4. W. Wilberforce, *A Practical View of the Prevailing Religious System of Professed Christians in the Higher and Middle Classes in This Country Contrasted with Real Christianity* (London, T. Cadell Junior and W. Davies, 1797), p. 298.

5. The first major statement was H. More, *Thoughts on the Importance of the Manners of the Great to General Society* (London, T. Cadell Junior and W. Davies, 1788).

6. E.P. Thompson, *The Making of the English Working Class* (Harmondsworth, Penguin, Pelican edition, 1967), p. 60.

7. For a very interesting discussion of the importance of the anti-slavery agitation in terms of a political transition, see D.B. Davis, *The Problem of Slavery in the Age of Revolution* (London, Cornell University Press, 1975).

8. R.I. and S. Wilberforce, *The Life of William Wilberforce,* vol. 3 (London, John Murray, 1838), p. 487.

9. For a good account of 1797, see E. Trudgill, *Madonnas and Magdalens* (London, Heinemann, 1976).

10. One of the best examples of this division is the Blagdon Controversy over Hannah More's running of Sunday schools. Cf. W. Roberts (ed), *The Life and*

Correspondence of Mrs Hannah More (London, R.B. Seeley and W. Burnside, 1834), and Ford K. Brown, *Fathers of the Victorians* (Cambridge, CUP, 1961).

11. For an interesting discussion of Wollstonecraft from a feminist perspective, see M. Walters, 'The Rights and Wrongs of Women: Mary Wollstonecraft, Harriet Martineau, Simone de Beauvoir' in J. Mitchell and A. Oakley (eds), *The Rights and Wrongs of Women* (Harmondsworth, Penguin, 1976).

12. H. More, *Strictures on the Modern System of Female Education*, vol. 2 (London, T. Cadell Junior and W. Burnside, 1799), pp. 186-7.

13. I. Pinchbeck, *Women Workers and the Industrial Revolution* (London, Frank Cass, 1969).

14. W. Cowper, *The Task*, in W. Benham (ed), *Selected Works of William Cowper* (London, Macmillan and Co., 1889).

15. J. Stephen, *Essays in Ecclesiastical Biography* (London, Longman, Brown, Green and Longmans, 1845), p. 510.

16. Halévy was the first to discuss the connections between Evangelicalism and Utilitarianism in *England in 1815* (London, Ernest Benn, 1913). That discussion is developed in Davis, *The Problem of Slavery*, and C. Hall, 'Evangelicalism and the Development of Bourgeois Values 1780-1820', unpublished MA dissertation, University of Essex, 1977.

17. Wilberforce, *The Life of William Wilberforce*, vol. 5, p. 77.

18. Cowper, *The Task*, Bk. 4.

19. H. More, *Essays Principally designed for Young Ladies* (London, R.B. Seeley and W. Burnside, 1777), p. 5.

20. In a letter to Hannah More, in Roberts (ed), *Life and Correspondence*, vol. 3, p. 453.

21. Wilberforce, *A Practical View*, p. 453.

22. Viscountess Knutsford, *Life and Letters of Zachary Macaulay* (London, Edward Arnold, 1900), p. 234.

23. H. More, *Coelebs in Search of a Wife*, vol. 1 (London, R.B. Seeley and W. Burnside, 1809), p. 23.

24. Ibid., p. 78.

25. Halévy, *England in 1815*.

26. T. Gisborne, *Duties of the Female Sex* (London, T. Cadell Junior and W. Davies, 1801).

27. Ibid.

28. Cf. F.R. Prochaska, 'Women in English Philanthropy 1790-1830', *International Review of Social History*, vol. 19, part 3, 1974, and Brown, *Fathers of the Victorians*.

29. More, *Coelebs*, vol. 2, p. 20.

30. Ibid.

31. N. McKendrick, 'A New Look at the Contribution of the Employment of Women and Children to the Industrial Revolution' in N. McKendrick (ed), *Historical Perspectives: Studies in English Thought and Society in Honour of J.H. Plumb* (London, Europa, 1974).

32. Cf. S. Alexander, 'Women's Work in Nineteenth-century London' in Mitchell and Oakley (eds), *The Rights and Wrongs of Women*.

2 A HOME FROM HOME
   — WOMEN'S PHILANTHROPIC WORK IN THE
   NINETEENTH CENTURY

Anne Summers

Philanthropy is a very broad term. In this chapter I shall be employing it in the sense of personal charitable dealings with the poor; and especially with the attempts made by individual women of the middle and upper classes to make contact with the poor and distressed, to visit them in their homes and bring material and spiritual comfort to bridge, as they hoped, the social and political gulfs between them. One can think of few topics more open to caricature and cliché than the house-to-house visiting of Victorian ladies, with their gifts of Bibles, tracts, lozenges, soup and good advice; the Lady Bountiful is a legitimate object of popular resentment and literary satire. Nevertheless, her work deserves rescuing from its invasive and condescending stereotype, if only because visiting was a social practice to which the utmost importance was attached by contemporaries, and which many might argue has been retained with few essential changes down to the present day. It is one of the tasks of feminist history to rescue women's work from oblivion and ridicule, and to demonstrate the effort, motivation and skills which a male-dominated society exploits and takes for granted. Nineteenth-century philanthropic organisations depended to a very great degree upon voluntary women visitors, and many of the earliest state welfare provisions of the twentieth century were predicated on the continuing existence of this work force.

This chapter is based on the premise that the voluntary visiting of the poor by leisured women of the last century was not just a dilettante fashion of passing free time, but an engagement of the self which involved the sacrifice of leisure and the development of expertise. The work of visiting, because it *was* work and not a pastime for so many women, in time created an informal interest group among them, which exercised significant political and social pressure on the direction and administration of official policies towards the poor. In asserting a particular feminine point of view, women philanthropists made an indirect contribution towards the emancipation of women of their own class. However, their philanthropic initiatives were often diametrically opposed to the emancipation of women in the social classes beneath

33

them.

It is not possible to give an exact account of the numbers of women involved in the work of visiting the homes of the poor in the nineteenth century. On the whole, charitable organisations of the period justified themselves to the world by the number of cases they helped, and not by the number of caseworkers they employed. The latter rarely figured in annual reports; and if they worked without payment, as middle-class visitors did, they were not mentioned in the audits either. The modern researcher experiences much the same frustration with philanthropic sources as L.M. Hubbard in 1893, when she circulated 1,164 institutions in an attempt to obtain figures of women philanthropic workers for the volume *Woman's Mission,* edited by Angela Burdett-Coutts. Only 290 sent usable returns; and from the figure of 84,129 voluntary workers at which she arrived, it is impossible for us to extract the number who would have been engaged as visitors.[1] By the same token, we cannot obtain any accurate picture of the regional distribution of visitors, but the fragmentary information to be obtained from Charity Organisation Society reports and elsewhere suggests that the great industrial cities did not necessarily supply the largest number of them. For example, the Manchester District Provident Society had 259 (mostly voluntary) visitors in 1835, a number which fell off almost completely in the next ten years; the number rose again to 25 in 1889, at a time when many small cathedral towns could boast larger totals.[2] An idea of the scale on which visiting was practised can be derived from the figures of some of the London charities. In 1835, the Congregationalist Christian Instruction Society fielded 2,000 voluntary visitors for over 40,000 families, who were called on twice monthly.[3] In 1843 the Bishop of London helped to found the Metropolitan Visiting and Relief Association, which recruited 1,000 visitors within twelve months. By 1873, the Association had 2,200 visitors.[4] In 1905 it was estimated that the London churches, chapels, missions and charities between them marshalled 7,500 voluntary and 900 paid visitors.[5] Between 1908 and 1914 Theodora Morton, Principal Organiser of School Care Committees for the London County Council, was able to enrol 10,000 voluntary visitors to support her work.[6]

Women visitors performed a number of different functions; the nature of these depended somewhat on the way the visit had been organised. In many small towns and country parishes, individual women worked on their own initiative. The wives, sisters and daughters of the vicarage assisted the sick and destitute, held scripture readings in their cottages, got their children to come to their Sunday schools, organised mothers' meetings, sewing and thrift clubs. In the larger towns, District Visitors did similar work in a more organised capacity on behalf of the church or chapel to which they belonged, reporting to it regularly on the work they had carried out and the individuals they had encountered in the section of the parish assigned to them. Very often these visitors were mostly concerned with strengthening and supporting the faithful within an existing parish. More ambitious Evangelical missions sought out the unknown and unconverted, the least respectable or conventionally 'deserving' poor. Towards the middle of the nineteenth century middle-class women who had gained experience in more salubrious spheres began to play a part in this work. Mrs Ranyard had been a visitor in Kent for the Bible Society before she married and moved to Bloomsbury; she recruited 'biblewomen', themselves of humble origin, to visit homes in desperately poor London parishes which had proved inaccessible to conventional mission work.[7] In Beckenham, where her father was rector, Catherine Marsh visited building and railway navvies in their lodgings and at their work, held prayer meetings with them, and banked their wages.[8]

Philanthropic enterprise and spiritual missions were, in fact though not in principle, almost inextricably intertwined in visiting work. Those who engaged simply in the relief of poverty and distress did so from a sense of Christian duty. And the sheer impossibility of preaching the gospels, where this was the primary aim, in front of those utterly destitute of food and warmth, would lead a missionary visitor to supply, or organise the supply, of money, bread, blankets and coal; later on, she might attempt to moralise, and to inculcate habits of providence and self-sufficiency. Material help was largely seen as a means to reach the hearts and minds of the poor; the idea that poverty could actually be eradicated by measures of social reform had very little currency among the charitable before the middle of the century, and was only slowly and partially adopted thereafter.

The Origins of Home Visiting 1780-1850

It might seem that in discussing the practice of visiting the poor we are dealing with the dateless and commonplace; but this is not so. The massive practice of house-to-house visiting in the nineteenth century must be understood in the specific context of social changes which had occurred less than a century previously. Both in the countryside and the towns in the eighteenth century, rich and poor had been growing residentially and socially distant from each other. The gap between squirearchy and tenantry widened, with a wave of enclosures driving many agricultural workers to the towns, and pressing hard on the live-lihood of those remaining. Rural clergy, once socially identified with their more humble parishioners, were after 1759 enabled to commute the payment of tithes and acquire larger holdings of land; they became socially absorbed into the gentry, and established their residences further and further away from their hungry sheep.[9] Their duty to visit parishioners on sick or death beds remained an inescapable charge, but little or no initiative was taken towards further contact with the poor.[10] It is significant that when Methodism came to challenge the established Church in the rural areas, its successes were achieved as much by prayer meetings in the labourers' own cottages as by the more celebrated open-air preaching.[11] The 'call to seriousness' on the part of Evangelical members of the established Church towards the turn of the century was a response to this Methodist challenge. Feeling themselves renewed by a sense of personal religious crisis, the Anglican Evangelicals sought to make their own church a better vehicle for the salvation of others. But if Anglicanism were ever to regain the ground stormed by Methodism, let alone preserve its territory from further encroachment, it needed, within the limits of propriety, to steal some of Methodism's clothes. Cottage prayer meetings came well within these limits; and visiting the poor became a weapon in the contest for social and spiritual supremacy in the countryside.

In the towns, a striking contemporary development was the separ-ation of the middle-class family residence from the middle-class work place. Merchants, manufacturers and employers of all kinds had pre-viously lived 'over the shop' in city centres, in close contact occupat-ionally and recreationally with their employees. In the early nineteenth century, Liverpool businessmen still lived 'opposite to or above their own offices and warehouses, and on fine evenings they took the air sitting by the dock side, while their children played at a safe distance from the deep water. . . .'[12] At the end of the nineteenth century Louisa Twining recalled how her father had maintained in the centre of London the working practices of the early 1800s:

'Not slothful in business, serving the Lord' might have been his motto: and here again I would note the changed habits of past and present. As long as we lived in Norfolk Street he frequently went out again after dinner at six o'clock, to his work in the Strand, for at least a time, returning to a late tea, thus far exceeding the hours now thought sufficient for all classes and ranks of workers.[13]

However, by the late eighteenth and early nineteenth centuries, many businessmen were beginning to invest a part of their growing profits in suburban homes. Employers and employees separated after working hours; working and leisure time and social space began to be more rigidly demarcated. The process of separation was observed in many of the older commercial centres, such as London, Liverpool and Bristol, and was also a feature of the newer industrial towns where, of course, social distance was a function of the increasing size and scale of the mechanised work place, as well as of the residential withdrawal. An apt comment on the process, in unconsciously Bunyanesque language, was that of Mrs Wightman, the temperance missionary. In 1858 she said of Shrewsbury's Butcher Row: 'The masters have mostly moved out into Pride Hill, a street which is also in our parish, but several of the men employed by them still reside in the Row.'[14] The withdrawal of the entrepreneurial classes' residences from the scene of their commercial or manufacturing operations was often repeated by successive generations of successful employers in the same city. For each such generation, the creation of social distance posed problems, often seemingly for the first time, or more acutely than ever before.

In the years following the first French Revolution of 1789, and in the economically unstable early decades of the new century, it was not enough to say 'the poor ye have always with you'. The unemployment and hunger of craftsmen made redundant by mechanisation and interruptions of trade, and the swelling population of the urban poor, were facts fraught with political menace. In 1800 Mrs Sarah Trimmer considered 'an assemblage of poor people, collected together without a regular plan in a tumultuary manner, each *demanding,* or at least expecting as *their right* a loaf of bread, or a bushel of coals, &c. is the next thing to a *seditious meeting,* and in times like the present they should be prevented'. Crowds which assembled for overtly political reasons could be physically suppressed; those which parish charity brought together at the vestry could be broken down into their component parts by kindness, in 'the interests of the deserving poor, who are seen to the greatest advantage in their own cottages, patiently struggling with the evils of poverty'.[15] The iron fist of coercion could be supplemented or even replaced by the velvet glove of friendship. Visiting the poor in their own homes could do more than demonstrate the benevolent and neighbourly intentions towards them of the rich; it could also help to isolate the poor from each other.

Why should it have fallen to the women of the upper and middle classes to perform these social functions? One obvious answer is that they were available, and we must allow some space for it. Women who had wealth enough to employ several servants had leisure for pursuits outside their own homes, the more so if they were spinsters. However, it is impossible to tell if there really were more spinsters involved in visiting the poor than married women, or more childless women among the latter group than mothers; there can be no strict connection established between degree of leisure enjoyed and degree of social concern. Leisure was a necessary condition for social work, not a sufficient one. Running through much contemporary criticism of the women 'do-gooders' of the time was what one might call the 'argument from boredom' — women busied themselves with the poor because they had nothing else to do. It is important not to fall into the trap of mistaking a necessary condition for a sufficient one. We know that many Victorian males of the leisured classes took up Parliamentary careers; it has never been suggested that their overriding motive for doing so was one of boredom. It is belittling and insulting to suggest that women had only a negative motivation for their actions, and that they might as easily have been beguiling the hours with playing musical instruments, exchanging visits with friends, eating chocolates, reading novels or having love affairs as with seeking to be of use to the poor in their neighbourhoods; and it is historically unhelpful to suggest that thousands of individuals acted without positive motivation or the exercise of choice.

As Catherine Hall has shown, women occupied an important place in the Evangelical movement. They showed great enthusiasm for personal and family religion, as opposed to the purely church-based ritual from which they were excluded; being so much outside a male-dominated institution, they were perhaps better placed than men to see its deficiencies, and their religious enthusiasm made them anxious to assist in repairing them. This was particularly true of the wives and daughters of Evangelical clergymen, so much so that by the mid-nineteenth century the Reverend Charles Kingsley was pronouncing rather sourly that the 'dogma' of the clerical wife's responsibility for a parish was 'much overstated'.[16] These women were very active in restoring pastoral contacts, especially in rural parishes. In the towns, Anglican Evangelicals had to compete with those outside the established Church. The urban population at the turn of the century was growing well beyond the reach and often beyond the ken of the Anglican parochial ministry; and Non-conformist employers — such as the Quakers in Birmingham, Unitarians in Liverpool and Congregationalists among many others in London — were foremost in the quest for social and spiritual influence among the radical or heathen poorer classes. In the Non-conformist communities, the distinctions between priest and laity were less pronounced than they were in Anglicanism, and the sphere of women was less narrowly confined. Unitarian women in Liverpool administered their own 'Ladies Charity', for example, established in 1796 to visit the sick poor, and set up, with the help of a separate Gentlemen's Committee, a Benevolent Institute for Reclaiming Women and Girls.[17]

These urban employers' wives and daughters approached the poor, not merely as spiritual missionaries, or as representatives of their menfolk, but as managers and employers of labour in their own right. The late eighteenth century appears to have been a period in which increasing numbers of households moved into the servant-employing category, and the servant class itself increased proportionately. This was particularly evident during the wars against Revolutionary and Napoleonic France, when it ceased to be the fashion to employ French or Italian servants; but independently of this change, large numbers of the poor were being drawn from agricultural and urban employment (or unemployment) into domestic service.[18] Women managers of households were thus establishing the closest residential contact with a relatively new class of employees at precisely the time that male employers were withdrawing from residential contact with *their* workers. Women were developing a pattern of personal relationships across class barriers at a time when men were losing the social element in relationships at work.[19] Relationships within the household offered a model for relations between rich and poor outside it: a model of the working class as economically and socially dependent, obedient, disciplined, clean and broken in to the daily methods and routines of the middle-class family unit.

What could be seen of the working classes outside the domestic service sector was in rude contrast to all this. Much of the content of home visiting in the nineteenth century can be seen as the attempt to transpose the values and relations of domestic service to a wider class of the poor. A process which some might wish to typify as 'social control' or the imposition of 'ideological hegemony' was almost certainly rooted in the more mundane and limited requirement of widening the field of recruitment for domestic service. We know that training establishments for servants were set up in this period,[20] but we know less about *recruitment* for training and service: there seem to have been few commercial agencies such as sprang up in the later nineteenth century. Retired servants were certainly visited in their homes, and it is likely that particular groups of families were cultivated as a way of ensuring a reliable reservoir of womanpower and manpower for one's own and one's relatives' domestic needs. This kind of visiting, practical and charitable in an unselfconscious way, would serve as a step towards more dynamic, and in some senses radical, Evangelical initiatives.

The state of research on the development of the servant class and on class relationships within households on the eve of the industrial revolution is not very far advanced. We must certainly be cautious of placing a greater weight on social interpretation of women's role as employers of domestic labour than the facts will yet bear. But it is worth quoting one male voice from the year 1855 which strongly and indeed effusively supports the account of women's changing role which I have advanced. In *Lectures to Ladies on Practical Subjects,* the Reverend J.S. Brewer, urging his audience to visit the inmates of work-houses, described the London workhouse poor as belonging[21]

mainly to a class which has never come in contact with the upper classes of society. They have not been domestic servants; they have been utterly removed in their sympathies, their training, their enjoy-ments, and their sorrows — in their whole lives, in short — from the upper ranks of society. They are chiefly drawn from the floating and working street poor of London, swelled by the country labourers who have left Ireland and been domiciled in the metropolis, hodsmen and their wives, basket-women, jobbing-smiths, gilders or cabmen.

Upon them the more fortunate classes have no hold, and exert over them no influence. Both are entire strangers to the others; the dislocation between them is complete. If you do not know what they do, neither do they know what you do. Remember, ladies, it is not so with any other poor. Over the classes just above them you have a power, and you are entrusted with a mission, of which it were to be wished that all ladies were fully sensible. Unwittingly, you are exercising in your own families a vast social and political power; you are educating the poor under you, it may be, without your own consciousness for good or evil, and instructing them in the most powerful, because the most unpretending way, in all that you your-selves know and practise. The female servants in your household, whom you have taken and instructed in their respective duties — whose manners you have softened — who have learnt from you how to manage a houshold — who have caught up from you, insensibly, lessons of vast utility, lessons of order, lessons of economy, lessons of cleanliness, lessons of the management of children, of household comfort and tidiness; these women eventually become the wives of small tradesmen and respectable operatives. They carry into a lower and a very extended circle the influence of your teaching and your training. Visit a hamlet or a village where the cottager's wife has been a servant in the squire's mansion, and you shall see the result immediately, in the air of comfort, order, and neatness which reigns around — in the gentle and respectful manner of the woman — in the tidiness and respectability of her children. Even her husband, though rude and habituated to rough toil, has caught something of the gentle manners of his wife. Go into the small butchers', bakers', green-grocers' shops in town, and the same result is observable. The woman . . . is not so good a specimen as the former, because she is not so unsophisticated; the town mansion and the management of servants in them have been somewhat different. Still from you she has carried lessons of inestimable value to her husband and her family . . . .

If then it were possible, in this or in the great manufacturing towns of this country, for the ladies of England to extend that influence over all classes of the poor which, for the great good of this country, they are extending over one large portion of the classes below them, I really believe the blessing to this nation would be inestimable. I know of nothing in the way of district visiting or missionary labours equal in its consequences, or fraught with any-thing like the same degree of advantage. You would find no invincible prejudices in the way of moral and sanitary improvement; you would not find large masses of the poor standing heedlessly and offensively on their rights and their independence, as jealous, and justly jealous, of having their freedom taken from them, but fearing that they could not assert it in any other way.

It would thus appear that by the middle of the nineteenth century women employers of servants established, through managerial activities in their own homes, and through visiting the homes of the poor, a model of class relations which suggested a remedy for present and future social ills. It was a limited model, which did not deal with industrial or commercial employees, and which in the first instance dealt almost exclusively with women; nevertheless, as the century wore on, and social breaches in town and country remorselessly widened, many male philan-thropists came to pin inordinate hopes on this sphere of women's work.

Practices and Theories

What was it like to be a visitor, or to be visited? The former question can be more readily answered than the latter, inasmuch as many visitors published memoirs and descriptive tracts; but visitors often worked amid a welter of conflicting assumptions, and it is not as simple as it might seem to give a straightforward account of their experiences.

Although I have indicated a possible natural progression towards philanthropic visiting of the poor from recruitment of domestic servants, I would not suggest that this step was an easy one for the visitor herself. Not every well-meaning woman was capable of entering the wretched tenement or hovel of a total stranger. Charles Kingsley thought it necessary for young unmarried ladies to find a philanthropic field which did *not* bring them 'in that most undesirable contact with the coarser forms of evil which house-visitation must do'; and a friend of Mrs Wightman's declared 'I am afraid of working men; if one happens to enter a cottage in my district, I walk out at once.' Ellice Hopkins recalled of her first cottage prayer meeting with men 'I doubt whether at that time a sheeted spectre had the same unknown terrors for me as a rough in the "too, too solid flesh".'[22] Such scruples and fears had to be overcome by something greater than an urge to recruit servants or tidy up squalid districts of the city, and more positive than the fear of revolution on the part of the unwashed and undisciplined proletariat. We are far from the conventional picture of the condescending 'do-gooder' in this reminiscence by Mrs Wightman. Her husband, the Evangelical rector of St Alkmond's, Shrewsbury, was anxious to reach the poorer men, as well as the women of his parish. He assigned her a mission to the Butcher Row to which I have already referred—an area where he himself had tried open-air preaching with little success. In 1859 she recalled:[23]

We have often laughed at my first start at night visiting in Butcher Row. After Charles had knelt in prayer with me, and I had gone out with a brave heart, as soon as I found myself alone in the street, a sense of fear came so overpoweringly over me, that I went like a shot past the men loitering near the public-houses in Butcher Row, turned down Pride Hill, retraced my steps hurriedly, and at last found myself at home within a quarter of an hour. 'What! have you forgotten anything?' said Charles, astonished to see me back so soon. Being agitated, I burst into tears, saying, 'I cannot go out at night; it's no use trying.' However, next day I managed better. Having first asked the wives if I might call at night, and my offer being thankfully accepted, I went with thorough comfort, feeling that I was expected; and from that moment I have never been timid. Often, unattended, I have been at ten o'clock p.m. a mile from home, and have never met with any incivility in the streets or elsewhere.

No matter how courageous or disinterested a middle-class woman might be, the visiting relationship was a very one-sided affair. The visitor offered the poor immediate material help, and the hope of it in future times of need — treatment at a hospital, for example, where the visitor was a subscriber—and could put individuals into employment, especially daughters into domestic service. The poor had nothing to offer in return except gratitude and good behaviour. Lower-class visitors such as the biblewomen might help the poor to organise themselves independently; Mrs Wightman's own temperance mission in Shrewsbury assumed something of a 'self-help' character, with working men encouraging each other's efforts at thrift and insurance as well as abstinence. But by and large the relationship was one of clientage; and as such it left the poor with very little dignity.

Victorian philanthropists nevertheless espoused some highly optimistic theories as to the social consequences of visiting. The practice was defined essentially as a mission from soul to soul, which permitted individual Christians of different classes to meet in genuine friendship. 'Woman's heart is alike in all ranks', was Kingsley's comforting slogan.[24] By means of the lady visitor, the divisive effects of class distinction and distance could be neutralised. However, there were many pitfalls in the enterprise. It was hard to map out the etiquette of visiting. One writer after another found it necessary to urge women to be *respectful* of the poor, to be courteous as well as pitiful. 'All may be nullified and stultified,' said Kingsley, 'by simply keeping a poor woman standing in her own cottage while you sit, or entering her house, even at her own request, while she is at meals.' C.P. Bosanquet found it necessary to advise against dictating to the poor, especially in front of their neighbours or children.[25] On the other hand, in the exhortation to neutralise class distinction, there was no suggestion that it be abolished. On the contrary: Catherine Marsh insisted that those following her and her navvies' example 'would find what cordial friendships could be formed *without losing their positions on either side* ...' (my italics) and Kingsley was a good deal more blunt in his advice. 'Be a sister to her. I do not ask you to take her up in your carriage. You cannot; perhaps it is good for her that you cannot.'[26]

In practice, many visitors must have resolved this hopeless dilemma by defining the task of bridging social gulfs simply as that of making the poor more like their betters. In 1869, a pseudonymous female writer claimed:[27]

Much of the apparent disrespect of the lower classes arises from ignorance and shyness. Teaching the children good manners, helps to teach the elders of a family. Miss James is particularly successful on this head. On entering a cottage, she makes a point of addressing, separately, each member present of the family, down to the youngest who can speak. She makes all the little ones rise from their seats, and the parents and elder children can scarcely remain seated when the little ones are made to rise. She breaks through the shyness of the poor little bashful creatures, by finding for them in the recesses of her bag, a penny toy, a sugar plum, or a biscuit. This will usually force, after repeated promptings by the mother, a whispered 'thank you'; but if the little tongue still refuses to speak, or the little head to bow, the toy, &c., is withheld till the next visit, or the next, till the child has spoken. When once the tongue has been loosed, the rest is easy, and after a few more visits the children speak properly, though they may require to be reminded to do so. The mothers have always seconded Miss James on these occasions.

It must be stressed that we are almost entirely without record as to the feelings of the poor on being visited. But we can infer from some philanthropic sources that the poor in their own homes were capable of putting up considerable social resistance to visitors, that they resented condescension, and maintained an independence of spirit while still on their own ground. The Reverend J.S. Brewer pointed out in 1855 that the great advantage of visiting the poor after they have been removed to the workhouse was that[28]

They are, mentally and bodily, in the same condition as the poor out of doors, except that they are more accessible in every way. Having no occupation, and allowed to exercise none, they are in a more suitable frame of mind to listen to you, more thankful for your attentions, more ready to confide in you, more unaffected and more natural. They are, moreover, almost entirely isolated from the rest of the world; many of them — far more than could be deemed possible — have not a single relative; they are strictly alone; they have outlived all their children, their friends, and their associates; and I therefore leave you to infer in what kind of value they would hold a lady's ministrations among them, where her offices of charity came in the place of all former ties, and reopened thoughts and affections buried but not forgotten.

Even more telling is the evidence of Mrs Ranyard, who recruited poor biblewomen because she realised that women of her own class were unwelcome visitors.

> Those who would be ashamed to be seen by a Clergyman, a City Missionary, or a Lady Visitor, have no objection to be a little cleared and set straight in their afflictions by one like themselves . . . .The 'woman' goes where the 'lady' might not enter. . . .[29]

The organisation of a corps of biblewomen, or 'native reformers' as Mrs Ranyard interestingly referred to them, in London and many provincial towns, did not by any means sound the death knell of middle-class visiting. Many ladies were quite content to deal with clients among the 'deserving poor' and were not ambitious to pluck brands from the burning; and some may have been too insensitive to know when they were not wanted. The belief died very hard that for members of a higher social class to visit members of a lower was a practical exercise in social conciliation. Obviously, many of the extravagant and contradictory beliefs on the subject were inspired by wishful thinking. If social problems really could be solved on a house-to-house basis, and by voluntary workers, then disturbing thoughts of structural change, or expensive reforms, could be conveniently shelved. However, there is a further aspect of this wishful thinking which is of particular interest from the point of view of women's studies. The male writers I have quoted did not think too deeply about the political dimension of women's visiting. Women were not considered political animals: they were the ornaments of the wealthy home, both aesthetically and spiritually. It was assumed that women graced the homes of the poor as they graced their own, exuding a wonderful and mysterious influence without abandoning an essentially passive role; certainly without dealing in threats and promises. It was not admitted that women, in dispensing material assistance and using influence on behalf of the poor, could not but exercise considerable leverage upon them. Visiting the poor, in fact, gave women a taste of power outside their own homes. Visitors constituted not an intangible spiritual force, but an important patronage group; and if all poor families did not barricade themselves in against the kind of ministrations I have described, or simulate drunken stupor or rigor mortis in self-defence, it was in order to gain the benefits of patronage rather than to accept the dubious and somewhat double-edged 'friendship' which was on offer.

Lady Visitors and Poor Law Reform 1834-90

The patronage which the lady visitor exercised must be assessed in the context of other forms of relief available to the poor in the nineteenth century. In particular, it must be seen against the background of changes in Poor Law policy. Before 1834, poor relief in Britain was administered on a parochial basis: poor rates were levied for the support of work-houses for the unemployed or unemployable; they were also distributed to poor individuals or families in their own homes; the latter system was known as outdoor relief or out-relief. In principle, the widowed, orphaned or elderly had a long-term claim to the charity of the parish, but not the able-bodied and employable poor. However, the economic dislocations of the Napoleonic wars and the post-war period, falling agricultural prices, and a generally low level of wages brought many parishes, especially rural ones, to the point of paying outdoor relief to those in regular, but ill-paid employment. With out-relief in aid of wages suggesting a quite limitless vista of parish responsibility, the rate-paying population took fright. The problem of poverty and its causes were much discussed by the propertied classes and an attractive solution seen in the abolition of out-relief. It was argued that employers were only encouraged to pay low wages because the parish topped them up; and that subsidised poverty was preventing the under-employed from uprooting themselves in search of proper work. Benthamite economic theory on the general need for a free and mobile labour force merged with the ratepayers' desire to keep down the rates, the employers' reluctance to pay more for labour, and the workers' legal incapacity to combine in the struggle for a living wage. The consequence was the Poor Law Amendment Act of 1834, which introduced the administrative construction of Poor Law Unions, grouping several parishes together, and the physical construction of workhouses large enough to admit all who sought poor relief. Out-relief was, in principle, to be abolished; and workhouse conditions were to be made so unpleasant as to deter all but the most desperate from seeking relief in the first place.

The patronage which women philanthropists had been exercising in the homes of the poor *before* the 1834 Act would almost certainly have come under the head of aid in relief of wages — and, indeed, of aid in relief of out-relief. In the case of the former, they could continue to subsidise a wage earner and his or her family, and would be the means of keeping them from applying to the parish and being swallowed up in the dreaded Bastille, as the workhouse was appropriately known.

Given the fact of this horrible alternative, women's patronage would in fact be more valuable than before 1834, and women's sense of social influence, and leverage over individuals, would correspondingly grow. But in the case of the latter form of aid, women would prove less, rather than more effective. With the curtailment of outdoor relief, women's charitable subsidies would now prove insufficient to maintain, for example, a poor pensioner in modest but independent comfort. Women thus began to lose some of their protégés to the workhouse, an institution over which they had no influence whatsoever.[30] Women's interest in workhouse reform in the nineteenth century springs directly from this chain of events. In the 1840s and 1850s individual women began to seek admission as visitors of workhouses in order to keep in touch with particular inmates whom they had known and patronised 'outdoors'. Elizabeth Twining recalled 'When I first obtained leave from one of the Guardians of the Poor in the parish where I had for many years visited in London, I went chiefly to follow out some whom I had known in their own little *homes* . . .' and her better-known younger sister, Louisa, wrote that 'In visiting poor people in a district, I had often heard of some who were going in. One poor old lonely woman, in whom I felt much interest, was obliged at last to break up her home and depart.' This old woman died six weeks later, and Louisa was so saddened by her own failure to visit her in what she at this time considered 'an inaccessible fortress', that she determined to gain admission to the workhouse when the next old friend should be forced 'indoors'.[31]

There are many printed sources on the New Poor Law, and this is not the place to discuss its workings in detail.[32] Suffice it to say that the squalor which women visitors found in many workhouses, the regimentation which prevailed in almost all of them, the enforced separation of husbands from wives, and mothers from children, the herding together of the whole and the diseased, moved them to pity and terror. Visiting by individuals gave rise to a Workhouse Visiting Society, formed in 1860 to generalise the practice, and later to a Society for the Promotion of the Return of Women as Poor Law Guardians; and women agitated in every sphere to which they had access for the more humane treatment of children and the elderly, the separation of sick and healthy inmates, the creation of a workhouse infirmary system, and many other reforms. Some of these reforms might have been achieved without specifically female pressure, some without any pressure beyond economic necessity; here I wish to single out for consideration those reforms and changes which throw light on women philanthropists as a distinct social and political grouping.

The agency which deprived the lady visitor of much of her social power and influence was a state institution, the Poor Law Board, set up under the 1834 Act. The Board had its paid officials in the Poor Law Unions, but for the most part its parochial administration was undertaken, much as before, by unpaid Guardians of the Poor elected from among the ratepayers. The burden of providing relief, and the responsibility for administering the poor rate and appointing workhouse officials, was in the mid-nineteenth century falling more heavily on a lower class of ratepayers. This was a direct consequence of the residential trend set out at the beginning of this chapter – the separation of social classes and in particular the withdrawal of wealthy families from the centres to the suburbs of cities. Those who could not quite afford to move away, the small tradesmen and shopkeepers of the city, formed the majority of those left to provide for the growing population of claimants. The financial strain which these poorer Guardians were experiencing had indeed had much to do with the call for Poor Law Reform before 1834. It was this class of Guardians whom the philanthropic women of the professional and upper middle classes tended to blame for the weaknesses and abuses of the Poor Law system as a whole. The contest for social patronage and influence was experienced as a contest between one class of women and another class of men; not as between women and men in general, much less as one between women and the state. In 1857 Louisa Twining wrote

> Everywhere we hear of gentlemen resigning their posts as guardians because of the opposition of the majority, whose ignorance and vulgarity cannot be tolerated by them. It is the same in the country as in towns; the ill-educated and narrow-minded have the upper hand, and generally succeed in their endeavours to get rid of their opponents. . . . It is justly asked, 'What co-operation could be expected in any system of lady visitors from such persons as these?'

In 1880, when reprinting this article, she recapitulated the argument, this time with regard to the appointment of gentlewomen as matrons and superintendents of workhouse wards.[33]

With such sentiments as these abroad, it is small wonder that C.P. Bosanquet, publishing his *Handy-Book for Visitors of the Poor in London* in 1874, thought it necessary to caution his readers: 'Do not start with a prejudice against Guardians or other parish officers. They have difficulties to contend with which you may not know of. Assume that they are doing their best till you know the contrary.'[34] Again and

again women were to plead for the men of their own class to return to
the social positions which they had vacated. As Octavia Hill wrote, 'what
might not the locality gain, if the administration of its affairs were
carried on under the influence of men of education!'[35] But they were
commanding the waves to recede: and since they could not persuade
their menfolk back into their former positions, they would have to fill
these positions themselves. The first woman Guardian was elected in
Kensington in 1875.[36]

As visitors and Guardians, women sought to infiltrate and improve
the administration of the Poor Laws, not to denounce them compre-
hensively. The 1834 Act and the legislation that followed in support
of it were not openly attacked: but they were often very effectively
subverted. Women consistently worked to reverse the most fundamental
tenet of the 1834 Act, the abolition of relief outside the walls of the
workhouse. They were concerned not only to visit their protégés who
had become inmates, and improve their living conditions, but also to
rescue them from the workhouse or, better still, save them from entering
it. In the 1850s, for example, Mrs Sheppard of Frome boarded deserving
paupers out of the workhouse in rooms which she hired in nearby
village homes; she often extracted a very small sum in out-relief from
the Guardians as well. She longed to be wealthy enough to establish
asylums for the aged poor. Louisa Twining found accommodation
outside the workhouse for old women who were on the point of
entering it. Elizabeth Twining had the parish almshouses restored near
her family's residence in Twickenham.[37] In 1868 Miss L. Boucherett
informed the editor of *The Englishwoman's Review* that as a result of
her pressures the Lincolnshire Guardians had resolved ' "That outdoor
relief should always be given, when possible, to women and children."
This Resolution is my greatest triumph . . .'[38] The first women to become
Guardians worked in the same direction. Mrs Charles of Paddington,
for example, found on her election in 1881 that no outdoor relief was
granted to widows in the Union; but after five years of her agitation,
out-relief was restored to them, as they were to their children.[39]

Possibly the best-known example of women's work against the grain
of the Poor Laws is the movement to board out orphan children under
the care and control of the Guardians. These were for the most part
maintained in the workhouses or 'district schools' of the Poor Law
Union in which they were born. From the earliest days of women's
organised workhouse visiting, it had been a stated goal to find family
homes for orphans within their Union and, if necessary, outside it;
and the corollary had been the formation of (largely female) committees

of visitors to inspect the homes chosen and supervise the fostering of the children. Societies such as the Birmingham Society for the Befriending of Pauper Children sprang up in several parts of the country in the 1860s; and in 1870 a petition on the subject bearing the signatures of more than 3,000 women was presented to the Poor Law Board, which by the end of the year issued an order sanctioning the practice of boarding out children wherever they could be adequately supervised.[40] By 1895 nearly 2,000 committees of visitors existed to supervise fostering.[41] There had also been some expansion of state administrative machinery to cope with the growth and diffusion of Poor Law responsibilities which the boarding-out system involved. By 1885 Miss M.H. Mason, previously a voluntary visitor of boarded-out children in Nottinghamshire, and a Vice-President of the Workers' Department of the Girls' Friendly Society, was appointed Local Government Board Inspector for boarded-out children.[42]

There was considerable friction between the local committees of voluntary visitors, and both the local Boards of Guardians and the Local Government Board department for boarded-out children. Some scandals came to light which redounded to the discredit of the former: foster-parents were discovered by state inspectors to have been grossly ill-treating children despite contrary assertions by local visitors. The inefficiency and sentimentality of local voluntary initiatives were condemned by the advocates of centralised and impartial state administrative practices. Women's expertise was said to have lagged behind progressive developments in social welfare. Today, having seen – too late – how a well-staffed state system can nevertheless let children like Maria Colwell slip through its fingers, we are probably less ready to condemn these voluntary local initiatives than the administrative reformers of the 1880s and 1890s; and we are better able to appreciate the good sense of many volunteers and the shrewdness of some of their criticisms of the burgeoning professionalisation of welfare work. Florence Hill, for example, wrote in defence of her own methods of inspection in 1889:[43]

It is very difficult to decide on a just standard of requirement. The most reasonable seems to be that the boarded-out child should be brought up as well in all respects as those of our respectable poor in the locality where such child is placed—for the gauge of well-being varies widely in different parts of the country. . . . It is impossible for the inspector to stay long enough in any one place to obtain accurate knowledge of the neighbourhood and the foster-parents;

yet without such accuracy he may be led entirely astray. . . . To differences of rank, education, and mental habit between inspector and inspected are added other items of complexity.

In the literature on nineteenth-century social work, boarding-out is among the best covered of women's movements for reform; I suspect that this is partly due to the fact that in dealing with children, women were occupying themselves in what has always been considered their proper sphere. We can see, however, that the boarding-out movement was part of a wider initiative by women which embraced the elderly, the widowed and that category of 'deserving poor' whose existence the 1834 Act had virtually decreed to be an impossibility, and certainly a contradiction in terms. In almost every sphere of their work women had undermined the inclusive principle of the New Poor Law; countered the tendency towards abolishing out-relief; and created conditions in which their own methods of work and the influence of their own social class could be reasserted.

Home Visiting in the Voluntary and State Sectors 1869-1914

The years in which women assumed positions of direct influence within the Poor Law system also saw the principles of 1834 being applied with a renewed intensity by the government. In 1871 the Poor Law Board was replaced by the Local Government Board, which forthwith campaigned for severer restrictions on outdoor relief. In its first report, the Board laid down that no out-relief should be paid to a deserted woman for the first twelve months that she was alone, and that widows should send their children into the workhouse and earn their own living outside it rather than receive the out-relief which would enable them to keep a family together. In 1870 the Metropolitan Poor Amendment Act had established a Common Poor Fund for the indoor relief of poverty in London. This measure distributed some of the burden of relief between rich and poor parishes, but left outdoor relief as the sole responsibility of individual Poor Law Unions: their Guardians were therefore additionally motivated to follow the Local Government Board's directives and cut down out-relief as far as possible. This renewal of the official onslaught on out-relief — against which, as we have seen, many women Guardians struggled successfully — was a reaction in part to the economic depression of the 1860s, which brought a growing number of people under the aegis of the Poor Law. Moreover, the population of cities continued to grow, and there was no slackening of the flight of wealthy citizens to the outer suburbs. The population in three East End parishes in which the Metropolitan Visiting and Relief Association took a particular interest grew from 60,000 in 1843 to 500,000 in 1901.[44] Neither the funds of Poor Law Unions nor the personnel of charitable organisations could show a corresponding rate of increase. The problems which had faced an earlier generation of reformers remained as intractable and frustrating as ever; and it was tempting to blame all failures so far on the imperfect application of an unimpeachable set of principles.

At the same time, new schools of thought were growing up on the 'poverty question', and new political groups were being drawn into the discussion. The second Reform Act of 1867, which enfranchised the male householder, and the Trade Union Act of 1871, which confirmed the legality of trade union organisation, brought a section of the working class into the established political system. In the 1880s, Bismarck's Germany offered a practical example of how measures of 'state socialism' might be introduced, which could free the working man's old age or sickness from the stigma of charity and pauperism. The demand would gradually grow for 'collectivist' state provisions in Britain, such as national insurance, old age pensions, free schooling and school meals. Even though almost all of this welfare legislation in fact waited until the election of the first Liberal government of the twentieth century, the collectivist/individualist debate was in the air for many decades before 1906. It was a threatening debate for the philanthropists. An increased provision of state welfare services would render voluntary social work superfluous and obsolete. Material benefits would be dispensed by impersonal state agencies, created out of tax revenue, not by visitors from another social class. The relief of poverty would lose its religious aspect. Neighbourliness would disappear, and so would gratitude.

The growing interest in collectivist solutions for poverty, as well as the rise of a socialist critique of the relations between classes in capitalist society, made personal charity appear, not as the humane alternative to Poor Law relief, but as its accomplice: providing temporary palliatives for social evils which it did nothing to destroy. One of the strongest reactions of middle-class philanthropy to this essentially working-class challenge was to deny its validity. It was reaffirmed that poverty was not a structural or economic problem for society, but a moral one. It was a function of pauperism, of *personal* failure; as such it would continue to be solved through the reform and help of individuals. The only structures allowed to have relevance to the argument were material ones. The urban environment was much studied; an interest in model housing was grafted on to an earlier concern with public sanitation. In the 1860s the young Octavia Hill bought up London tenements and supervised their improvement by the tenants from whom she collected the rent. She was much acclaimed and imitated. Here was a new framework for the old work of visiting, showing that it could move with the times: the days of tracts and lozenges were dead and gone; the personal ministrations of the fortunate classes could still provide constructive assistance to the poor and hence to the wider society.

Octavia Hill was one of the founding members of the Charity Organisation Society (often referred to as the COS), which was launched in 1869 in London and soon established branches in Birmingham and many other cities.[45] All historians of social work mark out the society as exerting a formative influence on modern practice, especially with regard to the work and training of home visitors. The Society's organisers claimed a philosophy and method of social work which would abolish the root causes of poverty by means of personal dealings between rich and poor. It was argued that if the poor could be trained to self-sufficiency, and weaned out of habits of dependence and improvidence, they would cease to need the helping hand of either charity or the state. While visiting was an indispensable adjunct to this process, it was now hedged about with reservations and cautions. All help given the poor must be as constructive and character-building as possible; material aid and cash subsidy should figure only as a very last resort; the visitor herself should never be the dispenser of relief, but should concentrate on rigorous investigative casework.

It is hard to agree with the Charity Organisation Society's own estimate of its work as innovatory. Its stated *raison d'être* was the urgent need to systematise and co-ordinate the vast number of competing and overlapping charitable ventures already in existence; similar attempts had been made in 1843, with the founding of the Metropolitan Visiting and Relief Association (MVRA), and again in 1860 with the formation of the Society for the Relief of Distress. Well-documented and reported casework had been a feature both of the MVRA, whose district visitors kept journals and communicated the particulars of all cases to their local committees, and of the earlier Christian Instruction Society.[46] The theories propagated by the COS certainly represented little more than a refurbishing of the 'deterrent' idea of 1834 in the language of the supportive home visitor. As before, people were to be bullied into independence and forced into economic mobility. But the Benthamite philosophy of economic individualism was now married to a time-hallowed philanthropic practice which had originated in the modest desire to 'soothe creation's groans', and had had few pretensions to eradicate their causes.

Unlike her predecessor of the 1850s and 1860s, the COS visitor did not officially espouse a social policy other than that of the state, and exercised no independent influence over the poor. Where a previous generation of philanthropic visitors had exercised their patronage on a stick and carrot basis — with fear of the workhouse balanced by some hope of material assistance — the COS visitor's power would rest mainly on stick. With the hope of material help pushed as far as possible into the background, applicants for any kind of relief were warned that the workhouse was waiting for them if they failed to follow the improving advice they were given. Octavia Hill wrote in 1874 that the connection between parish visitors and the Poor Law system enabled them 'to use with much greater effect and with much greater frequency the lever which distaste for the "house" puts into their hands'.[47] In the same year, C.P. Bosanquet in his *Handy-book for the Visitors of the Poor* instructed his readers:[48]

> Should you meet with persons in receipt of out-door relief who, from incapacity to take care of themselves or for other reasons, would be better off in the Workhouse, you should send word of this to the Relieving Officer. You should do the same if you find that persons receiving out-door relief are in the habit of drinking to excess, begging, or otherwise show themselves unworthy of what unquestionably is a favour.

There is no longer any conflict in principle between voluntary social workers and the officials of the state, and the former were now to provide a sort of free clearing-house service for the latter.

The fact that the COS was continually pressing for this transformation of the voluntary woman visitor into an unpaid handmaiden of the Poor Law authorities does not necessarily mean that it was universally successful. The Society's literature complained of the opposition met with from the ranks of other organisations, whose visitors could not bear to pass a poor household without giving some material aid; from the 'lady from the west end who liked to do a little good one day a week'; and from the mission or biblewomen of the lower classes. A branch secretary in 1903 recalled the early difficulties of the COS in Kent:[49]

> The idea of *inquiry* was particularly terrible, and we were told it was quite unnecessary, when the mission woman 'knew every one so well'. This mission woman was herself no small difficulty, her

spiritual work and relief work having got hopelessly mixed, a state of things which resulted in great deceit and hypocrisy among the cadgers of the parish.

In 1905 a member of the COS Council declared that the battle was only just beginning: 'Before anything could be done to systematise visiting, the occupying forces must either be routed or captured or converted.'[50]

Paradoxically, while advocating the most punitive treatment of those poor who might have the temerity to seek material relief, the Society continued to believe, with an earlier generation of philanthropists, that the mission of the visitor was essentially one of friendship. The precepts of previous generations of visitors were incorporated wholesale, with, for example, the *Lectures to Ladies on Practical Subjects* of 1855 (from which we have quoted the advice of Brewer and Kingsley) featuring on the recommended reading list of C.P. Bosanquet's *Handy-book* of 1874. Hoary injunctions and hoarier hopes were repeated. The function of the visitor was to make friends with the poor, to bridge the gulf between classes. As the representative of the more fortunate classes, the visitor would grace and bring happiness into the life of the poor:[51]

> You, who know so much more than they, might help them so much at important crises of their lives. You might gladden their homes by bringing them flowers, or, better still, by teaching them to grow plants; you might meet them face to face as friends; you might teach them; you might collect their savings; you might sing for and with them; you might take them into the parks, or out for quiet days in the country, in small companies, or to your own or your friends' grounds, or to exhibitions or picture galleries; you might teach and refine them and make them cleaner by merely going among them.

Octavia Hill's *A Few Words to Volunteer Visitors,* written in 1876, breathes the spirit of Mrs Sheppard's *Sunshine in the Workhouse,* published almost 20 years earlier.

Given the claims to pioneering rigour voiced by the COS, this emphasis on intangible and purely personal qualifications for effectual charity is rather startling. It was the corollary of the Society's increasingly hysterical insistence that the question of poverty should be divorced from that of economics, and that the poor must be helped on a personal basis: neither as workers engaged in the class struggle nor as so many units of the electorate or the national work force but essentially as individuals and members of families. Visiting the poor made it possible to continue to focus on the family unit rather than the work place, and subordinate the issue of wages to questions of personal conduct and domestic behaviour; it was the practical expression of the COS's resistance to collectivism and the working-class movement. Octavia Hill extolled 'the great human ground, older than theories of equality, safer than our imaginings of fresh arrangements for the world, and fitter to inspire the noblest and simplest sense of duty'[52] and asked '. . . what is it we look forward to as our people gradually improve? Not, surely, to dealing with them as a class at all, any more than we should tell ourselves off to labour for the middle class, or aristocratic class, or shop-keeping class. Our ideal must be to promote the happy and natural intercourse of neighbours . . .'[53]

The implications for women social workers were conservative in the extreme. The teachings of the 1850s were meted out to a rising generation which had university education and professional appointments in its sights. The rallying cry 'It is in the homes of the poor that you must reach them' demanded social workers' dedication to the notion of home and family as sacrosanct. Women social workers should embody the domestic ideal, and indeed be bound by it; otherwise their work would be self-contradictory, and would cancel itself out. Octavia Hill rejected women social workers' growing demand for professional status with the question: 'how are we to teach and help in the family, if the sacred duties to parents, to brothers and sisters — if the old household claims — seem to us of little moment, and to be easily thrown aside for others?'[54] and drew an explicit connection between an ideology of domesticity in respect of women and of individualism in respect of the poor.

> . . . I have heard persons who give their whole time to the poor speak a little disparagingly of these fleeting visits, and young girls themselves, fevered with desire to do more, talk rather enviously of those who can give their time wholly to such work; but have they ever thought how much is gained by her who is not only a visitor of the poor, but a member of a family with other duties? It is the families, the homes of the poor, that need to be influenced. Is not she most sympathetic, most powerful, who nursed her own mother through the long illness, and knew how to go quietly about the darkened room; who entered so heartily into the sister's love and marriage; who obeyed so perfectly the father's command when it was hardest? Better still if she be wife and mother herself, and can enter into the responsibilities of a head of a household, understand

her joys and cares, knows what heroic patience it needs to keep gentle when the nerves are unhinged and the children noisy. Depend upon it, if we thought of the poor primarily as husbands, wives, sons, and daughters, members of households, as we are ourselves, instead of contemplating them as a different class, we should recognise better how the house training and high ideal of home duty was our best preparation for work among them.[55]

Octavia Hill's anxieties were hardly justified. Her ideal of the unpaid guardian of the hearth acting as the unpaid guardian of the status quo was threatened by the growing movement for women's emancipation; but it was not greatly threatened by the rise of professionalism in social work. True, women were being appointed to public positions, as inspectors of midwives, boarded-out children and so forth; they were also finding more appointments as paid secretaries of voluntary organisations. But the volunteer army was in little danger of being transformed into Regulars. The number of public posts was limited by the exigencies of national and local budgets; and since voluntary women workers *were* available in such large numbers to support the work of public officials, there was no great incentive to increase the number of the latter: witness the single public appointment of an inspector of boarded-out children in 1885 to supervise the work of thousands of voluntary visitors.[56] Unpaid women bore much of the cost, and indeed concealed much of the cost of the measures of state intervention which were adopted before the First World War. They assisted inspectors of midwives in their efforts to instruct mothers in the causes of infant mortality,[57] acted as supervisors where school meals were provided,[58] became visitors for School Care Committees,[59] and performed a host of other functions which nowadays would have a wage attached to them. The introduction of state welfare services was predicated upon the existence of this vast, unpaid work force. Women were recruited as state social workers, but in a manner which confirmed their domestic status and their financial dependence upon men.

Women's Philanthropy and Women's Emancipation

In my title I have described women's philanthropic work as a 'home from home'. Visiting the poor was a practice in part intended to transpose the values of the visitor's home to the working-class environment. The work confirmed the visitor herself in her own domestic role, and prevented her from finding a different status in society. The ideology of domesticity played a vital part in the development of social work, strengthening its conservative functions by treating social problems on an individualistic basis rather than subjecting them to structural and economic analysis. Does it then follow that women's philanthropy was, both for the women themselves and for society in general, a wholly reactionary phenomenon? At least as far as the former are concerned, I think the answer must be no.

There is always a sense in which a missionary is one who leaves home. There were contradictions inherent in the practice of visiting which were fruitful in consequence for the middle-class women's movement of the nineteenth century. In the earliest writing by and about women philanthropists, there is a clearly discernible tension between charitable enterprise and domestic duty. In the 1830s and 1840s 'tea and Bible' ladies were accused of neglecting their homes, and 'thereby causing more moral mischief than all their exertions could eradicate among the poor'.[60] (The implication being that if the existence of a servant class was a necessary condition for philanthropic work it was still not sufficient to lower the claims of husbands and children.) The criticism voiced by less outgoing women seems much like that aimed at the working wives and mothers of today. There was, however, an added dimension to the criticism of nineteenth-century women philanthropists. The outward movement of the visitor, while in one sense designed to strengthen the middle classes by propagating their values in a wider sphere, was in another sense a threat to those classes—many of whom preferred to keep the poor at a safe distance, and had withdrawn to the suburbs for precisely this reason. Women who took up charitable work were tacitly or openly condemning this withdrawal and the growth of a self-contained bourgeois culture. The constant reminders to which visitors were subject, that they must *not* gloss over distinctions of class, reflected the fear that acts of charity might rebound on the charitable by calling the whole structure into question.

A great many of the women who visited the poor in the mid-nineteenth century were anguished by tugs of loyalty between the homes of their birth and the homes of their vocation. Florence Nightingale's agonised struggles to escape the confines of her family home, with its superfluous and contrived 'duties', are well known. This was, in fact, a fairly common struggle of wills and consciences, as is indicated by the movement of the 1850s to establish orders of Anglican deaconesses, intended to provide a safe 'home from home' from which women could with propriety exercise to the full their Christian vocation to social work. Such a solution could hardly hope to find wide acceptability within the ultra-Protestant milieu which produced so many women philanthropists, but its advocates demonstrated how acutely they and their contemporaries experienced the problem of reconciling their family relationships and domestic identity with their work for a wider social good. In the 1890s, women's university settlements fulfilled rather similar functions to these deaconesses' orders.

This conflict between the claims of home and work did not necessarily imply a sense of identity between women social workers and their lower-class sisters. The lady visitor, although she frequently spoke of herself as contributing a distinctive female element to social work, offered help and patronage from a social height which precluded any specific sense of female solidarity. Indeed, with a narrow and instrumental perspective common to middle-class men and women, she often saw the poorer woman as the potential agent of domesticity, the means by which working men might be brought home off the streets, out of the pubs and more into line with their functions as fathers, husbands and sons. The lady visitor therefore put pressure on the poorer woman to increase her obligations and her work-load. The bourgeois concept of family life and the sexual division of labour was propagated no less avidly by the lower-class biblewoman delegated to visit the poor by the lady superintendent. 'Marion B.' ministered to married women in the St Giles parish of London who were occupied in the same way as their husbands, in selling watercresses, fruit, fish and flowers, hare and rabbit skins; and who kept their own earnings from the family hop-picking season in their own hands. Complaining, with their babies in their arms, that they had 'bad husbands', they were told that they were to blame for this and that a wife 'who sits about dirty and idle, and never has a clean hearth or a nice cup of tea for him when he comes in from his work, need not wonder if he goes to the public-house, and spends there in one night what would keep the family for a week'.[62]

Most of the women whom I have quoted in this paper were ardent Christians who espoused deeply conservative political principles; and many were, indeed, explicitly anti-feminist. Nevertheless, the philanthropic impulse which inspired them could not but raise questions of fundamental and even revolutionary importance for women. 'From the very strength of our family instincts', wrote Ellice Hopkins, 'our family selfishness is the hardest thing we have to overcome. The hardest thing is not to give up ourselves, but to give up our dear ones to God, to let them run counter to the world and be talked about, and encounter evil and impurity with only the God we profess to believe in to keep them safe, while they are about their Father's business.' Her biographer indicates the conflict over this issue within Miss Hopkins's own family:

'Having the old ideas as to woman's work, Mrs Hopkins shrank from publicity for women, and was herself very gentle, quiet and domestic. Hence it must often have been a severe trial to her that her daughter should take up work which led her along such thorny roads, and into such a glare of publicity, and even of opprobrium.'[63] Philanthropic enterprise brought wives and daughters to discuss the privatisation of middle-class life and the confinement of women to domestic and familial roles, not in academic journals, but round the fireside, and with fathers, brothers and husbands. Social work of the humblest and least spectacular nature brought to light many of the tensions and contradictions in the roles assigned to women by Victorian middle-class society.

In 1889 Octavia Hill wrote:[64]

Long ago hardly a woman I knew had any opportunity of devoting time to any grave or kindly work beyond her own household or small social circle. Now there are thousands who achieve it, in spite of interruptions and difficulties in settling to steady work; and there are comparatively few parents who do not recognise for their daughters the duty of sympathy and of rendering such service as other claims permit. With the different ideal of life, customs have altered in a marked manner; it used to be difficult for a girl to walk alone, and it was considered almost impossible for her to travel in omnibuses or third-class trains. The changes in custom with regard to such matters have opened out fresh possibilities of work.

It may be argued that the practice of visiting in the nineteenth century has merely opened out fresh possibilities of visiting in the twentieth; that women's philanthropy gave employment opportunities for a very few women at a relatively low level of welfare work; and that it helped to divide women from each other. Emancipation is a movement made up of many, sometimes opposing currents. We have seen that women visitors of the poor were conscious of advancing themselves to functions in society which were being vacated by men of their own class. Their personal influence, with that of their class, was threatened first by the changing social composition of the cities in the early decades of the nineteenth century, and then by the extension of the male suffrage after 1867. Their initiatives were therefore both progressive *and* reactionary: progressive in that they were reaching out for more power for women; and reactionary in that they sought to prevent that power from passing from a restricted social group to a wider one. In this, if not in many other particulars, they resembled many of the middle-class suffragettes; we must leave as an open question how far they resemble either the feminists or the social workers of the present day.

Notes

I wish to thank Jill Liddington, Tim Mason and Raphael Samuel for their advice and comments on the first draft of this paper; they bear no responsibility, of course, for the outcome.

1. Angela Burdett-Coutts (ed), *Woman's Mission* (London, Samson Low and Marston, 1893), pp. 361-2.
2. H.C. Irvine, *A Short History of the Old D.P.S. 1833-1933* (Manchester, Manchester and Salford DPS, 1933), pp. 9-12; *Register of Charity Organisation and Related Societies in correspondence with the London Charity Organisation Society* (London, Charity Organisation Society, 1893), p. 29.
3. A.F. Young and E.T. Ashton, *British Social Work in the Nineteenth Century* (London, Routledge and Kegan Paul, 1956), pp. 88-9.
4. Rev. J.C. Pringle, *Social Work of the London Churches* (London, Oxford University Press, 1937), p. 182.
5. *The Charity Organisation Review* (London, Longmans, Green & Co., December 1905), pp. 305-6.
6. Pringle, *Social Work*, p. 226.
7. K. Heasman, *Evangelicals in Action* (London, Geoffrey Bles, 1962), p. 36; LNR (Mrs Ranyard), *The Missing Link* (London, James Nisbet, 1859), pp. 11-15, 28-31.
8. L.E. O'Rorke, *The Life and Friendships of Catherine Marsh* (London, Longmans, Green & Co., 1917), pp. 133-4.
9. W.R. Ward, *Religion and Society in England, 1790-1850* (London, Batsford, 1972), p. 9.
10. G. Kitson Clark, *Churchmen and the Condition of England 1832-1885* (London, Methuen, 1973), p. 196.
11. Ward, *Religion and Society*, p. 47.
12. E.F. Rathbone, *William Rathbone* (London, Macmillan, 1905), p. 56.
13. Louisa Twining, *Recollections of Life and Work* (London, Edward Arnold, 1893), pp. 25-6.
14. Rev. J.M.J. Fletcher, *Mrs Wightman of Shrewsbury* (London, Longmans, Green & Co., 1906), p. 53.
15. Sarah Trimmer, *The OEconomy of Charity* (London, T. Longman, 1801), vol. II, pp. 57-8.
16. Rev. Charles Kingsley, 'The Country Parish', in Rev F.D. Maurice (ed), *Lectures to Ladies on Practical Subjects* (Cambridge, Macmillan, 1855), pp. 55-6. Maurice was the chief founder of the London Working Men's College in 1854. These lectures were delivered there as part of a 'Plan of a Female College for the Help of the Rich and the Poor'. Maurice's theories of 'Christian Socialism' were influential within a clerical and literary circle which included Kingsley, Ruskin, Louisa Twining and Octavia Hill.
17. M. Simey, *Charitable Effort in Liverpool* (Liverpool, Liverpool University Press, 1951), pp. 21, 63.
18. Simey, ibid., p. 62; F. R. Prokaschka, 'Women in English Philanthropy 1790-1830', *International Review of Social History*, vol. XIX, part 3, 1974, pp. 434-9. See also J. Jean Hecht, *The Domestic Servant Class in Eighteenth*

Century England (London, Routledge and Kegan Paul, 1956), and D. Marshall, *The English Domestic Servant in History* (London, Historical Association, 1949).

19. Brian Harrison, *Drink and the Victorians* (London, Faber and Faber, 1971), p. 40.

20. Prokaschka, 'Women in English Philanthropy', p. 434.

21. Rev. J.S. Brewer, 'Workhouse Visiting' in Maurice, *Letters to Ladies*, pp. 273-7.

22. Kingsley, 'The Country Parish', in Maurice, ibid., p. 58; Fletcher, *Mrs Wightman*, p. 80; R.M. Barrett, *Ellice Hopkins* (London, Wells and Gardner, 1907), p. 17.

23. Fletcher, *Mrs Wightman*, p. 81.

24. Kingsley, 'The Country Parish', p. 64.

25. Kingsley, ibid., p. 63; C.P. Bosanquet, *A Handy-Book for the Visitor of the Poor in London* (London, Longmans, Green, Reader and Dyer, 1874), p. 17.

26. O'Rorke, *Life and Friendships*, pp. 133-4; Kingsley, 'The Country Parish', p. 62.

27. Lois, *Pleas for those who Greatly Need Them: Three Letters on Helping and Visiting the Poor. Addressed to a Lady* (London, W. Mackintosh, 1869), pp. 30-1.

28. Brewer, 'Workhouse Visiting', in Maurice, *Lectures to Ladies*, p. 264.

29. LNR, *The Missing Link*, pp. 276, 269.

30. It seems that neither before nor after the 1834 Act were women visitors officially barred from workhouses: see Trimmer, *The OEconomy of Charity*, vol. II, p. 56; their admission was entirely at the discretion of the all-male Board of Guardians of each individual Poor Law Union. As is known from the career of Elizabeth Fry, women visited prisons from the early years of the nineteenth century.

31. E. Twining, *Leaves from the Notebook of Elizabeth Twining* (London, W. Tweedie, 1877), p. 82; Louisa Twining, *Recollections of Workhouse Visiting and Management* (London, C. Kegan Paul, 1880), Appendix I, pp. 91-2.

32. A particularly helpful collection of recent papers is D. Fraser (ed), *The New Poor Law in the Nineteenth Century* (London, Macmillan, 1976).

33. Louisa Twining, *Recollections*, Appendix VI, p. 192; and p. 76.

34. Bosanquet, *Handy-Book*, p. 23.

35. O. Hill, 'A Word on Good Citizenship', in O. Hill, *Our Common Land* (London, Macmillan, 1877), p. 102.

36. E.M. Ross, 'Women and Poor Law Administration 1857-1909', unpublished MA thesis, London University, 1956, pp. 217-18; on most Boards, the women Guardians were of a higher social class than the men.

37. Mrs G.W. Sheppard, *Sunshine in the Workhouse* (London, James Nisbet, 1859), pp. 26-30; Louisa Twining, *Recollections of Life and Work*, pp. 179, 190; *Dictionary of National Biography*, vol. XIX, p. 1315 (London, Smith and Elder, 1909), entry for Richard Twining.

38. Quoted in F.D. Hill, *Children of the State* (London, Macmillan, 1868), p. 190.

39. Ross, 'Women and Poor Law Administration', pp. 175, 233.

40. F.D. Hill and F. Fowke, *Children of the State* (London, Macmillan, 1889), pp. 182-4.

41. Young and Ashton, *British Social Work*, p. 137.

42. Ross, 'Women and Poor Law Administration', p. 246.

43. Hill and Fowke, *Children of the State*, pp. 205-6.

44. Pringle, *Social Work*, pp. 191-3.

45. On the COS see H. Bosanquet, *Social Work in London 1869 to 1912*

(London, John Murray, 1914); C.L. Mowat, *The Charity Organisation Society, 1869-1913* (London, Methuen, 1961); D. Owen, *English Philanthropy* (London, Oxford University Press, 1965), pp. 215-47.

46. Pringle, *Social Work*, pp. 184-6; Young and Ashton, *British Social Work*, pp. 88-9.

47. Parliamentary Papers, 1874, xxv, O. Hill, Report of 10 January 1874 in the Third Annual Report of the Local Government Board, 1873-4, Appendix 12, p. 128.

48. Bosanquet, *Handy-Book*, p. 24.

49. *The Charity Organisation Review*, December 1903, pp. 58-9.

50. Ibid., August 1905, p. 175.

51. O. Hill, 'A Few Words to Volunteer Visitors among the Poor', in *Our Common Land*, pp. 59-60.

52. O. Hill, 'Trained Workers for the Poor', *The Nineteenth Century*, January 1893, p. 38.

53. O. Hill, 'District Visiting', in *Our Common Land*, p. 26.

54. O. Hill, 'Trained Workers for the Poor', p. 37.

55. O. Hill, 'District Visiting', pp. 24-5.

56. Ross, 'Women and Poor Law Administration', pp. 250-1.

57. Mary Leslie, *Through Changing Scenes* (Beaconsfield, Mary Leslie, 1972), p. 60; Anna Davin, 'Imperialism and the Cult of Motherhood', *History Workshop Journal*, no. 5, Spring 1978, pp. 1-60; L.V. Shairp, 'Leeds' in Mrs B. Bosanquet (ed), *Social Conditions in Provincial Towns* (London, Macmillan, 1912), pp. 75-6.

58. F.G. D'Aeth, 'Liverpool' in Mrs B. Bosanquet, ibid., p. 44; E.H. Kelly, 'Portsmouth', ibid., p. 10.

59. Pringle, *Social Work*, p. 226.

60. Prokaschka, 'Women in English Philanthropy', p. 436; I. Bradley, *The Call to Seriousness* (London, Jonathan Cape, 1976), p. 151.

61. Fletcher, *Mrs Wightman*, p. 81.

62. LNR, *The Missing Link*, pp. 34-5.

63. Barrett, *Ellice Hopkins*, p. 23.

64. O. Hill, 'A Few Words to Fresh Workers', *The Nineteenth Century*, September 1889, p. 454.

3 THE SEPARATION OF HOME AND WORK? LANDLADIES AND LODGERS IN NINETEENTH- AND TWENTIETH-CENTURY ENGLAND

Leonore Davidoff

There is a long-standing belief that urbanisation and industrialisation necessitated the 'separation of home and work'. It can be argued, however, that this division as we now know it was not simply the inevitable result of technological developments or even a side effect of the emergence of first a bourgeoisie and then the working class. On the contrary, particularly in the period 1780 to 1850, the definition of masculinity and femininity, together with their social location in work and home, became an arena of conflict.[1] The process of redefinition was taking place throughout the society, although it was interpreted in different ways by different class groups.

It was undoubtedly the urban middle class who were the most zealous in promoting the separation of spheres, proseletyzing their message to both the upper and developing working classes. The central belief that emerged during this period was that of a male breadwinner gaining a livelihood through work and maintaining his female (and child) dependants within the home, as well as representing them in political activities appropriate to his station. In this view, husband and wife were the archetype, but father and child, brother and sister, uncle and niece, master and servant reproduced the relationships of clientage and dependency. These expectations were not only themes in contemporary commentaries; they were embodied in important new legal codes such as the Poor Law of 1834.

Historians have tended to accept the prescriptive literature on the separation of spheres and the domestic ideal as a description of reality, partly because the sources for historical analysis are cast in these terms.[2] But it is equally necessary to ask what people were actually doing, how and where they were living, and whom they were living with.[3]

Whatever the expectations within the domestic ideal, in an increasingly urban as well as cash-dominated society, women had to find ways to earn income in lieu of or in addition to support from father, husband or other male relatives. Family ties precluded residential domestic service except for the young and single. Factory work was often problematic,

64

both practically and morally, and in many areas simply not available. One alternative was outwork — from squalid, miserably-paid fur-pulling, matchbox making, etc., to respectable work such as tinting Christmas cards. The other major sources of income were activities like casual cleaning, child minding, washing in other people's homes, taking in washing into their own homes or providing houseroom and domestic services to lodgers and boarders. In the middle class, similar strategies included becoming companion to an older woman or resident teacher of young children. For all classes of women, these surrogate family activities could contain maternal or sexual elements, evident in roles as diverse as housekeeper or prostitute. It could be argued that these marginal activities were part of an inevitable 'transitional' stage of the economy, on the way to a more clearly demarcated and rationalised labour system. But such sweeping and deterministic assertions often obscure many times and places where the outcome was by no means certain. By looking at one of these activities — the provision of lodging and boarding[4] — it should be possible to throw some light on the formation of both gender and class divisions.

Landladies, Lodgers and Social Observers

Historians, as well as other social commentators, have tended to regard lodging as an insignificant phenomenon in recent history. When they have noticed it at all, it has been treated primarily as a housing category. Urban sociologists, following social investigators of the late nineteenth and early twentieth century, have equated the existence of boarding and lodging with urban decay, a practice often located in a 'twilight zone' within the city.[5] Family sociologists have confirmed this picture. 'The demonology of boarding is characteristic of the entire theory of family breakdown under the impact of industrialisation and urbanisation.'[6]

Recently this view has been challenged by both urban and family historians who have seen lodging as a housing arrangement particularly suited to migrants[7] and as a phase in the family life-cycle.[8] According to the most detailed study of boarding and lodging to date, this type of living arrangement contributes to the conclusion that under the impact of industrialisation, 'the family was not fragile, but malleable'.[9]

While this perspective has added greatly to the understanding of family patterns and urban development, it still suffers from the disadvantage of seeing the family as a unit interacting functionally with the economy in a process of 'modernisation'.[10] Although divisions within the family are recognised, there is a prior assumption of equality between all family (and household) members. This assumption, in turn, underlies the rational choice models which are used in these studies.[11] It is significant that, within this framework, the Haraven and Modell study of boarding and lodging reproduces the division between home and work by explicitly excluding boarding and lodging *houses* from their discussion and in this they follow other historians.[12] This exclusion limits the historical analysis even before it begins.

Recent Marxist theory, too, emphasises the boundary between domestic and socialised labour (wage work). Indeed, the whole notion of 'domestic labour' is premised on the existence of a fully developed system of capitalist enterprise with a proletariat (who is included in that term is immaterial for this argument) living in nuclear family homes run by housewives. In this way, the 'domestic labour debate'[13] as a whole seems to be not only ahistorical but couched at a level of abstraction which must overlook the intermediate forms of enterprise where women were so often located.[14]

Similarly, it is becoming evident that an analysis based on individual occupations, as in the concept of 'occupational segregation', also takes the division between home and work, the private and the public, as given.[15] 'The emphasis . . . is on the structure of the labour market and the question of men and women's place in the family in this paper is relegated to the status of an explanatory factor.'[16]

In both schemes, all activities carried out within the home are assumed to be for consumption by the family. The women who do this work are not directly related to 'the economy', since the economy by this definition is located *outside* the home. The conceptual limitations of this division between the labour market and the home are clear when trying to analyse a situation such as residential domestic service: the largest single occupation for women, numbering over 1,000,000 well into the 1930s. This activity was viewed by employers as familial (and therefore particularly suitable for young women). Servants, on the other hand, despite the fact that they were performing domestic tasks in a domestic setting, stressed that they were selling their labour as in any other occupation, and where possible they rejected the paternalistic features of the situation. This divergence should prompt us to enquire what kind of an organisation this entity called a household was, and what were its goals?

Such an approach is akin to the analysis of the form and size of the enterprise in the analysis of the Third World today.[17] As in these countries now, in nineteenth-century England it was not at all clear whether subsidiary household tasks were for producing a profit. Nor, in fact, was it clear that members of the household regarded themselves as engaged in profit-making activities. Rather, an activity such as the housing and feeding of lodgers can be understood as a kind of subsistence employment, one of a variety of forms of labour existing side by side or even carried on by the same people: a way of life, as much as making a living.

The creators of the census in the nineteenth century were aware of the contradictions in dealing with domestic activities. Some discussion of this problem can be found in the introduction to every decennial census. In the development of the census over the century, statistical categories were successively changed in the direction of a stricter demarcation between domestic and market activities. New instructions in 1911 tried once and for all to eliminate the ambiguity with regard to the occupations of women:

> The occupations of women engaged in any business or profession including women regularly engaged in assisting relatives in trade or business must be fully stated. No entry should be made in the case of wives, daughters or other female relatives wholly engaged in domestic duties at home.[18]

The ambiguities in the position of those people performing these domestic duties, however, presented even greater difficulties. For several decades Class II was the Domestic Class of the occupational census, subdivided into Orders 4 and 5:

> The persons in this class are all employed, if they are employed at all, in houses. Some supply simply service, others with it supply board and lodging. They are paid wages (servants) or they are paid for the board and lodging and attendance they supply (inn-keepers, etc). Wives perform at home for the bulk of the population the same kind of duties as persons in Order 5 perform, but they are not paid directly in money for their services as they form a part of the natural family, and consequently they are distinguished in a separate Order 4, ...The Fourth Order consists entirely of women; it embraces the majority of the women engaged in the most useful of all occupations, that of wife, mother and mistress of a family . . . and includes daughters of 15 and upwards at home.[19]

The implication of this statement is that within the family these activities are carried out only by women.[20] In turn, one of the results of such a definition was the construction of a concept: 'the natural family'.[21]

Lodging, Boarding and the Domestic Ideal

There have always been strangers or 'sojourners' living with the basic nuclear family, although the definition of who belongs to this category has varied. In the seventeenth century an elderly yeoman explained that 'his wife being dead and his children grown up, he now lived as a soujourner with one of his sonnes'.[22] In eighteenth-century London, rented furnished rooms probably formed the main type of housing; an arrangement which shaded off into the 1d per night common lodging house, lowest in the finely graded social scale of housing. This 'custom was by no means confined to the poorer sort; there were furnished lodgings for all classes and the letting of lodgings was a great industry, besides being, as Adam Smith pointed out, a by-industry of London shop keepers'.[23] The importance of this living arrangement increased as the custom of having living-in farm servants and apprentices slowly died out. This involved not just a change in housing, but an important shift in authority patterns. 'With the breakdown of the paternalistic practice of apprentices living in their master's houses in the late 18th century, the number of lodgers living in a household but not under the control of its head must have increased considerably.'[24] This shift was part of the substitution of cash payments for labour, instead of paying by providing training and payment in kind. While it appealed to the theorists of political economy, in practice many middle-class house-holders feared the consequences.

From that period on, lodging and boarding began to carry moral opprobrium. On the part of both lodger and householder it came to be considered a necessary evil and a sign of the loss of genteel status. In memoirs, novels and official reports alike there are ambiguous, mostly negative reactions to the practice. George Gissing, the lower-middle-class novelist, was particularly attuned to the social meaning of living arrangements. In his novel, *In the Year of the Jubilee,* Mary Woodruff is the ex-servant of the main character, Mrs Nancy Tarrant. Mary has been left a small income by a former master and rents an unfurnished house in Harrow-on-the-Hill. She lets the two front rooms furnished to Nancy Tarrant, who is living with her child, apart from her husband. While Nancy writes her novel, Mary takes care of the child and much of the housework is done by a very young residential servant kept by Mary. Nancy Tarrant was considered a lodger, in Gissing's words 'seeing that she paid a specified weekly sum for her shelter and maintenance; in no other respect could the wretched title apply to her. To occupy furnished lodgings is to live in a house owned and ruled by servants; the least tolerable status known to civilisation.'[25]

Taking in lodgers acted as a social indicator throughout the nineteenth and early twentieth century. The daughter of an ex-nursemaid married to the manager of a grocery shop remembers how her mother's experience in genteel service meant that her own childhood was dominated by ideas of respectability which kept her family very isolated. She and her siblings were not allowed to play with the children of a neighbouring family that took in lodgers, even though the family was materially better off than her own.[26]

In reality, the ability to take in lodgers on a regular basis and provide even basic services for them could only be managed at a certain level of income and organisation. This was at least tacitly recognised within the working class, where the condemnation of lodging was by no means widespread. In fact, the decline of an area in Camberwell from 1871 to 1881 is characterised by the fall in the proportion of households with lodgers, from 15 per cent to 4 per cent. 'Few indexes of poverty and overcrowding could conceivably be more significant than the inability to sub-let even sleeping room.'[27]

Middle-class failure to recognise this fact, and disapproval of lodgers who were less firmly under the control of the head of the household than apprentices had been, do not, however, explain why there was such a change in middle-class acceptance of the practice in the early nineteenth century. Nor was it simply a recognition of the sanitary and medical effects of overcrowding. Admittedly, in the eighteenth century in the middle class 'it was a matter of custom that the family lived in two rooms and rented out any excess space as furnished lodgings. The cramped way of life of the comfortably-off classes is illustrated by the popularity of beds concealed in various articles of furniture . . . .All classes lived so much at coffee-houses, ale houses or clubs that house-room was a secondary consideration. The necessary 'good address' was provided by the coffee house or tavern.'[28] But at the end of the eighteenth century a new consciousness of privacy began to be stressed — a privacy which would keep the family inviolate behind the walls of the home.[29] As the Registrar General said in the introduction to the Census of 1851: 'The possession of an entire house is strongly desired by every Englishman; for it throws a sharp well-defined circle round his family and hearth — the shrine of his sorrows, joys and meditations.'[30]

Living in lodgings, then, with its sharing of part of someone else's house, was a sign that the family could no longer be kept private and implied a loss of caste. In a mid-century tract, when loss of income forces two spinster sisters to live in lodgings, the elder admonishes her sister to resignation: 'Look at all the comforts we have in these respectable lodgings where we can be all by ourselves' and the sisters have stipulated (improbably) that the couple with whom they lodge shall not take any other lodgers with whom they would have to mix.[31] Mrs Craik, the author of the best seller, *John Halifax, Gentleman,* summed up this repugnance when one of her characters says:

> . . . not temporarily, but permanently sitting down to make one's only 'home' in Mrs Jones's parlour or Mrs Smith's first-floor, of which not a stick or a stone that one looks at is one's own . . . .To people with family feeling living in lodgings is about the saddest life under the sun.[32]

Privacy was necessary for genteel status because it kept 'the family' free from the taint of the market place. If family relationships became commercialised, there would be no way of maintaining the careful facade of strict sexual divisions and, by extension, no way of enforcing sex and age hierarchies. For both men and women, the fear was that all the vaunted domestic felicities might not in reality stand up to the temptations of being able to live in situations where cash could buy most, if not all, of the 'comforts of home' without assuming the long-term obligations and emotional entanglements of marriage and domesticity.

Since men had both greater freedom of action and greater financial resources, the pull of independence which such an arrangement promised was more threatening for them. The definition of masculinity which stressed the responsibilities of the male breadwinner also had an escape clause which maintained that the 'natural inclinations' of the male could, at least occasionally, allow him to slough off these responsibilities with impunity. The way this masculine prerogative operated across classes is brought out in Booth's discussion of common lodging houses in London:

> The provision to be found in the Metropolis for those who are 'homeless' — or perhaps it would be more accurate to say, those who enjoy no family life — has a wide range. From the luxury of the West End residential club to the 'fourpenny doss' of Bangor Street is but a matter of degree. The club loafer of Piccadilly or Hyde Park Corner, and the unkempt and ill-clad vagabond sleeping away the summer day on the grass of St James Park, are often influenced by much the

same desire — to attain the advantages of the associated life without the cares of housekeeping — and the election which the one has to undergo to pass a 'clubable' man finds its counterpart in the unwritten law which makes certain common lodging houses accessible only to the 'game'uns'.[33]

The idea that lodging was an evil, although possibly a necessary one, acted as a powerful force in middle-class attitudes towards working-class housing and living arrangements. The necessities of working-class life, as well as its cultural traditions, resulted in a great deal of mobility and flexibility in living arrangements of a kind incomprehensible, if not downright immoral, in middle-class eyes. The extent to which people lived 'on the road', even slept out in the open despite the English climate, is hard for us from a twentieth-century vantage point to understand; it was a practice hounded by the authorities throughout the period.[34] This mobility implied a casualness of relationships, the mixing of age, sex and social groups which was also viewed with revulsion by Victorian middle-class observers who were hypersensitive to social boundaries. The drive to eliminate all forms of living arrange-ments except the nuclear family (with servants) was, then, in part a continual effort to strengthen current definitions of masculinity and femininity, to separate sexual as well as class groups. Given this context, it is not really surprising that one of the first and most punitory inter-ventionist pieces of Victorian legislation was the Common Lodging Houses Act of the early 1850s (subsequently modified by later legislation). The immediate aim of these acts was to control both the sanitary and moral living conditions of this mobile population; particularly in the large cities, the 'working of an Act of Parliament reaching to the homes and health of the people benevolently intruding on their habits . . .'[35]

One of the main reasons put forward for the introduction of this legislation was to control the problem of overcrowding that undoubtedly existed in the fast-growing cities of the early Victorian period. However, as in much subsequent nineteenth-century housing legislation, over-crowding was often understood as synonymous with taking in lodgers. In evidence taken from Birmingham, for example, a witness reported that 'there has never been any serious overcrowding within the limits of the borough. The habits of the people are to have separate houses; they do not to any very considerable extent take in lodgers.'[36] This view is similar to the opinion held in America, where social observers 'explain the dangers of overcrowding just as though biologically related persons required less space than unrelated individuals. Social, not physical, space was the question.'[37] In reality, crowded living conditions were directly related to low wages and the condition of the labour market.[38]

The Common Lodging House legislation gave specially appointed agents of the Metropolitan police (and soon afterwards their provincial counterparts) the right of entry and search at any time of the day or night to check on the numbers of people sleeping in a house, the sanitary state of the building and the mixing of the sexes in sleeping arrangements. Lodging houses were seen as 'the great source of contagious and loathsome diseases, the hot-beds of crime and moral depravity' in the words of Captain Hay, one of the most assiduous of the commissioners, who used 2 a.m. raids to catch his elusive quarry.[39] Ironically, the overcrowding which was believed to be caused by lodging was really feared because it, in turn, was believed to lead to incest, a preoccupation of middle-class Victorians, although one which was seldom openly acknowledged.[40] In an inspection by the special police it was reported that 'in many cases the law is no doubt evaded; lodgers and landlord falsely asserting relationship of parties occupying the same room . . . Where such relationships really exist and many adults are herded together night and day, in the narrowest limits, all decency must be lost and frightful evil is the consequence.'[41]

Since the private home was sacrosanct by both law and custom, this type of draconian measure could only be taken against what were presumed to be the larger lodging houses. But no definition of a Common Lodging House was ever laid down, so that people taking in lodgers might find themselves open to inspection and regulation. It was quite clear, however, as with much other interventionist legislation, that the authorities had specific groups in mind:

> The opinion of the law officers of the Crown with regard to lodging houses does not give any definite idea as to what constitutes a common lodging house and we have very great difficulty in discriminating. All they said was that private hotels and houses to let to the upper and middle classes do not come within the provisions of the Act.[42]

It was where paternalistic schemes existed, often with additional controls through tied housing, that the prohibition against lodgers could be most effectively enforced. On the Duke of Cleveland's estate, where 500 cottages were let to lead miners, lodgers were not permitted

and the bailiff informed the agent if anyone went into lodgings. The
Duke of Bedford owned 1,830 cottages on his estates, which were
inspected annually. Where there was room to spare, and with permission, a lodger could be taken.[43]

Lodging, in fact, is an excellent illustration of a familiar Victorian
dilemma where moral commitments and the wish to control the lives
of the working class ran counter to the free play of market forces.
At the start of the large-scale municipal housing programmes after
the First World War, this contradiction was brought out into the
open:

> House room is a commercial commodity and in the absence of
> express restrictions its conversion at the will of the possessor into
> money or money's worth can hardly occasion comment. But the
> free exercise of any such right is presumably contrary to the intention
> of municipal housing estates . . . .[44]

The prohibition or, at least, regulation of lodging was regarded as only
a partial solution. As with many other Victorian social problems,
proscription was to be softened by charity. Model lodging houses were
to be built on land donated by the municipality, the best-known of
these schemes being the Lord Rowton Houses for homeless men in
London. Permissive legislation passed in 1851 — the Labouring Classes
Lodging Houses Act — conferred on local authorities the power to
borrow money on the rates and apply it to the erection of lodging
houses; in effect the earliest form of municipal housing in Britain.[45]
While some authorities did take up this option, most did not, and many
of those who did ended up providing single family units.[46] The truth
was that private enterprise could not provide sufficient housing for the
population, and lodging was a sensible, flexible arrangement, no matter
how it outraged middle-class sensibilities.[47]

Both municipal and charity schemes were deliberately aimed at the
'casualities' — those considered to be outside the ideal family structure.
They were never intended to be an alternative living arrangement, and
many of them had punitive regulations which made them all too
reminiscent of that ultimate lodging place — the workhouse. Their
character is also reflected in the fact that many more places were
provided for men than for women and children.

Indeed, by now it should come as no surprise to discover that
women and girls in lodgings were considered even more reprehensible
than men. There was an expectation that girls should be living at home

under the control of their parents, or in domestic service under control of their employers.[48] Part of the distaste for factory work for girls was that it often meant they had to go into lodgings to be near their work and thus, in Dr Barnardo's words, developed that 'precocious independence' so inimical to home life.

In Nottingham in the 1880s, when lace work began to offer increased employment for girls, there were schemes to lay on special trams to take them to lodgings in the suburbs. There was such a public outcry against this in the town that employers and philanthropists joined in building about ten barrack-like Homes for Working Girls in the city centre.[49] Even where it was recognised that such housing must be provided, attempts were made to domesticate the inmates. The Duchess of Marlborough, addressing the National Conference on Lodging House Accommodation for Women, stressed the need for providing moral and hygienic lodgings for women and girls, with someone on the premises to teach the duties of home life and motherhood in such surroundings.[50] Some felt, however, that such girls should be urged to 'start earning their own living by domestic service rather than in the precarious employment of the mill and factory' for 'any arrangement which, by supplying cheap accommodation encourages young women to leave the shelter, however poor, of their own home and offers them an opportunity of living without any restrictions or oversight . . . exercises a decidedly harmful influence'.[51]

The Problem of Definition

Before going on to discuss the practice of lodging in detail, three points about Victorian and Edwardian living arrangements must be understood. First, pre-industrial patterns of production and service included the bringing of raw materials to the craftsman by the customer, to be made up or finished. So also in lodgings, many people provided their own food, even fuel, either to cook for themselves or have others cook it. Fires were lighted in any hearth in the house, not just for heat but to make tea, toast or even meals. Artifacts such as toasting forks, wash stands to which water had to be carried, chamber pots which had to be emptied, show that the division of function and space within the house was not yet entirely fixed. This was true for all levels of society. The poor would cook wherever they could get access to a fire; hence the large communal kitchens in common lodging houses. (This also goes part of the way to explain the intense dislike of the workhouse practice of ladelling out the 'skilly' [gruel] individually to the inmates, giving them no choice or control of their diet.) The wealthy too could have cooking and serving done for them in their own 'rooms' when in lodgings or in inns (the forerunner to room service). They could provide their own linen, plate, etc., as well as bringing their own servants to wait on them, providing they could afford to pay for their keep. On census night in 1871, the Clifton Ville Hotel in Margate had 32 adult and 4 child guests. They were waited on by 42 servants, 11 of whom had been brought as private servants by the guests.[52] Further, middle-class families and individuals expected – and could pay for – an extraordinarily wide range of services from working-class people, particularly women and children, much in the manner of Third World countries today. This was the day-to-day face of class interaction, in the street as well as in the home. These were not just regular domestic services, but casual errand running, lifting and carrying everything from luggage to messages. Working-class people's *time* as well as labour was at their disposal.

In a similar manner, so too were the facilities of working-class homes. Many middle-class people felt that they had the right to enquire into the lives and enter the homes of the working class in the name of charity; how much more they assumed service and attention on working-class premises if payment were offered. For example, a French mid-century tourist explained how, on leaving London by train for an excursion to the country, he got out impulsively in a small village. He stopped on the edge of the common and knocked on a door at random. He was shown by the woman of the house into a 'modest room but very well furnished. "If monsieur needs a little apartment this parlour and one or two rooms are free." Climbing the stairs she showed me a bedroom as fresh and comely as the parlour. "How much do you want for them and will you be able to feed me?" "Yes", she said "22 shillings per week for board and room and I promise you that you will be satisfied".' He decided to stay several weeks 'in this solitude'.[53]

Note that some of the great social investigators of the late nineteenth and early twentieth century made full use of this prerogative. Charles Booth made a regular practice of living in working-class lodgings in the East End, proclaiming that he preferred their diet and timetable to the upper-middle-class routine of his own nine-servant establishment.[54] George Orwell, Stephen Reynolds and others used lodgings for shorter or longer periods to give flavour, favourable or otherwise, to their commentaries on working-class life. Intellectuals like E.M. Forster, among many others, could dip into working-class culture in this way, believing that they understood it from the inside. Note, too, that almost all these examples are single males who could use the freedom and flexibility of lodging to its greatest advantage.

Finally, the division of the sexes and the creation of a special domestic sphere with higher standards of cooking, cleaning, laundry and mending, had promoted male expectations of being 'serviced' by women; not only by mothers and wives, but also daughters, sisters, nieces, aunts, cousins, female servants and even neighbours. Hence the colloquial phrase that has now almost completely disappeared: 'to *do'* for someone.[55] Unless a man was living at home with his mother, or married, or employing paid servants, enquiry would be made about his living arrangements: 'who does for him?'. In extreme conditions, for example, as a widower, a man could 'do' for himself and even his children, but this was felt to be an unnatural arrangement. When Hannah Munby's aunt died, a cousin of hers who had been a lady's maid in London had to give up her place and go back to Shropshire to 'do' for her uncle, as he could not look after himself.[56] This element of personal female service is crucial in understanding the special relationship of landladies (and their servants) to boarders and lodgers. For lodging was in some ways only semi-commercialised. Note for example, the connotations of the word *landlord* (one who owns property and collects rent) as compared to *landlady* (one who, usually living on the premises, provides houseroom and services for cash). Such a relationship, just as in domestic services, could include covert sexual services. There was, after all, a deeply rooted expectation that any man living with a woman would provide support, as a husband did, in return for services; the position of housekeeper very easily ran into common-law wife.[57] Some Poor Law Unions, in fact, imposed a rule under which no woman receiving outdoor relief could take in a *male* lodger without permission from the relief committee.[58]

It is not surprising, therefore, that not only the Special Commissioners of the Metropolitan Police found difficulty in defining the categories *lodger* and *boarder*. Historians, too, have been known to give up the attempt and list them as 'residuals', together with visitors, etc., in their analysis of household structure.[59] 'There are two problems here. One is to overcome the varying practice of the [census] enumerators in discriminating between lodgers and either tenants or independent households at the same address . . . .The second problem in classifying lodgers is more fundamental. When is a lodger not a lodger?'[60]

Nevertheless, ambiguities, which might appear to be a methodological disaster, especially when using statistical sources such as the census, may point to important historical insights. For example, the confusion in the census between *visitor* and *lodger* is revealing. When Hannah

Munby, general servant, was not employed, she would move in with friends for a few days or weeks and help to pay for food in cash and/or do extra cleaning, wash curtains or whitewash a scullery, in return for her keep. But when she was in a town where she had no friends, she lived for a while on exactly the same basis with a woman whose house she had found simply by knocking on the door.[61]

The problem of definition in the nineteenth century was partly a creation of the Registrar General's Office itself. The basic unit in the census was taken to be the family, whatever actual living arrangements may have been, for example, kin who paid cash for services, house sharing by kin, unrelated people or even fictive kin.[62] From the beginning of the census, the convention was adopted that boarders were part of the family of the occupier but lodgers were to be counted as single families having their own separate census schedule:

> The family in its complete form consists of a householder with his wife and his children; and in the higher classes with his servants. Other relatives and visitors sometimes form a part of the family; and so do lodgers at a common table who pay for their subsistence and lodging [e.g. boarders].[63]

Enumerators would persist, however, in confusing the two, as well as being inconsistent among themselves. Reviewing the situation in 1851, the Registrar General observed gloomily:

> Mr Rickman (the first Registrar General) adverts to the difficulty of defining in an Act of Parliament, the degree of connection between the head of a family and lodgers who reside under the same roof. For in the Census of 1831 it had been stated that: 'those who use the same kitchen and board together are to be deemed members of the same family. But he (Rickman) proceeds to say, 'even then remains the question whether a single person inhabiting a house solely, or lodging, but not boarding, in another man's house is to be deemed a family. This admits only of an unsatisfactory reply 'that it cannot be otherwise' and by this negative paralogism is decided in the affirmative'. A lodger, then, who did not board in the house in which he lived, was by this decision 'a family'. Whether a family can be constituted by a person who lives alone in a house or a lodger who either boards in a family or only occupies the chamber in which he sleeps and, as in Paris or London, lives in the daytime at coffee houses, clubs or other places, may be disputed.[64]

This period, when the shape of the private household was thus being officially defined, was also the time when large institutional units were being created for all those who did not come under the domestic rubric: workhouses, hospitals, orphanages and purpose-built barracks for soldiers. It is significant that, in his task of creating categories, the Registrar General specifically saw the *lodging and boarding house* as an 'intermediate form between the institution and the private family'.[65]

The difficulty in defining lodging goes back to the status of the tenancy of the occupier, in both custom and law. Most houses were occupied by tenants; that is a relationship created simply by the acknowledgement that one party was the tenant of the other, who was the owner of the property. A lodger, on the other hand, was one who resided with the landlord (landlady) on the premises. Of course this landlord may have been – indeed probably was – himself or herself also a tenant. The question of who actually was the lodger and who the tenant was important, but could be problematic. According to law, the occupier had to 'retain his quality of master, reserving to himself the general control and dominion over the whole house. If he does, the inmate is a mere lodger' (Marle, J. in *Tom* v. *Luckett* (1847)). The position of master, then, ultimately depended on who had control over the outer door (Willes, J. in *Smith* v. *Lancaster* (1869).[66] In this context it should be remembered that the franchise had always been based on property qualifications. But in 1867 it was extended to every man who occupied the same lodgings for twelve months if the yearly value of the premises, unfurnished, was over £10. Nevertheless, this recognition of lodging as a normal part of working-class life was in name only, as it was generally acknowledged that the 'lodger's franchise' remained a dead letter because of complicated registration procedures.[67]

The Demand for Lodging

Some of the concern over lodging may be due to the belief confirmed by historical research, that lodgers tended to be the 'semi-autonomous young persons'[68] who have always made authorities anxious. Their abundant energy with potential for both work and violence, their budding sexuality with its potential for 'unregulated' reproduction, have made problems of control over this group seem particularly acute. In rural and pre-industrial society, living-in farm service, apprenticeship, as well as peer group sanctions, had provided much of this control.[69] But by the nineteenth century, the masses of young people flocking into cities, combined with a relatively high age of marriage, created a new situation. Residential domestic service for girls was seen as one solution, while young men went into lodgings. A witness to a government enquiry in the 1880s said 'I suppose it would lie between a young unmarried man of 20 living at home with his family or becoming a lodger with some family or getting married'.[70] In fact, male lodgers usually outnumbered female by between two or three to one.[71] According to this view, domestic service may be seen as an alternative to lodging, with apprenticeship as a situation halfway between the two.[72]

The demand for certain types of labour greatly increased the numbers of people, particularly young people, constantly on the move. For example, railway employees needed lodgings at the end of the line if they could not return home after a journey. At first the companies rented room and board in private households, but eventually built their own lodging houses.[73] One of the greatest areas of employment throughout the century was in building, from private housing to the huge public buildings which transformed Victorian cities. Building needed labour for irregular periods of work; both labourers and craftsmen moved from site to site and were affected by the seasons. 'At Kinson, Dorset in 1865 . . . many of the men were employed in building work at Bournemouth. Some came home only weekly, living in lodgings while away.'[74] Others would stay on until the work was finished. When a journeyman stonemason came to London to seek work, he found lodgings under the same roof as his foreman. He describes the foreman's 'good lady' as a stout, burly woman:

> . . . pretty clean in herself and her household, a pretty good cook and of an exceedingly mild and willing disposition never seeing it a trouble to cook or do anything for us even if it happened out of the common way so that we were quite at home here, although there were eight men lodging in the house, six of the number working together with me.[75]

As in this case, occupational links between landlord and lodger could be as important as place of origin (see Table 3.1).

Moving about the country was a well-established part of many trades or even a way of life. 'Tramping was not the prerogative of the social outcast, as it is today; it was a normal phase in the life of entirely respectable classes of workingmen; it was a frequent resort of the out-of-work; it was a very principle of existence for those who followed itinerant callings and trades.'[76] Lodgings were the fixed points in these circuits and certain streets in every town were known for their lodging houses for travellers. One of the greatest benefits that the card-holding 'tramping artisan' gained by his membership in a trade organisation was the contact that provided respectable, comfortable lodgings in a strange town, either at the pub where the local chapter met or with the families of local fellow artisans, where the wife (or daughter) provided service. This institutionalised arrangement was not available to women or girls, as they were usually ineligible for union membership and, in any case, not often found in the type of occupation that provided such benefits. The few young women who had seasonal occupations − such as the herring girls from Scotland who followed the catch to East Anglia − made full use of the freedom from parental and community surveillance whilst in their lodgings.[77]

Table 3.1:   Household 1: 146 High Street, Margate, 1871

John Hyland	Head	Married	Age 33	Bricklayer
Clara Hyland	Wife	Married	Age 22	Coffee House Keeper
May Hyland	Daughter		Age 1	
Charles Hyland	Son		Age 9	
Mary Higgs	Visitor	Single	Age 18	Domestic Servant
Frederick Jones	Boarder	Single	Age 23	Bricklayer

In the first half of the century, pubs and inns were important way-stations for all classes of lodgers, including billeted soldiers. 'Drink-sellers provided lodgings for homeless or itinerant working men, and sheltered lodgers whose landladies allowed them on the premises only to sleep.'[78] Pubs also provided lodgings for sailors and seamen, occupations which created a steady demand for temporary accommodation, a demand undoubtedly associated with prostitution. Prostitution, in turn, included 'private lodgings where they [prostitutes] were more likely self-employed and less physically segregated from a general working-class neighbourhood ... Prostitutes tended to reside in dwellings with two or three other women, often run by an older woman but in a capacity as landlady, not "madam".' This accommodation was scarcely distinguishable from low-class lodging houses or, often, even 'externally respectable establishments', and seems to have been an example of a strong female network resulting in good fellowship and sociability among the prostitutes, physically located in these female lodging houses.[79] Significantly, the use of such temporary lodgings might very well not show up in the census figures, for they were often the result of seasonal or migratory patterns, while the census was always taken on one night at the end of March or beginning of April.[80]

There were, however, less peripatetic groups, such as clerks and shop assistants who came to the cities, particularly London, and filled the respectable lodging houses or lived as lodgers in private households in districts such as Kennington or Camberwell. In those areas where little housing was available, the provision of lodgings helped to attract young, single workers. In rural Essex a scheme was established by the silk manufacturing firm of Courtauld whereby their purpose-built housing was let to their workers on a sliding scale, provided the tenant also lodged the single girls who often returned to their families in the villages on Saturday and walked back to Halstead on Monday morning. It was even possible for the tenants to be paid a small sum or at least live rent free, as in the case of Miss Greer who housed 10 lodgers.[81]

All the activities associated with travel greatly expanded as a result of the railways, better road surfaces and river and coastal steam traffic. With this increased travel came demand for overnight or longer-stay lodgings. There were special occasions when middle-class people were on the move: parents visiting sons at college or boarding school, staying near relatives for festivities or in times of illness when they could not stay with kin. There were the groups of kindred spirits who booked rooms for a few weeks at a time to pursue common interests, such as the reading parties of the famous Cambridge 'Apostles'. Lytton Strachey, on one such occasion, wrote from Penmenner House in Cornwall: 'We are quite close to the sea. The house seems very comfortable. We have two sitting rooms. There is another party of young gents from Oxford in the house.'[82] Race meetings, royal occasions, or any other public event would bring a rush of people to the area.

Above all, there was the increase in holidays, first in spa and seaside towns, later in the country, for which medical ideas about rest, recuperation and good air provided part of the justification. The period of growth of middle-class resorts was from the mid-eighteenth century to 1820 and 'once the reputation of a resort was established, people were willing to build lodging houses, shops and other amenities to cater for the visitors'.[83] Later in the century the better paid, more regularly employed, of the working class joined in, at first only for day excursions by rail, but later for weekends and even whole weeks. At the heart of a city created to cater for holiday-makers (Blackpool, for instance) was the seaside boarding house.

What Was Provided

The basic services provided in lodgings seem to have been 'attendance, light and firing'. 'Attendance' included services such as cleaning, carrying water and coal, emptying slops such as waste water and chamber pots, making fires, running errands (with the kiss on the stairs if the lodger could snatch it).[84] In furnished lodgings, the lodger could supply some of his own effects, or alternatively, the arrangement could be 'all found', virtually as in an hotel.

Anderson found that most of the working-class lodgers in Preston had room, candles and coals provided, paying extra to the landlady for washing or for washing materials.[85] A report from London confirms that 'in furnished rooms the "keeper" provides the bedding as a rule, but it is generally understood that the lodger is responsible for washing bed linen'. Either coppers were provided for the tenants or 'women made use of the public wash-houses'.[86] This indicates that male lodgers might receive (and pay for) more services than female; Anderson cites a report that 'single women ordinarily pay a sum per week for cooking their own food'.[87] Most often lodgers ate at the same table with the family, whether or not they had provided their own food, with the exception of lodgers who themselves formed a family unit, where they would probably have had a separate room, even though cooking was still often done by the landlady.[88] Middle-class lodgers, of course, could command a higher standard of service and more privacy. One bachelor lodger in the 1880s (with an annual income of £300 a year, paying 30 shillings a week 'all found') complains of the new servant being moody and dour, who 'shuts her eyes' when he gives his orders to 'fetch coals or water or beer, post letters, cook a steak or bring up tea'.[89]

A variety of arrangements was found in holiday accommodation. Wives on holiday in Margate sent letters with minute instructions for bringing groceries by the 'Husbands' Boat' which came down from London on Saturdays: coffee, tea 'and a breast of veal from Fleshby's because Margate butchers are asking preposterous prices'.[90] According to the *Tourist Hand Book to the British Isles* for 1880, as much as £2 to £6 per week could be paid for staying in the West End of London. However, the writer notes that private lodgings may always be had by the week in nearly every part of the metropolis. Cards for 'furnished apartments' are almost always placed in the windows of houses where there are rooms to let:

The price of apartments includes attendance in most cases. Extra charges are made for light, use of kitchen fire and washing of bed and toilet linen and usually of boot cleaning.

But the warning is added:

> Strangers should be careful to have a clear understanding as to prices
> and to fix upon an arrangement which will include all extras. Lodgers
> may make their own purchases of provisions or the housekeeper will
> make them, rendering weekly accounts with the bill (p. 138).

Supply of Lodgings

If many lodgers were young and single, then it should follow that
landlords and landladies would be married or widowed middle-aged
people, and this does seem to have been the case:

Table 3.2:   Lodger Households by Age of Household Head:
Colchester, 1851

Age of household head	Lodger household	All households
Under 30	16%	16%
31-50	38%	61%
Over 50	46%	23%
Total	100%	100%

Attention has been drawn to the taking in of lodgers as a way of providing
a livelihood for widows or other women left without support.[91] In
Colchester in 1851, while women made up 19 per cent of household
heads in the city as a whole, they constituted 30 per cent of household
heads who took in lodgers. For example, in 1861, Emma Bond, a
widow aged 57, lived with her son, a bookbinder aged 20, and a lodger
aged 24. By 1871, the son had moved out and been replaced by two
additional young artisan lodgers.

It could be further argued that such a resource was important for
married women living with their husbands, particularly those with
very young children who did not yet take up much houseroom or,

on the other hand, could not make any financial contribution to the household:

Table 3.3:   Household 2: 19 Long Wyre Street, Colchester, 1851

John Bennington	Head	Married	Age 31	Writer and Grainer
Elizabeth Bennington	Wife	Married	Age 29	
2 sons aged 3 and 1				
Frederick Morris	Boarder	Single	Age 16	Apprentice Writer and Grainer

For couples in late middle age, lodgers would once again fill the beds and supply the income in lieu of grown-up children who had left home. This cyclical pattern is analogous to the domestic economy of peasant households, where the labour of living-in farm servants was used when the children were very young and again after they had grown up and left home.[92] In both cases, household resources and space were balanced by the presence of non-kin at certain times in the family cycle.

The hatter Fred Willis, who lived in Camberwell in the 1900s, rented a house for 12s 6d per week with six rooms and a scullery. At that time he had four children ranging in age from six to thirteen years old. When he first married, the whole top floor was let unfurnished, but as the family increased, the lodgers decreased. The compositor who inhabited the front room upstairs and who shared supper and all his meals on Sunday with the family, was the last, they hoped, but he was clean, quiet and orderly and they couldn't give up the 10s a week he brought in. Interestingly enough, he also was able to get an apprenticeship in his own trade for the eldest boy, thus demonstrating how lodging could increase the network resources of a nuclear family.[93]

It could be further argued that the taking in of lodgers would be particularly attractive to ex-domestic servants who had neither the experience nor contacts necessary to find factory work or even, in some cases, outwork.[94] A building worker in London said of his landlady: 'Mrs Jennings had been in service as a cook in a gentleman's family. In order to improve their scanty income, she took in a little washing, and she also washed for myself and fellow lodger.'[95]

Although in one sense taking in of lodgers was seen as being incompatible with middle-class gentility, on the other hand it was a way of supplementing income without the women in the household having to work in public. On these grounds alone, it would appeal to both ex-domestic servants and respectable working men alike. It was also a resource which could be used by middle-class women left without means of support, particularly after the First World War, when gentility was more loosely defined and the euphemism 'P.G.' (paying guest) softened the idea of taking strangers into the house for cash.

An early nineteenth-century American visitor to London gives a vivid picture of a household where he had to supply a character reference to his middle-class landlady:

> I am now comfortably and quietly settled in lodgings with an elderly lady who has good blood in her veins . . . Comfort, neatness and economy distinguish her household from the cellar to the garret. Nothing is wasted, nothing is wanting. . . . This economy is neither the offspring of meanness nor of avarice, but the rational result of a determination to preserve her independence. Her means are just sufficient with this rigid economy, to enable her to appear with that sober sort of gentility, which is her pride and delight to exhibit. Were she to relax in any one respect, the nice system would lose its balance and fall to the ground.[96]

Taking in lodgers could not only maintain gentility; it could also support dependants at a time when women's wages were often below subsistence level for themselves alone. Elderly parents, younger brothers and sisters, or even illegitimate children could at least be provided with a roof over their heads:

Table 3.4:   Household 3: 30 Priory Street, Colchester, 1851

Ann Dunningham	Head	Widowed	Age 63	No occupation
Rachel Dunningham	Daughter	Single	Age 29	Machinist
Charles Dunningham	Grandson		Age 10	
Jabez Dunningham	Grandson		Age 6	
Female Lodgers ages 19, 19, 19, and 22 - all tailoresses				

It is difficult to know when taking in a couple of lodgers became the sole support of a household or individual when in effect it might be considered running a boarding house. In Colchester in 1851, of those households where lodgers were kept, 70 per cent had only 1, 17 per cent had 2 and 13 per cent had 3 or more. Only one household had 5, which was the highest figure in the sample. These proportions are confirmed by Anderson's findings for Preston. From examining the manuscript census, it seems clear that some enumerators used the category 'lodging house keeper' to designate a household head who happened to have one or two lodgers and no other declared occupation; but some enumerators seem to have used this practice much more widely than others. In fact, as Charles Booth knew from his study of London, the line was very difficult to draw. The 1931 Housing Report tried to lay down guidelines for making a distinction between a private household where lodgers were taken in and a lodging house:

> In the case of business establishments and boarding houses, where any doubt has arisen in regard to the nature of the occupation, the residents have been included in the private family class when the number of business assistants or boarders was not greater than the number of members of the employer's or householder's family (including domestic servants).[97]

A legal case decided in 1978 put the matter most succinctly. The issue was whether a single woman providing breakfast, tea and Sunday lunch for her five lodgers (as her mother had done in the same house) was, in effect, running a business and thus subject to the Landlord and Tenant Act rather than the Rent Act:

> No one factor was decisive; all the factors — the number of lodgers, the money, the size of the house, had to be looked at. She was not reaping any commercial advantage. She was doing it probably because she liked it and no doubt she was good at it.[98]

The proportion of men listed as 'inn keepers' in the census throughout the nineteenth century is 80 per cent, compared to 20 per cent women, while almost exactly the reverse percentages of the sexes are listed as 'lodging house keepers'. While, undoubtedly, men found it much easier to obtain the licence and raise the capital to become an inn keeper, it is possible that the sex of the householder may have influenced the enumerators' description. Certainly this definitional distinction is clear in the separate list of inn keepers' *wives* (61,553 in 1871); of course there is no category of lodging house keepers' husbands.

If the initial capital and/or housing could be found, there were several advantages for women in taking in more lodgers — in effect running a lodging house. Not only could dependants be supported, but enough might be saved for retirement. A somewhat romanticised version of this is the theme of Arnold Bennet's novel *The Old Wives' Tale* (1908), where the heroine, having been abandoned by her philandering husband in Paris, sets up and runs a select boarding house for English visitors and eventually retires in triumph to her native town in the Potteries. In real life, Mrs A.P. Patchett's furniture and fittings for her Nottingham lodging house (three public rooms and nine bedrooms) were valued at £131 1s 6d in 1885.[99]

The 'production' of services to lodgers, however, was by no means the only form of using women's labour at home to augment income or promote the family enterprise. The 1931 Housing Report noted that, as with the definition of a lodging house cited above, a similar rule was applied to 'exceptional families of like character e.g. a doctor with resident patients, a tutor with resident scholars'. But in the nineteenth century, such households were not so exceptional. In Colchester in 1851 there were more households with apprentices than lodgers. Other categories would include tradesmen's wives who serviced residential shop assistants, doctors' wives caring for resident medical students (the standard form of training for general practitioners), and clergymen's wives watching over the young boys boarded and taught by their husbands. While a general servant might have performed the heavier work in such households, the mistress often did light cleaning, the cooking and serving herself, as well as overseeing the provision of clean laundry and other managerial tasks. The necessity for the wife's (or her substitute's) contribution is made clear in the dilemma of Dr Gibson, the widowed country practitioner in Mrs Gaskell's *Wives and Daughters,* who had to cope with two resident students and a lively daughter in her early teens — a situation which propelled him into a second and unhappy marriage. There were also joint enterprises such as the rural pub run by the wife and daughters of the carter who was often away from home in the course of his trade. Not only did the pub increase household resources, but it provided more houseroom for the family and thus directly raised their standard of living.[100]

Similar enterprises are found in those, often all-female, households where middle-class women added their only other meagre asset — education. In Margate in 1871, in Hawley Square and the two streets running off it, there were nine small private schools, every one of them run by women, who were for the most part unmarried.[101]

Table 3.5:   Household 4: 'Egerton House', 38/39 Hawley Square,
Margate, 1871

Mary Brooks	Head	Single	Age 50	Headmistress
Martha Brooks	Sister	Single	Age 46	Schoolmistress
Jane Brooks	Niece	Single	Age 23	Schoolmistress
Laura Brooks	Niece	Single	Age 15	
Thurza Hill	Governess	Single	Age 22	Schoolmistress
3 female servants, aged 56, 21 and 16				
12 female pupils aged 7 to 17 years				

Often an elderly relative and/or boarder was added to the household.
In fact, many of these establishments were little more than private
homes surviving through taking in boarders or fostering children; for
example, 'Anglo-Indians' — that is children sent home without their
parents from insalubrious parts of the Empire. An advertisement of the
1880s says: 'Two ladies residing in a pretty cottage would be happy to
take charge of a young child. Education, including music etc. if afterwards required.' An advertisement in a newspaper by the wife of a
retired naval captain in Southsea resulted in a boy aged six and his
three-year-old sister being sent from India to board for three years in
what later became known to the world as 'The House of Desolation' in
Rudyard Kipling's famous story 'Baa Baa Black Sheep'.[102]

Table 3.6:   Household 5: 30 Goodwin Road, Margate, 1871

Clara Searles	Head	Widow	Age 45	Schoolmistress
Helen Searles	Daughter	Single	Age 17	
Annie Culver	Servant to school mistress	Single	Age 15	
Catherine Brown	Boarder	Widow	Age 26	
1 boy aged 2				
5 boys aged 7-8				
1 girl aged 10				
Sarah Goodall	Servant to School	Single	Age 19	

In addition to the convenience and respectability of being able to earn income within the four walls of the house, the provision of domestic services to boarders, lodgers, pupils and others did not require the exercise of any authority except over servants and children, both categories falling within a legitimate feminine domain. However, the correlative assumption that the feminine domain was gentle and uncommercial does not tally with the facts: especially where such activities were the only support of the household, and in particular where lodgings were supplied on a scale large enough to produce a profit, the lot of these servants could be very hard indeed. The lowest form of domestic service was the 'slavey' in a lodging house and was often the fate of young girls from workhouses or orphanages.[103]

In summary, then, rather than investigating the supplying of lodging and boarding in isolation, it should be seen as part of a continuum of positions: wife or female relative helping to service apprentices, pupils, and others, child-minding or fostering children, taking in boarders or lodgers, keeping a small school, running private apartments, a lodging house or hotel.

The Meaning of the Landlady—Lodger Relationship

The fact of having strangers in the house could be seen as — and, undoubtedly often was — a heavy burden for the landlady, who had not only to provide the material comforts of home but also to keep the emotional atmosphere on an even keel, to apportion scarce resources of time as well as things, to sooth ruffled feelings and to arbitrate between lodgers, servants and her own family. On the other hand, an enlarged household brought the added interest of contact with the outside world, bringing colour into what might otherwise have been an exceptionally narrow, meagre life. This was particularly true in the case of boarding where meals were served, although one need not go as far as the flippant journalist who said: 'My general experience of boarding houses leads me to think they are kept not so much for profit as for society'.[104]

The importance of these contacts is brought out in an autobiographical novel which gives a detailed account of a middle-class lodging house in the Tavistock Square area of London in the 1890s. The author was a dentist's assistant earning £1 per week. At first she had only room and 'attendance', surviving on boiled eggs and toast at an ABC cafe, for like many upper-middle-class girls of the period she did not know how to cook. After about a year, the widowed landlady decided to change over to boarders. She is quoted as giving the following reason:

It will give my chicks a better chance. It isn't fair on them living in the kitchen and seeing nobody . . . What others have done I can do; something for the children. Mrs Reynolds has married three of her daughters to boarders. I know it's a risk but if you get on it pays better. There's less work in it and you've got a house to live in.[105]

There was always a certain ambiguity involved in extracting payment for the services that would be expected from mothers, wives and other female relatives. Unlike the relationship with a servant, however, the lodger was not on his own home ground; the landlady had considerable control over the conditions of his life. Partially because of this equivocal status, landladies have, on the whole, received a 'bad press'. This may also be due to the fact that the relationship has usually been seen from the point of view of the lodger, the young single hero, while the landlady has shared the generally negative image of the older woman.

On the other hand, the landlady was thought to be too inquisitive and demanding because she was afraid of not being paid enough or because she lived vicariously through her boarders, prying and listening at key holes, examining the sheets of the honeymoon couple. The most devastating portrait we have of that negative, pleasure-denying image is Dylan Thomas's imaginary seaside village, where Mrs Ogmore Pritchard presides over Bay View Cottage, a house for paying guests, 'in her iceberg white holily laundered night-gown under virtuous polar sheets and before she raises the blinds to let the sun in, tells it to mind and wipe its shoes'.[106]

On the other hand, the landlady was seen as the equivalent of the 'tart with the heart of gold', a source of nurturing, always ready to do that little extra without thought of self. This expectation lies behind the patronising tone of the artisan lodger who said of his landlady: 'I have many times felt sorry to observe that she had gone beyond her means in making a pie or tart, perhaps a custard, merely for the satisfaction of asking me to have a bit'.[107] Thomas Wright, the engineer, remembered the young journeyman from the country, employed in the same place as his father, who lodged with his family: 'As is often the practice of this class with their landladies he calls her "mother" and he strikes her as being like what her first born boy would have been had *he* lived to be three and twenty.'[108] The overtones of the relationship were not only maternal, as Roberts remembers about his local community in the Salford of the 1900s:

The very word lodger stood, so to speak, pregnant with meaning.

In plain fact, of course, many single men spent all their mature lives in other people's homes in a relationship which, despite close quarters, always remained platonic. But circumstances offered scope for scandal and malicious tongues made the most of it. 'Three evils' one learned judge had said, 'most commonly break up marriages: they are selfishness, greed and lodgers'.[109]

There was a feeling that the lodger had access to all sorts of hidden extra privileges through his special relationship to his landlady (and/or her servant and daughter); yet he was never a full masculine adult, a householder.[110] Indeed, an index of this indeterminate status was the *de facto* disenfranchisement of a man who remained in lodgings throughout his adult life. 'In the metropolitan boroughs the number of lodgers [eligible to vote] was estimated at between 200,000 and 300,000 but the number on the electoral register in 1872 was 4,000 in the whole of London.'[111]

The lodger gained these privileges at the expense of the 'legitimate male head of house'.[112] Thus the maternal and sexual came to be fused in a well-recognised if semi-licit relationship between an older woman and younger man, further confused by the handing over of cash for service rendered. The tensions such a relationship produced, including its Oedipal implications, may at least partially account for the jokes, songs and stories with a 'Roger the Lodger' motif.[113]

Conclusion

Historians have recently pointed out that the experience of lodging must have been much greater than our 'snapshot' type of statistical data would suggest: as a child growing up in a house with lodgers, occasional or more permanent; as a young person living in lodgings, or a servant waiting on lodgers; as a married householder letting out lodgings. All these positions might have been maintained for relatively short periods, but they gave a variety of household living experience very different from our own nuclear family dominated lives.[114]

With the decline of house building and massive movements of population during the First World War, the twentieth century saw a temporary increase in lodging and house sharing. By the early 1930s this had been reversed as the demand for lodging slackened. There was less geographical mobility as enterprises became more bureaucratised and occupations more settled. The development of short-distance transport — trams, buses and bicycles — meant that young, single people could live at home and still get to their work. In any case, with a fall in the age of marriage, they were more likely to try and set up independent households at an earlier age.

The growth of the building society meant that owner-occupation was increasing. Building societies were attracted to houses designed for nuclear families only. Furthermore, it was much more difficult for a woman to raise a mortgage to buy a house, as opposed to getting control of a tenancy.[115] Municipal housing, too, was more carefully controlled than private lettings had been. On the whole, councils were opposed to the sub-letting of rooms and, where it was allowed, additional charges were often made. Taken together, these developments meant that the flexibility which had been an especial advantage to women was being removed from the housing market.

The amount of general service expected by the middle class declined after the war, despite the continued high levels of women occupied as domestic servants. Working-class women were being urged rather to take better care of their own families and menfolk, as emphasised by the new moves to scientific motherhood and domestic teaching in schools. The inter-war period was the time when advertising promoted consumption within an 'Ideal Home' where there was no social space for the lodger. The 'final and definite transition' to the small, nuclear family household (mean 3.04 in 1961) is said to have occurred between the 1920s and 1940s.[116]

Of course lodging for shorter or longer periods has continued, but even among those groups where it was once almost universal, such as students or holiday-makers, it has rapidly declined in the last ten or fifteen years. As a recognised social experience it has, like residential domestic service, almost disappeared. Similarly, family enterprises, from small shops to small schools, have declined numerically, and with them the unpaid labour of wives (and children), while even clergymen's and doctors' wives are increasingly entering the labour market rather than contributing to their husband's work. The one form of family surrogate work which remains in the home and has, if anything, increased is child-minding, in the forms of both fostering and boarding-out children who are in the care of the state or private daytime child care. This is in keeping with the emphasis put on the nuclear family as the natural and best place for children to live.

It has been stated repeatedly that the post-Second World War period has witnessed an 'explosion' in the proportion of married, particularly older, women working: from 8 per cent in 1921 to 60 per cent in 1976. But perhaps what we are seeing is a shift in the location and, to a lesser extent, the kind of work that these women are doing.

This shift may ultimately affect the women's view of themselves as it brings them into contact, even if only as 'part-timers', with large-scale private or state enterprises. However, the expectation that this move would, in some way, fundamentally change their consciousness, does not, as yet at least, seem to have materialised, despite a considerable increase in women's trade union membership.[117] This may be partly explained by the fact that in some sense the shift may be seen as a loss of autonomy as the ladlady becomes the supermarket employee. The rise of lodging and boarding did not only structure opportunities: women actively helped to shape this alternative or supplementary arena, where they could at least gain a measure of financial and social independence. If it is impossible ever to weigh up the gains and losses, at least this examination of the recent past should be a reminder that there is no natural or fixed separation between a private and a public sphere.

Notes

I should like to thank Sandra Taylor, Judy Lown, Anna Davin, Diana Barker and Diana Gittins for help and suggestions in the writing of this paper. Support for the research came from the Gulbenkian programme of Lucy Cavendish College, Cambridge.

1. B. Taylor, 'The Woman Power' in S. Lipshitz (ed), *Tearing the Veil: Essay on Femininity* (London, Routledge and Kegan Paul, 1978).

2. D. Crow, *The Victorian Woman* (London, Allen and Unwin, 1971).

3. D. Schneider, *American Kinship: A Cultural Account* (Englewood Cliffs, NJ, Prentice-Hall, 1968).

4. All examples from Colchester are based on a 1 in 8 sample of the 1851 manuscript census. Colchester was a market town in East Anglia with a population of 20,000.

5. R. Park, E.W. Burgess and R. McKenzie, *The City* (Chicago, Chicago University Press, 1967); J. Rex and R. Moore, *Race, Community and Conflict: A Study of Sparkbrook* (Oxford, OUP, 1967).

6. T. Haraven and J. Modell, 'Urbanisation and the Malleable Household: An Examination of Boarding and Lodging in American Families', in T. Haraven (ed), *Family and Kin in Urban Communities 1700-1930* (London and New York, New Viewpoints, 1977), p. 182.

7. J. Lee, 'Aspects of Urbanisation and Economic Development in Germany 1815-1914', in P. Abrams and E.A. Wrigley (eds), *Towns in Societies: Essays in Economic History and Historical Sociology* (Cambridge, CUP, 1978); B. Laslett, 'The Family as a Public and Private Institution: A Historical Perspective', *Journal of Marriage and the Family*, no. 35, August 1973.

8. M. Katz, *The People of Hamilton, Canada West: Family and Class in a Nineteenth-Century City* (Cambridge, Mass., Harvard University Press, 1975); M. Anderson, *Family Structure in Nineteenth-Century Lancashire* (Cambridge, CUP, 1971).

9. Haraven and Modell, 'Urbanisation and the Malleable Household', p. 182.

10. For a critique of this view, see W. Breines, W. Cerullo, and J. Stacey, 'Social Biology, Family Studies and Anti-Feminist Backlash', *Feminist Studies*,

February 1978.

11. Anderson, *Family Structure*; J. Humphries, 'Class Struggle and the Persistence of the Working-Class Family', *Cambridge Journal of Economics*, vol. 1, 1977.

12. Haraven and Modell, 'Urbanisation and the Malleable Household', p. 183; A. Armstrong, *Stability and Change in an English County Town: A Social Study of York 1801-1851* (Cambridge, CUP, 1974).

13. J. Gardiner, D. Himmelweit and M. Mackintosh, 'Women's Domestic Labour', Bulletin of the Conference of Socialist Economists, vol. IV, no. 2, 1975.

14. 'It is this necessity — to do concrete, historically specific research from a feminist perspective — which could be described as the most important thing that we have learned from our last few years.' Women's Study Group Centre for Contemporary Cultural Studies, 'Women's Studies Groups: Trying to do Feminist Intellectual Work', *Women Take Issue* (London, Hutchinson, 1978).

15. M. Blaxall and B. Regan (eds), *Women and the Workplace: The Implications of Occupational Segregation* (Chicago, University of Chicago Press, 1976).

16. R.D. Barron and G.M. Norris, 'Sexual Divisions in the Dual Labour Market', in D. Barker and S. Allen (eds), *Dependence and Exploitation in Work and Marriage* (London, Longman, 1976), p. 47.

17. A.M. Scott, 'Who are the Self-employed?', in R. Bromley and C. Gerry (eds), *Casual Work and Poverty in Third World Cities* (London, Wiley, 1979).

18. *Census*, 1911, General Report, p. 51.

19. *Census*, 1873, General Report, p. xii.

20. In 1871 Order 4 contained 4,014,044 women over the age of 20 or 62 per cent of the total female population (*Census*, 1871).

21. For an examination of the way statistical categories help to shape social reality see B. Hindess, *The Use of Official Statistics in Sociology: A Critique of Positivism and Ethnomethodology* (London, Macmillan, 1973).

22. M. Spufford, 'Peasant Inheritance Customs and Land Distribution in Cambridgeshire from the Sixteenth to the Eighteenth Centuries', in J. Goody, J. Thirsk and E.P. Thompson (eds), *Family and Inheritance: Rural Society in Western Europe 1200-1800* (Cambridge, CUP, 1976), p. 174.

23. M.D. George, *London Life in the Eighteenth Century* (Harmondsworth, Penguin, 1965), p. 100.

24. L. Stone, *The Family, Sex and Marriage in England 1500-1800* (London, Weidenfeld and Nicolson, 1977), p. 28.

25. G. Gissing, *In the Year of the Jubilee* (London, Watergate Classics, 1947), p. 401.

26. SSRC Oral History Archive, no. 116.

27. H.J. Dyos and O. Reeder, 'Slums and Suburbs', in H.J. Dyos and M. Wolff (eds), *The Victorian City: Images and Realities*, vol. I (London, Routledge, 1973), p. 375.

28. George, *London Life in the Eighteenth Century*, p. 103.

29. L. Davidoff, J. L'Esperance and H. Newby, 'Landscape with Figures: Home and Community in English Society', in J. Mitchell and A. Oakley (eds), *The Rights and Wrongs of Women* (Harmondsworth, Penguin, 1976).

30. For the origins of these ideas, see Catherine Hall's article in this volume.

31. Society for the Promotion of Christian Knowledge, *The Lodgers* (London, 1901), p. 18.

32. C. Craik, *Mistress and Maid* (London, 1863), p. 108.

33. C. Booth, 'Common Lodging Houses', in *Life and Labour of the People of London*, vol. 1 (1898), p. 206.

34. R. Samuels, 'Comers and Goers', in Dyos and Wolff (eds), *The Victorian City*.

35. *Parliamentary Papers*, 1852-3, LXXVIII, Common Lodging House Act, Report to the Secretary of State for Home Department, p. 528.

36. *Parliamentary Papers*, 1884-5, XXXI, Housing of the Working Classes, First report of HM Commissioners, Q 12, p. 359.

37. Haraven and Modell, 'Urbanisation and the Malleable Household', p. 166.

38. Dyos and Reeder, 'Slums and Suburbs'.

39. *Parliamentary Papers*, 1852.

40. A. Wohl, 'Sex and the Single Room: Incest Among the Victorian Working Class', in A. Wohl (ed), *The Victorian Family: Structures and Stresses* (London, Croom Helm, 1978).

41. *Parliamentary Papers*, 1859, XXII, Accounts and Papers, W. Harris in Report of the Assistant Commissioner of Police on the Condition of Single Rooms Occupied by Families in the Metropolis.

42. *Parliamentary Papers*, 1887, LXXI, Housing of the Working Classes, Report of HM Commissioners, Q4147.

43. Ibid., 1884-5, Rural Report, Housing of the Working Classes.

44. *Census*, 1931, Housing Report.

45. A. Sherwell, *Life in West London: A Study and a Contrast* (London, Methuen, 3rd edn., 1901).

46. Fabian Society, *Homes for the People*, Tract no. 26 (London, 1897).

47. E. Gauldie, 'The Middle Class and Working Class Housing in the Nineteenth Century', in A.M. MacLaren (ed), *Social Class in Scotland: Past and Present* (Edinburgh, Donaldson, 1976).

48. L. Davidoff, 'Mastered for Life: Servant and Wife in Victorian and Edwardian England', *Journal of Social History*, vol. 7, no. 4, Summer 1974.

49. Sandra Taylor, private communication.

50. National Association for Women's Lodging Homes, *National Conference on Lodging-House Accommodation for Women* (London, 1911).

51. Mrs B. Booth, 'The Need for Real Homes for Women', *National Conference on Lodging-House Accommodation for Women* (London, 1911).

52. Manuscript Census, Public Records Office, RG 10.

53. Count C. de Rémusat, *La Vie de Village en Angleterre Ou Souvenirs d'un Exilé* (Paris, Didier, 1862), p. 31.

54. T.S. Simey and M.B. Simey, *Charles Booth, Social Scientist* (Oxford, OUP, 1960).

55. E. Partridge, 'Do — Hence to please, to meet the requirements of a person', in *A Dictionary of Slang and Unconventional English*, vol. 1 (London, Routledge, 1937), p. 226.

56. A.J. Munby, Diaries 1861-1875, quoted by permission of the Master and Fellows of Trinity College, Cambridge.

57. This expectation remains as in the Department of Health and Social Security's 'Co-habitation Rule'.

58. M. Finer and O. McGregor, 'The History of the Obligation to Maintain', *Report of the Committee on One Parent Families*, Cmd. 5629, 1974, Appendix 5, p. 126.

59. Armstrong, *Stability and Change*, p. 180.

60. H.J. Dyos and A. Baker, 'The Possibilities of Computerising Census Data' in H.J. Dyos (ed), *The Study of Urban History* (London, Edward Arnold, 1971), p. 102.

61. Munby, Diaries.

62. Anderson, *Family Structure*.

63. *Census*, 1863, vol. LIII, p. 33.

64. *Census*, 1851, General Report, p. xxxiv.

65. Ibid.

66. *Tom v. Luckett* (1847) 5 C.B. 23; 12 J.P. 6; 11 Jur. 993; 136 E.R. 781. *Smith v. Lancaster* (1869) L.R. 5 C.P. 246; 1 Hop. & Colt 287; 39 L.J.C.P. 33; 21 L.T. 492; 18 W.R. 170.

67. C. Seymour, *Electoral Reforms in England and Wales: The Development and Operation of the Parliamentary Franchise 1832-1885* (New Haven, Yale UP, 1915).

68. Katz, *The People of Hamilton.*

69. J. Gillis, *Youth in History: Tradition and Change in European Age Relations, 1770 to the Present* (New York, Academic Press, 1974).

70. *Parliamentary Papers*, 1884-5, Q 15, p. 203.

71. The Colchester sample produced 49 lodgers: 12 female and 37 male. A special sample of 14 sub-districts of the general 1851 census showed that 66 per cent of lodgers were male.

72. Katz, *The People of Hamilton.*

73. F. McKenna, 'Victorian Railway Workers', *History Workshop Journal*, Spring 1976.

74. R. Samuels, 'Village Labour', in R. Samuels (ed), *Village Life and Labour* (London, Routledge, 1975), p. 16.

75. J. Burnett, *Useful Toil: Autobiographies of Working People from the 1820's to the 1920's* (London, Allen Lane, 1974), p. 284.

76. Samuels, 'Comers and Goers', p. 152.

77. T. Vigne, P. Thompson and A. Howkins, personal communication.

78. B. Harrison, *Drink and the Victorians: The Temperance Question in England 1915-1872* (London, Faber and Faber, 1971), p. 47.

79. J. Walkowitz, 'The Contagious Diseases Acts and their Repeal', unpublished manuscript, 1978, p. 51.

80. For a critique of the 'snapshot' approach to historical statistics, see L. Berkner, 'The Uses and Abuses of the Census for Family History', *Journal of Interdisciplinary History*, vol. v, no. 4, 1975.

81. Essex Records Office, D/F 3/3/22 and 56.

82. M. Holroyd, *Lytton Strachey: A Biography* (Harmondsworth, Penguin, 1971), p. 204.

83. C.W. Chalkin, *The Provincial Towns of Georgian England* (London, Edward Arnold, 1974), p. 53.

84. Munby, Diaries.

85. Anderson, *Family Structure*, p. 47.

86. Medical Officer of Health, *Report on Kensington 1899* (London), Appendix 2.

87. Anderson, *Family Structure*, p. 47.

88. Ibid; R. Tressell, *The Ragged-Trousered Philanthropist* (London, Panther, 1955).

89. Anonymous, *Looking for Lodgings and Other Tales* (Brussels, 1885).

90. *All About Margate and Herne Bay* (1865, publicity pamphlet).

91. Anderson, *Family Structure*; Armstrong, *Stability and Change*; Haraven and Modell, 'Urbanisation and the Malleable Household'.

92. L. Berkner, 'The Stem Family and the Developmental Cycle of the Peasant Household: An Eighteenth Century Austrian Example', *American Historical Review*, vol. 77, 1972.

93. F. Willis, *101 Jubilee Road: A Book of London Yesteryears* (London, Phoenix, 1948).

94. Davidoff, 'Mastered for Life'.

95. Burnett, *Useful Toil*, p. 285.

96. A New England Man, *A Sketch of Old England* (New York, Wiley, 1822), p. 10.

97. *Census*, 1931, Housing Report.

98. *The Times*, Law Report, 14 April 1978.

99. Nottingham Archives, PL/111/275.

100. M. Winstanley, 'The Rural Publican and His Business in East Kent Before 1914', *Oral History*, vol. 4, no. 2, Autumn 1976.

101. Here was one of the ways in which 'surplus' women were surviving. It is questionable whether the problem of surplus women in the mid-nineteenth century was demographic so much as social, and public concern may have been at least partially due to the publicity given to certain findings of the 1851 census. W.R. Greg, 'Why are Women Redundant?', *Literary and Social Judgements* (London, Trübner, 1868).

102. A. Wilson, *The Strange Ride of Rudyard Kipling: His Life and Works* (London, Secker and Warburg, 1977).

103. 'Toilers in London', *British Weekly*, London, 1897; Munby Diaries.

104. 'Juloc', *Boarding-House Reminiscences, or, the Pleasure of Living with Others* (London, T.F. Unwin, 1896).

105. D. Richardson, 'Interim', *Pilgrimage*, vol. II (London, Dent, 1938), pp. 286-7.

106. D. Thomas, *Under Milk Wood: A Play for Voices* (London, Dent, 1966).

107. Burnett, *Useful Toil*, p. 285.

108. T. Wright, *The Journeyman Engineer* (London, 1867), p. 210.

109. R. Roberts, *A Ragged Schooling* (Harmondsworth, Penguin, 1978), p. 82.

110. 'The Landlady's Daughter' a music hall song of the late nineteenth century:

> Where I'm lodging, oh dear me?
> The daughter of my landlady
> She's a perfect little treet
> Not quite 19, and so neat!
> Talk about a fellow when
> He's made to feel quite easy
> I never knew what comfort was
> Until I met Miss Squeezy. (*Fred Earle Songbook*)

111. Seymour, *Electoral Reforms in England and Wales*, p. 364.

112. This was essentially a working-class image. It is striking that the other semi-licit sexual stereotype of Victorian society, the older middle-class man and the young working-class girl (often a servant), gains its piquancy by crossing class lines. It too, of course, involves a cash relationship which masks an Oedipal situation. How far either of these reflected reality is very difficult to say.

113. In rhyming slang, a lodger was *artful dodger*: 'The lodger was the butt of many late nineteenth and early twentieth century jokes – now almost all obsolescent due to the vast change in post-war social conditions.' J. Franklyn, *A Dictionary of Rhyming Slang* (London, Routledge, 1969), p. 34.

114. Katz, *The People of Hamilton*; Haraven and Modell, 'Urbanisation and the Malleable Household'.

115. P. Wilmott and M. Young, *Family and Kinship in East London* (London, Institute of Community Studies, 1957).

116. P. Laslett, 'The Decline of the Size of the Domestic Group in England. A Comment on J.W. Dixon's Note', *Population Studies*, vol. 24, November 1970.

117. F. Engels, *The Origin of the Family, Private Property and the State* (London, Lawrence and Wishart, 1972); W. Seccombe, 'The Housewife and Her Labour Under Capitalism', *New Left Review*, no. 83, 1974.

4 WOMEN COTTON WORKERS AND THE SUFFRAGE CAMPAIGN:[1]

The radical suffragists in Lancashire, 1893-1914

Jill Liddington

The radical suffragists were an extraordinary group of women who ran a grass-roots campaign for the vote in the Lancashire cotton towns at the turn of the century. Since then, they have been virtually written out of history. Today, the story of the suffrage campaign is usually told in terms of Mrs Pankhurst, Christabel and the suffragettes in the Women's Social and Political Union who organised a militant, and sometimes even violent, suffrage campaign; less usually it is told in terms of Mrs Fawcett and her giant, peaceful, non-militant organisation of suffragists, the National Union of Women's Suffrage Societies. The industrially-based campaign run by working-class women is almost always forgotten; the documentary evidence the women left behind was scarce and, until recently, easily dismissed as unimportant; their story has now been pieced together only by patiently sifting local records and by recording the stories told by the radical suffragists' descendants.

Lancashire must occupy a special place in the minds of feminist historians. The radical suffragists sprang from an industrial culture which enabled them to organise a widespread political campaign for working women like themselves. Lancashire was one of the few parts of the country where it was commonplace for women to go out to work, to earn wages comparable to men, and to join a trade union. No less than 280,000 Lancashire women went out to work in the cotton mills each day at the turn of the century — and together they comprised more than two-thirds of the industry's work force.[2]

The majority of these women were young and single; yet it was quite usual for a woman to keep on working after she got married, some taking only a few days off work each time they had a child. Married women's work flourished particularly strongly in the weaving towns well to the north of Manchester — Preston, Burnley and Blackburn. Here, three out of four single women worked, and of these, about half continued working after they got married.[3]

Why did so many Lancashire women go out to work? By the turn of the century economic factors had become further reinforced by three generations of social conventions. It became almost unthinkable for women not to work. Financially, working-class families depended heavily on the wages a mother or daughter brought home each week, for their wages averaged about 19 shillings each, at least 5 shillings more than the national average for women workers. At the same time, the men of the family who worked in the mill averaged 28 shillings, about a shilling less than the average male wage.[4] Women weavers — of whom there were about 150,000 in Lancashire, compared to only 60,000 men — were particularly well paid and could earn up to 25 shillings a week. Equally important, they were proud of their skill at the loom; one woman from Blackburn, whose mother, Ethel Derbyshire, became a weaver in 1889, described how her mother's economic status rested on far more than merely high wages:

> That was a big thing, they used to talk about, the cotton workers, 'You've a *trade* in your hands, a wonderful trade, a weaver. A trade in your hands if you learned to weave.' So [her elder brothers and sisters] said, 'Well she ought to go in and learn to weave, she'd always have something in her hands.'[5]

Ethel Derbyshire started work in one of the local weaving sheds when she was ten; when she was twelve she joined the Blackburn Weavers' Association. This was by no means unusual. Most women who worked in the mills seem to have joined the appropriate cotton union as young adolescents. Indeed, the majority of the members of these unions were women; their weekly dues were collected by house-to-house collectors and, as a woman who worked in one of the Lees' mills near Oldham makes clear, union membership was accepted as part of normal female behaviour in the cotton towns:

> It was as well to be in a union, you know ... my sisters worked in the mill then; Betty's mother was a twiner-piecer, and my other sister, she was a reeler. ... I joined because they were in, you see. This collector used to come, and my mother put me in. ... We'd find him the card and the money.[6]

Lancashire women, trade unionists on a massive scale unmatched elsewhere, were organised, independent and proud; it was these strengths that underpinned the local suffrage campaign at the turn of the century. But the demand for the vote for working women was an integral part of a wider political movement as well. During the 1890s a strong socialist culture had begun to develop, centred largely on Keir Hardie's new Independent Labour Party, the ILP, formed in 1893. Local ILP branches mushroomed in all the cotton towns and were supplemented by a whole range of complementary socialist groupings – Labour churches. Socialist Sunday schools and Clarion Clubs – offshoots of the immensely popular socialist newspaper, the *Clarion*. None of these was wholeheartedly committed to women's suffrage, but nevertheless they provided an invaluable political education and network of local support for working-class suffragists. For instance, Ethel Derbyshire, who used ILP platforms for demanding votes for women, used to go with her family and the local ILP branch to the Clarion Clubhouse near Blackburn—as her daughter describes: 'We always had what you call a field day there. It was an outing—you took your own food, and made your tea, and we had races, you know, winning the races at the Clarion. Yes, they were members of the Clarion, was father and mother.'[7]

Selina Cooper, one of the most active and effective suffrage campaigners, had much in common with Ethel Derbyshire. Born in 1864, she started work when she was ten, and worked as a winder preparing the spun threads for the weavers. She joined the Burnley Weavers' Association around the late 1880s and in the 1890s became a member of her union committee and a member of the local ILP branch; in 1897, she joined the Women's Co-operative Guild, a politically-minded organisation for working-class wives that had developed as a spin-off from the larger co-operative movement in 1883. By the turn of the century, women like Selina Cooper and Ethel Derbyshire had become numerically so significant in the cotton towns that they began to have considerable impact on the existing suffrage movement.

Women Weavers' Right to Vote

Since 1867, when John Stuart Mill introduced his women's suffrage amendment to the Second Reform Bill, regional suffrage societies had grown up in all the large towns – including Manchester. Here, the local society was organised during the following two decades by the energetic and efficient Lydia Becker, a well-educated, middle-class spinster. The various suffrage societies were run in polite, ladylike fashion, lobbying well-placed sympathisers to support votes for women 'as it is or may be' given to men. This was, of course, a property-based vote, as defined by the successive 1832, 1867 and 1884 Acts. Demanding a property-based vote made great sense to potentially qualified voters like Lydia Becker, but had little appeal for working-class women like Ethel Derbyshire or Selina Cooper. Even if their fathers or husbands were householders, they certainly were not; nor would they be likely to qualify for the franchise through, say, the £10 lodger provision.[8]

Yet tens of thousands of women cotton workers like Ethel Derbyshire or Selina Cooper provided the cornerstone of Victorian Britain's prosperity. They produced the cloth that was exported from Liverpool right round the world — in particular to India, then a colony, which alone bought 3,000 million yards of British cotton each year. They stood at their looms next to men who encouraged them to join the local Weavers' Association, but who saw little point in demanding votes for their womenfolk. To them it was sufficient that there were sympathetic MPs in the Commons who were prepared to protect the cotton workers' interests. That the majority of the cotton trade unionists were disenfranchised seemed to them less important. Yet trade union questions were increasingly becoming politicised and, as Selina Cooper put it, women union members lacked the vital lever of the ballot box:

> I carefully watched the proceedings and the policy pursued by such great unions as the Miners, the Cotton Spinners, and the Engineers, who all pressed for state interference with the object of improving their industrial conditions. I was compelled to recognize the power of Parliament. . . . Those well-organized industries had the ballot box as a lever to raise their standard of life, but the women workers, however well they combined, had no such lever to help them in their demand for the redressing of their grievances.[9]

Selina Cooper was not alone in recognising how politically disadvantaged even the well-paid, well-organised women cotton workers were; in the mid-1890s the injustice of keeping disenfranchised such a large group of industrial workers came to a head. In 1893, the middle-class suffrage societies, realising that the last 30 years of discreet lobbying had made little real headway, decided on a new strategy: a Special Appeal, a monster petition for votes for women, to be signed only by women. Within a year, a quarter of a million women — including one in four of the Women's Co-operative Guild members — had signed. But before long the appeal had been forgotten by all except suffrage *afficionados*, and had become merely another dusty paragraph in the histories of the genteel suffrage societies. Only in one area of the country, Lancashire, did events take a different and more exciting turn. Here, the Special Appeal was the signal for a new campaign, based on support from industrial women workers, which was to battle for the vote for the next 21 years.

The Cotton Workers' Suffrage Campaign

A young, middle-class graduate called Esther Roper had recently taken over Lydia Becker's position as Secretary of the Manchester Suffrage Society. For reasons that are still not altogether clear (she was an extremely reticent woman, and left only a few elusive clues about herself for the historian), she decided to direct the Special Appeal specifically towards the voteless women working in the local cotton mills. To do this, she adopted what must have appeared positively revolutionary tactics to the old stalwarts in the Manchester Society. 'The women were visited in their homes as well as at factory gates', she wrote, 'and a large quantity of women's suffrage literature was given away.'[10] She departed even further from the Becker norm by appointing two working-class women to work as organisers to help her in the gargantuan task of contacting some quarter of a million women. Sadly, the way in which they went about their work has not been documented; all that is recorded is that one, Mrs Winbolt, had worked as a handloom weaver in the local silk industry for over 20 years, and had been originally won over to the women's suffrage movement by Lydia Becker in the 1880s; the other, Annie Heaton, was — like Selina Cooper — a winder from the Burnley area.[11]

The response they met in the cotton towns was most encouraging, and over the next seven years more and more local women were drawn into the suffrage campaign. By 1900 this head of steam had grown so powerful that Esther Roper and her friends decided to organise a petition to be signed exclusively by women working in the Lancashire cotton mills. The petition campaign, launched with maximum impact on May Day 1900 at an open air meeting in Blackburn, was an immediate success. The women's rights journal, *The Englishwoman's Review*, reported in its columns that the summer of 1900 was

> quite an experience. . . . Canvassers in fifty places — one, two three or four in each, according to the numbers of the factory population — were soon at work.
> The method of canvassing has been chiefly that of going to the homes of the workers in the evening, after factory hours. . . . Some employers allowed petition sheets in the mills, and others allowed canvassers to stand in the mill yards with sheets spread on tables so that the signatures could be got as the women were leaving or returning to work.[12]

The following year, 1901, the cotton workers' petition, with no fewer than 29,359 signatures, was taken down to Westminster by a deputation of 15 cotton workers, including Selina Cooper and Annie Heaton. The next year, another giant petition was taken down to Westminster, this time by the textile workers of Cheshire and Yorkshire; the 16 delegates were greeted in London by 10 MPs and were taken on a tour round the House of Commons by Keir Hardie MP, one of the most ardent champions of women's suffrage. Later that day, a public meeting was held in Chelsea Town Hall, at which Hardie readily gave labour's endorsement of the radical suffragists.

Spurred on by this success, more and more working women began demanding the vote for themselves and mobilising local labour groups behind them. For instance, the President of the Wigan Weavers' Association, a socialist called Helen Silcock, approached the Trade Union Congress for its support in 1901 and again in 1902. Sarah Reddish, a textile worker since the early 1860s, who was President of the Bolton Women's Co-operative Guild, helped persuade the national Guild to give its valuable backing to votes for women. Other women canvassed and won the support of men who ran the local cotton unions, and some even managed to persuade the influential Secretary of the 80,000 strong Weavers' Amalgamated Association to push a women's suffrage resolution through the 1904 Conference of the Labour Representation Committee (as the fledgling Labour Party was then called). In addition, women all over Lancashire drummed up support at Guild and ILP branches, as well as at factory gate and cottage meetings.

By the early 1900s these women — like Selina Cooper, Sarah Reddish, Helen Silcock, Annie Heaton and Mrs Winbolt — comprised a distinct and effective pressure group. They can be called the 'radical suffragists', for they seemed marked out from all other suffrage activists in two important ways. First they were, unlike the Pankhursts and the suffragettes, non-militant; instead of disrupting meetings, attacking unsympathetic politicians and relying on sensationalism to attract attention, the radical suffragists worked exclusively through the labour and industrial organisations from which they had sprung. Second, they put forward a political programme that was far more radical than that of any other suffrage group. They recognised that the parliamentary vote was just one aspect of a far wider political campaign. For instance, Esther Roper was particularly active in defending the rights of various groups of women workers — like barmaids and pit brow lasses (the women who worked at the pit heads) — when their jobs were threatened by proposed legislation; both Helen Silcock and Sarah Reddish worked through the Women's Trade Union League to try to improve the wages and conditions in local trades. Selina Cooper was elected to the Burnley Board of Guardians in 1901 and one of her first challenges as a Guardian was to try to double the meagre two ounce butter allowance that the 25 workhouse children were allotted. Overall, the radical suffragists campaigned for a whole spectrum of women's rights, stretching from equal pay to better maternity and child-care facilities for working mothers.

The radical suffragists realised that in order to make their campaigns effective, they would have to organise themselves into a distinct and identifiable pressure group. So in the summer of 1903 – some months before Mrs Pankhurst gathered a handful of women to her house elsewhere in Manchester in order to form the Women's Social and Political Union – the radical suffragists created a new organisation to spearhead their efforts. It was called the Lancashire and Cheshire Women Textile and Other Workers' Representation Committee, an awkwardly cumbersome title which had the sole advantage of focusing attention on the logic of their demands as industrial workers. They had witnessed the rapid growth of the Labour Representation Committee over the previous three years. If working-class men could demand to be represented in Parliament, why, they argued, couldn't working-class women?

The original Lancashire Women Textile Workers' Representation Committee had five members, three of them working-class women. One was Selina Cooper. The second was Sarah Reddish from Bolton. The third was Sarah Dickenson, an ex-mill worker from Salford; she had begun work in 1879 when she was eleven and, not long after this, had brought the girls she worked with out on strike, in protest against the twopence charged by the employers for the stools they were now legally obliged to supply. In 1895 she had become Co-Secretary of the Manchester and Salford Women's Trade Council, and so was now excellently placed to fuse together the local labour and suffrage campaigns. Esther Roper and her friend, the Irish poet Eva Gore-Booth, made up the fourth and fifth. Together, they won increasing support for their demands and local groups of like-minded women began to grow up in Nelson, Bolton, Oldham and other cotton towns in 1903-4.

Working-class Suffragists

Sadly, no reports or minute books of these local groups have survived from this early period and it is difficult to reconstruct how the groups were run. However, we know that the Nelson group used to hold its meetings in Selina Cooper's front room. Her daughter, Mary Cooper, still has the Society's book of accounts (though dating only from 1912) that her father, a weaver and a keen suffragist, kept to record the members' subscriptions. No member subscribed more than a shilling a year, most paid threepence or sixpence, and some not even that. 'Some of them were so poor — they didn't — that's only a record of payments. . . .' Mary Cooper explained. 'They came whether or no. . . . They just managed to pay for the coffee.'[13]

Mary Cooper also recalls how, as a small child, she used to be rather puzzled by the strange goings-on in the front room:

> There was always something. 'Cos I remember listening at the key-hole, you know what I mean, listening at the door. I was puzzled by it, couldn't understand it. But—there was always some resolution going before a trade union, or they were going to go and march somewhere, or go and help—they used to help candidates that were suffrage.[14]

Oral testimony like this provides invaluable evidence to supplement the few documentary records left behind by the radical suffragists. Mary Cooper was able to give us a vivid picture of a suffragist stronghold like Nelson, and Ethel Derbyshire's daughter could describe the difficulties that constantly confronted her mother in Blackburn, where there was no strong local base:

> She did speaking for the movement in Blackburn on the market . . . They used to have speakers on the market-place, and the ILP had taken it for a meeting, you see. . . . And they would drag her off, try to drag her off. Well, of course, the other members, they would get round her and that; and they used to have to really guard her or else she would have been hurt. And she did it quite a few times and then she said she realized if she did get hurt, what would happen to her three young children. You see, there was me and two brothers then. And she said, well, in spite of what she really believed in, she'd have to keep quiet a bit.[15]

So Ethel Derbyshire, a working-class woman with three children, had to give up campaigning because of the violent opposition to votes for women. Had she been hurt, she could not have fallen back on the kind of convenient arrangements a middle-class woman could rely on. There were no servants to look after the children or cook the meals. If a mill worker became too interested in the suffrage question, she knew that her job — and so her valuable wages — might well be jeopardised. Oral evidence indicates how little sympathy most employers had with political aspirations among their women workers; one woman, from one of the small wool weaving villages on the Lancashire side of the Pennines, recalled how she and her workmates got into trouble when they left their looms for a few minutes to go and listen to travelling suffrage speakers:

> I can see them now, up back of that mill . . . with these big hats on and long trailing skirts. And us workers, you know, we—then boss fetched us in. We copped it for going out. When we went back to us work, us shuttles had gone. They took shuttles off and this made us play.[16]

(With her shuttle gone, of course, a piece-worker lost her wages.)

If it took courage for a working woman even to listen to a suffrage speaker, it took considerably more guts for her to get up on a soap box and demand votes for women like herself. The very idea offended all Victorian notions of female propriety and domestic order, and provoked crowds to heckle the speaker with 'Go and wash the pots', 'Go whoam an' mind yer babbies', and 'Wot about the old man's kippers?' There must have been countless women like Ethel Derbyshire who had to give up in the face of local hostility. Less usual were the courageous working women who kept on battling away, despite all the jeers and threats. This aspect of the suffrage story is particularly poorly documented, and the historian has to rely heavily on oral testimony. For instance, Mary Cooper retains a clear memory of the time when her mother was savagely heckled at Howarth, the Pennine village where the Brontë sisters had lived:

> My mother — she's slow to rouse, but when my mother was roused I was scared stiff of her. She was right slow to rouse; my father was stiff-tempered. Anyhow my mother went out, and she stood on this cross, and she said, 'I'm stopping here, whatever you throw, so go and fetch all the stuff you've got to throw, because', she says, 'I'm going to speak to you, I've come here to speak. And', she says, 'this blooming village would never have been known about but for three women — the Brontës.'[17]

The Radical Suffragists and the Labour Party

One of the major ways in which the radical suffragists placed themselves in the firing line was by putting their own labour-suffrage candidates up for election. They fought both the 1906 General Election and the January 1910 General Election, though in neither case was their man elected. In 1906 the Wigan man did manage to beat the Liberal candidate, but was unable to dislodge the Tory MP; in Rossendale in 1910 their candidate polled a pitiful 639 votes and came bottom of the poll. On occasions like these, the radical suffragists found that they always came up against important and influential groups of working men who had no sympathy with women's suffrage. They were untouched by the arguments of working women like Selina Cooper or Ethel Derbyshire, and held steadfastly to their traditional view that 'votes for women' was a bourgeois deviation from the central issues of interest to the working class: electing independent labour representatives to Parliament, combating unemployment and introducing a badly-needed programme of social reform. So, the radical suffragist candidates got no support from the powerful local miners in Wigan nor from the thousands of weavers in Rossendale. Nor was either man able to win the support of the local trades council or the growing Labour Party.

Indeed, the radical suffragists were isolated from the Labour Party for seven important years, from 1905 to 1912. During that time the party, due to an odd but effective anti-feminist alliance between Marxist-socialists and conservative trade unionists, rejected women's suffrage motions time and time again, in favour of all-or-nothing adult suffrage resolutions. The conflict between adult suffragists and women suffragists emerged clearly at the 1905 Conference; Selina Cooper, as an ILP delegate, stood up to second the resolution in support of the Women's Enfranchisement Bill that had recently been introduced into Parliament. She held the views she did, she said,

> because I am a working woman. . . . I speak on behalf of thousands of women engaged in the textile trades, to whose class I belong. . . . In the Clitheroe Division alone, 5,500 women have signed a petition in favour of women having the vote on the same terms as men, and I would impress upon you not to think that women want the vote merely as women. We are as keenly alive to the needs of the people as anyone, and if we have the vote we will be able to use it in the interests of reform.[18]

She was immediately opposed by Harry Quelch, a socialist and a delegate to the Conference from the London Trades Council. Quelch was an implacable opponent of women's suffrage and was convinced that the only franchise reform that Labour should support would be a bill that demanded 'one adult, one vote', and nothing less. 'Mrs Cooper has appealed to the sentiment of sex,' he claimed, 'but I repudiate that there is any sex antagonism. Mrs Cooper has placed sex first; but it is not the place of the [Labour Representation] Committee to place sex first; we have to put Labour first in every case.' Mrs Pankhurst and others rose to support Selina Cooper's appeal, but Quelch's allegation that suffragists 'placed sex first' found a receptive audience among the delegates. When it came to voting, Quelch's amendment was carried by 483 votes to 270, an unequivocal rejection by Labour of the Women's Enfranchisement Bill.[19]

So for the next seven years the radical suffragists were cut off from the Labour Party. During these years of isolation, they found that Mrs Fawcett's giant non-militant National Union of Women's Suffrage Societies provided them with useful backing. The London-based union, a federation of largely middle-class suffrage groups, had funds enough to employ a few working women as salaried organisers. In return, the women offered invaluable organising and speaking skills, based on their years of experience in the cotton mills, local trade unions, Women's Trade Union League and Women's Co-operative Guild. Selina Cooper, for instance, worked for the National Union from 1906 until war broke out. Sarah Reddish from Bolton and Sarah Dickenson from Manchester were also employed, though only on a part-time basis; and in about 1911 they were joined by two other working-class women, Margaret Aldersley from Burnley and Ada Nield Chew from Rochdale.

At a time when the militant suffragettes in the Women's Social and Political Union were escalating their militant tactics to the point of arson, these five Lancashire women travelled the country for the National Union, covering by-elections, speaking at open meetings and drumming up support. While the Pankhursts largely relied on negative attacks on unsympathetic politicians, the radical suffragists organised a more positive campaign, based on their links with the labour movement. At the 1912 Conference, the Labour Party finally came round and voted in support of women's suffrage. A few months later the National Union decided to forego its traditional policy of political neutrality, and instead to support sympathetic Labour candidates at forthcoming elections. So, for the next two and a half years, until war broke out, the radical suffragists were in great demand as speakers wherever a by-election was imminent. Ada Nield Chew's daughter recalls how busy her mother was then. 'Labour women were very much sought after at that time,' she said, 'because they could appeal to the ordinary working man or woman — working man mainly, the ones with the votes.'[20]

Their busy timetable meant that they were often away from home for weeks at a time, not an easy undertaking when children were involved. The women coped with the problem in different ways. Margaret Aldersley, who had four children, was heavily criticised by her family for leaving home at all, and in the end seems to have succumbed to their reproaches and given up her job. Selina Cooper was perhaps more fortunate. She was provided with a living-in housekeeper, a friend of the family called Mrs Holt, while her daughter was small; and later on, whenever she had to go away, she made her absences into a game for her daughter:

> Oh, my mother used to put under this map all the menus when she went away for a fortnight that I'd to get for a week — menus written on the back, on a paper stuck on the wall under the map. And I had to go and get this and I had to buy so-and-so at the weekend and — roast it, you know. I could do a roast. I couldn't do much but I could do a roast. My father used to help too, you see, and then during the week I had to come home from school and there were all shops around about that sold potato pie and different . . .[21]

Ada Nield Chew, who had worked as a tailoress during the 1890s and later as an organiser for the Women's Trade Union League, also had only one daughter. She used to take her with her whenever she went away on National Union work, and her daughter recalls that:

> She always had hospitality, and I suppose it was an understood thing that if people gave her hospitality, they had to give it to me too. And I was left in the house while she went out and did her organizing and speaking. I wasn't taken round to meetings or anything like that. I have just disjointed memories of meeting other children, and people's things that I envied, like a beautiful theatre or a toy shop.[22]

The radical suffragists found that they were often in an anomalous social position. Although they themselves were working-class women, they found that they were now involved in an organisation with an exclusively middle-class pedigree, epitomised by Mrs Fawcett herself. Outside Lancashire, there seemed to be no groups of working-class women which could match the radical suffragists' campaign. Indeed, the radical suffragists may have been slightly denigrated by the middle-class suffragists in the National Union. Ada Nield Chew's daughter recalls that her mother 'liked them, and she admired them, and she respected them. But she thought that a few of them looked down on her because she had to be paid for what she did and she resented that very much.'[23] Selina Cooper used to receive letters putting pressure on her to drop socialism and just stick to votes for women; one suffragist she had met when she went to speak at Tunbridge Wells (a town of classic middle-class respectability) wrote urging her:

> not to let that class-hatred and bitterness come into your heart again.
> . . . *None* of us can help society being broken up into classes, and
> therefore if we cannot help it, why hate each other for it. . . . Let us
> try and find out where we can all help each other regardless of class,
> as at the Suffrage meeting on Thursday.[24]

Lancashire Versus the Rest of the Country

The radical suffragists failed in the end to achieve the political impact they sought. The reforms for which they campaigned — of which the most important was the parliamentary vote — demanded the backing of the national legislature at Westminster. Thousands of working women in the Lancashire cotton towns supported their campaign, and cotton workers represented five out of six of all women trade union members. No other group of women workers could match their level of organisation, their (relatively) high wages and the confidence they had in their own status as skilled workers. Their strength, however, was regional rather than national, and when they tried to apply their tactics to working-class women elsewhere or to the national political arena, they met with little success. Ultimately the radical suffragists' localised strength proved to be a long-term weakness.

Yet the importance of the radical suffragists goes far beyond the success or failure of their immediate tactics. They have a wider significance. Although their central demand was for the vote, they never fell into the trap of seeing it as an end in itself. Even after the vote was won, they continued working locally for child allowances for mothers, for better child-care and maternity provisions, and for improved wages for the cotton workers, who now faced a major slump. The radical suffragists were the only group of working women to sustain a campaign for the parliamentary vote for women like themselves, on the basis of their own industrial muscle. As such, they comprised the vanguard of working-class women in the twenty years leading up to the First World War.

Notes

1. This article is based on material in J. Liddington and J. Norris, *One Hand Tied Behind Us* (London, Virago, 1978).
2. 1901 census.
3. 1901 census; 33.8 per cent of married women in Burnley, 30.5 per cent in Preston and 38 per cent in Blackburn were recorded as working.
4. All wage rates are for 1906 and are based largely on H.A. Clegg, A. Fox, and A.F. Thompson, *A History of British Trade Unions Since 1889* (Oxford, Clarendon Press, 1964), pp. 480-2.
5. This and the interviews noted below were recorded by the authors of *One Hand Tied Behind Us*. This interview was recorded by the authors in September 1976.
6. Interview recorded by authors, July 1976.
7. Interview recorded by authors, September 1976.
8. The number of working-class women who would be enfranchised if the existing franchise laws were to apply to women was hotly debated by contemporaries and is still difficult to unravel; for further discussion see C. Rover, *Women's Suffrage and Party Politics in Britain 1866-1914* (London, Routledge and Kegan Paul, 1967).
9. Interview with Selina Cooper, *The Queen*, 17 April 1909.
10. *Manchester National Society for Women's Suffrage, Annual Report 1894-5.*
11. There is no direct evidence of Annie Heaton's job, but one of the meetings she is known to have addressed was the Burnley Women Winders on 17 October 1900.
12. *Englishwoman's Review*, 15 April 1902.
13. Interview recorded by authors, June 1976.
14. Interview recorded by authors, March and June 1976.
15. Interview recorded by authors, September 1976.
16. Interview recorded by authors, May 1976.
17. Interview recorded by authors, March 1976.
18. *Labour Representation Committee, Annual Conference Report, 1905;* indirect speech has been transcribed as direct speech.
19. See also the *Clarion* 16 December 1904 and following issues for another example of a confrontation between an adult suffragist (Ada Nield Chew) and a woman suffragist (Christabel Pankhurst).
20. Interview recorded by authors, March 1976.
21. Interview recorded by authors, June 1976.
22. Interview recorded by authors, March 1976.
23. Interview recorded by authors, March 1976.
24. Susan Power to Selina Cooper, letter dated 28 October 1906.

5 MILITANCY AND ACQUIESCENCE AMONGST WOMEN WORKERS

Kate Purcell

Introduction

It is one of those taken-for-granted assumptions that women, and particularly women workers, are generally more placid, stable, fundamentally exploitable than men. An unconscious parody of the stereotype involved may be found in an article on industrial disruption by C. Northcote Parkinson.[1] He advised managers wishing to avoid industrial relations disputes to employ a high proportion of women workers on the grounds that:

> industrial peace is clearly characteristic of trades in which women constitute a third (say) of the labour force and is still more characteristic of those in which they actually predominate. The reasons for this difference between male and female behaviour are clearly basic, women being more concerned about their children's welfare than about loyalty to a trade union or to the working class. Historically, the trade union is an essentially male institution . . . The militance of a union has something in common with the enthusiasm which pervades the supporters of a football team. Male emotions are involved in which women share to only a limited degree. As for loyalty to the working class, women are usually without it. They have a sneaking regard for the upper class as is shown by their urge to follow the current fashion in dress. One sometimes sees adjacent doors in a public place labelled respectively 'Ladies' and 'Men'. This usage symbolises the fact that the abolition of the gentleman, a proper trade unionist goal, does not mean the abolition of the lady. To down tools is unladylike — a good housewife would at least put them tidily away. Quite apart from that, to strike on a point of principle (as when coming out in sympathy with others) is something which no woman would advocate. More practical than her husband, she would rather have the money for food and clothes.

Like all parodies and stereotypes, this both reflects and distorts reality. Underneath the humour lurks a covert set of beliefs about the differences between men and women, which is widely held.

112

It is important that the actual and potential roles of women in employment are not obscured by such stereotypes, since they form, as well as reflect, women's and men's attitudes to themselves and each other. As part of the demystification of patriarchal clichés, I think that it is necessary to re-examine what I will call the passive woman worker thesis. To do this, we may proceed in the following way. First, we look at the cultural scaffolding that supports the thesis that women are more passive employees than men. Second, we examine the composition and distribution of female labour in order to see precisely whom we are talking about when we generalise about women workers. Third, we spend some time looking more closely at the concept of militancy and its relationship to behaviour in, and views about, the work place. And finally, we reassess the passive woman worker thesis in the light of empirical evidence concerning female action which has been labelled militant, acquiescent or counter-militant.

The Myth of the Passive Woman Worker

There are three main sources of supporting evidence for the passive woman worker thesis. The first, and most obvious, is the political invisibility of women workers. Female strike leaders, trade union officials and political activists do exist, but they are a small minority of both women and activists. Women workers are less likely to be trade union members than their male counterparts, and they are less likely to be active within their union if they are members. The evidence for this, and some reasons why it is so, are discussed later, in the section of this chapter that deals with the composition of the female labour force.

The second source of evidence frequently referred to in the matter-of-fact explanation of the passivity of women workers is the general psychological profile of womankind deriving from personality tests and tests designed to measure specific characteristics, such as aggressiveness. King[2] summarises the psychological material with reference to a widely used personality test, the Sixteen Personality Factor Questionnaire (16PF) and emphasises the overlap between men and women. For example,

men are more assertive, more aggressive, more competitive, more stubborn, more independent than women (though about 20% of the women are higher on this factor than half the men) . . . women are more careful, more conventional, more regulated by external realities, more practical than men (although about 40% of men are higher on this factor than half the women)

Obviously, we could take virtually every one of the characteristics listed and question both its validity as a concept and the validity of the means used to measure it, but my purpose at the moment is not to challenge either psychological methodology or its specific findings concerning sex and gender: merely to illustrate the sort of findings that emerge from psychological investigations, and to point out that such findings of differences in the *average* scores of men and women become reified as *sex* differences, despite the extensive overlap found between men and women. It may be that men and women respond to tests such as these by conforming to what they perceive as the appropriate gender stereotypes to be. In so far as they do this, both in the tests and in everyday life, we are likely to find that the majority of males are assertive, aggressive, etc. and the majority of women mild, accommodating, conforming, etc. But do we? For the purpose of this chapter, I am not going to enter into the debate about how far gender differences reflect socialisation and how far they reflect innate sex differences; I am not attempting to unearth a sort of Hobbesian natural woman, but rather to look at specific patterns and examples of female behaviour, taking socialisation as given.

The third source of support for the common-sense notion of women workers as passive is the sexual division of labour within the family, wherein the main job for the majority of women is presumed to be that of wife and mother. Any other employment undertaken by women is assumed to be a secondary interest, entered into solely for a little extra money. This being so, women's commitment to work itself is assumed to be much weaker than men's, and their interest in pay and conditions is assumed to be less liable to provoke industrial conflict because their work is seen as temporary, or at least as subsidiary to their main concerns, their earnings being basically an inessential bonus undertaken for what is commonly termed 'pin money'. Apart from their lower commitment to work, the corollory of their greater investment in the family and their role as consumers has been taken to predispose them to be privatised, individualistic and essentially a reactionary brake to working-class revolutionary zeal. According to this thesis, women defuse the pressures built up by social inequalities in two major ways. In the long term, they pass on their privatised, individualistic values to the next generation in their role as the main socialising agents of children; and in the short term, they exert pressure on husbands to avoid militant action which threatens the family income and stability.[3]

These beliefs about women's nature and priorities support the impression that the stereotypes of man the breadwinner and woman the home-maker are somehow part of the natural order and any deviation from the gender roles prescribed is a distortion of Nature. In fact, the sexual division of labour does not conform to this complementary, asymmetrical pattern, as an examination of the work force will indicate.

The Composition of the Female Work Force

Although over 90 per cent of people marry at some stage and the majority of these become parents, the sexual division of labour within the family rarely conforms to the stereotype, although in some cases and at some stages of the family-building cycle it may do so to a greater or lesser degree. Forty-one per cent of the economically active (i.e. wage-working) population are women,[4] and of these, approximately 62 per cent are married women with husbands who are also economically active.[5] In 1977, nearly nine million women worked outside their homes[6] and this can be safely taken to be an underestimate of wage-working women, since at the lowest-paid end of the labour market (particularly in cleaning, child care and homeworking, which are almost exclusively done by women) the size of the 'hidden', undeclared and untaxed working population is known to be considerable. Of working women included in the official statistics, over one-third work part-time. The proportion of part-time women workers varies considerably among the groups of industries designated in the Standard Industrial Classification: from 57 per cent in miscellaneous services to 18 per cent in coal and petroleum products. There was a significant increase in part-time female employment between 1966 and 1976, whilst the figures for full-time female employment actually fell between 1972 and 1976.[7] It is important to examine the age structure of the female labour force, especially of married females, which indicates a clear relationship between paid work and child-bearing and rearing responsibilities: women drop out of the labour market from the birth of their first child until child care ceases to be a full-time job, most commonly when the youngest goes to school. According to 1971 census figures, married women's activity rates varied considerably according to age, from a highest point of 59 per cent for wives between 45 and 49, to a lowest point of 36 per cent for wives between 25 and 29. Further evidence of the relationship between women's economic activity and their family-building patterns suggests that the existence of dependent children is a critical element in determining whether or not women work outside the home.[8]

Table 5.1:   Distribution of Women in Employment

Industry (Standard Industrial Classification)	Women as a proportion of work force	Part-time women as a proportion of women employed in the industry	Proportion of total female work force
Agriculture, forestry and fishing	25.92	41.96	1.10
Mining and quarrying	4.2	24.14	0.16
Food, drink and tobacco	39.98	34.86	3.08
Coal and petroleum products	10.7	17.5	0.04
Chemicals and allied industries	28.09	22.08	1.32
Metal manufacture	11.36	20.82	0.60
Mechanical engineering	15.46	21.27	1.59
Instrument engineering	35.75	22.92	0.59
Electrical engineering	36.63	21.01	2.99
Shipbuilding and marine engineering	7.35	22.48	0.14
Vehicles	12.03	12.93	0.99
Metal goods not included	28.03	25.48	1.63
Textiles	45.15	21.51	2.42
Leather, leather goods, fur	43.58	27.75	0.19
Clothing and footwear	75.63	19.16	3.07
Bricks, pottery, glass and cement	23.1	20.13	0.67
Timber and furniture	19.38	24.9	0.56
Paper, printing and publishing	31.72	23.6	1.90
Other manufacturing industries	36.2	28.72	1.30
Construction	8.03	36.5	1.14
Gas, electricity, and water	19.63	21.69	0.75
Transport and communications	17.51	21.69	2.84
Distribution	55.68	50.68	16.60
Insurance, banking and finance	50.87	28.85	6.16
Professional and scientific	67.93	47.33	27.01
Miscellaneous services	57.48	56.90	14.46
Public administration and defence	37.53	24.48	6.63

Source: 1976 Census of Employment, *Department of Employment Gazette*, November 1977.

Table 5.1 shows the distribution of women in employment. From an examination of the fourth column, it can be seen that women's economic activity is highly concentrated, most women being employed in one of five sectors of the work force, and more than half working in the three service sectors of distribution, professional and scientific, and miscellaneous services. In manufacturing, which employs approximately a quarter of all women working outside the home, half of these women are concentrated in four industries: clothing and footwear, textiles, food and drink manufacture and electrical engineering. The remaining areas of concentration of women are insurance, banking, finance and business, 51 per cent of the work force of which is female.

The final two characteristics of the female labour force to which attention needs to be drawn are levels of skill and authority and levels of pay. In all sectors of the labour force quoted above, women are further concentrated in the lower-skilled, lower-paid ends of the industries. The proportion of female manual workers who are classified as skilled has been gradually declining throughout the century: 24 per cent in 1911 to 14 per cent in 1977; whereas the proportion classified as unskilled has risen in the same period from 15 per cent to 27 per cent.[9] Allied to this, few women are employed in jobs where there is a possibility of upward mobility. Even where such a possibility exists, such as in insurance, banking or teaching, women tend to be promoted much less often than male colleagues with similar qualifications. Indeed, in banking and finance, men are usually referred to as 'the career staff'.[10] Despite the Equal Pay Act, average gross weekly earnings for full-time men and women in April 1977 indicate that women's wages are considerably lower than men's, even in industries where female employees predominate. For example, in food, drink and tobacco the average weekly wage for men working full-time was £72.6, whereas for women working full-time it was £46.4; in electrical engineering the male wage was £71.2, the female wage being £47.6; in clothing the figures are £58.1 and £38.8 respectively, and in the distributive trades £60.5 and £38.7.[11] In male-dominated industries the discrepancy between male and female earnings tends to be even larger. Added to this, the majority of part-time workers are women, and part-time work tends to be badly paid. Since the Equal Pay Act is built around the principle of comparability with equivalent male workers, it is of no relevance to the large number of women in jobs exclusively done by women, as the very low rate of success of equal pay cases in industrial tribunals shows. It is particularly difficult to consider the problem of low pay amongst part-time women workers in terms of the Act, since part-time workers are almost all women doing jobs where there are no male counterparts, and comparison with full-time workers is fraught with legal difficulties. In addition, protective legislation relating to permitted hours of employment effectively ensures that most overtime and financially advantageous shift work, especially night shift working, is done by men and gives employers a loophole through which to avoid the provisions of the Sex Discrimination Act. A parallel pattern of pay-ment rates is found in the employment of professionally-qualified men and women, even where equal pay has technically been in force for many years. Women are the part-timers and junior staff, men the senior staff. A good example of this is the medical profession.[12]

Barron and Norris[13] and others have hypothesised the operation of a dual labour market, 'consisting of a primary sector containing relatively well-rewarded and stable jobs and a secondary sector, containing lower-paid and insecure occupations'. They argue that the former consists mainly of men and the latter mainly of women, and that women generally provide a second-class, reserve labour force which is utilised more or less according to different economic needs. The best illustration of this is the old one of the change in demand and supply of women workers during wartime, when women were drafted into the work force to replace men engaged on military service; but different regional patterns of economic activity bear testimony to it and an historical analysis of recruitment to the teaching profession over the last few decades might provide an interesting case study of the effect on an occupational group of fluctuations in supply and demand.

I should like to emphasise four points from this brief analysis of women's employment patterns. First, there is a tendency for the majority of women to experience breaks in the continuity of their employment, which are related to family-building patterns and indicate their dual role as domestic workers and members of the labour force. Second, over one third of women workers work part-time, and this is where the greatest increase in women's employment has taken place in recent years. Third, the majority of women in employment work in the tertiary sector of the economy: they provide services rather than products and represent the greater part of the growth in white-collar employment over the last two decades. It needs to be remembered, too, that a high proportion of the women employed in manufacturing are engaged in clerical and administrative work, constituting the service sector *within* the industry. Fourth, women in employment tend to have lower average hourly earnings than men in the same industry, to be graded as having less skill, and to have less authority. Most women in employment are classified as semi-skilled. In terms of dual labour market theory, they tend to be concentrated in the secondary sector. Finally, it should be pointed out that there are significant regional variations in the structure and size of the female labour force. According to the 1971 census, female economic activity ranged from 45 per cent in the West Midlands to 36 per cent in Wales, and obviously there is concentration within such large areas, which leads to greater variations between communities, particularly between urban and rural areas. A recent study of the labour force participation of married women[14] concludes that the *demand* for labour in a given region is probably the most influential factor in determining the level of economic activity (which includes counting registered unemployed as economically active): where jobs for women are few, the 'discouraged worker' effect operates and married women do not bother to register as unemployed. It is clear that traditions of female employment and current rates of economic activity affect not only women's activity *per se*, but also their attitudes to, and experience of, employment. The married women I interviewed in Stockport,[15] where female activity rates are 45 per cent[16] and have always been high, define their work as normal and necessary, whereas those women interviewed in the course of a similar exercise in Hull, where the widespread employment of married women is more recent and male unemployment rates are higher, frequently made references to the fortuitous nature of their work, which was mostly badly paid and devoid of obvious intrinsic satisfactions.[17]

Women in Trade Unions

The final characteristics of women in employment with which we shall concern ourselves is their membership of trade unions. Over one-third of all female employees in 1976 were trade union members, an increase of 58 per cent from 1966. Women comprised approximately one-quarter of the membership of unions affiliated to the TUC over the same period, and almost two-thirds of new recruits were women. Some unions have recently become more conscious of the membership potential of women workers and have adjusted their recruitment policies accordingly, in line with the current increased interest of the TUC in issues concerning women in employment. The bulk of the increase, however, is explained by developments in the tertiary sector, notably the expansion of white-collar unions in local and central government administration, office work and the National Health Service. As the concentration of women's employment would lead one to expect, women's trade union membership is similarly concentrated. The TUC-affiliated unions where women formed a majority of the membership in 1976 are shown in Table 5.2.

Table 5.2   Women as a Proportion of the Membership of TUC Affiliated Unions

Union	Female Members %
Union of Shop, Distributive and Allied Workers	59
National Union of Tailors and Garment Workers	88
Association of Professional, Executive, Computer and Clerical Staff (APEX)	55
Tobacco Workers' Union	66
Confederation of Health Service Employees	74
National Union of Teachers	75
Civil and Public Services Association	68
Inland Revenue Staff Federation	56
Ceramic and Allied Trade Union	53
National Union of Hosiery and Knitwear Workers	73
Amalgamated Society of Textile Workers and Kindred Trades	58
Rossendale Union of Boot, Shoe and Slipper Operatives	64
Amalgamated Association of Felt Hat Trimmers and Wool Formers	100

Source: TUC Congress Report, 1976

The most interesting point which emerges from this list is that all these unions except APEX are essentially one-industry unions, so it makes sense to look for an explanation of militancy or lack of it in factors inherent in the organisation and character of the industry concerned; the predominance of women in the industry is only one factor.

Militancy

The *Shorter Oxford Dictionary* definition of militant as an adjective is 'engaged in warfare, warring' and as a noun 'one engaged in war or strife'. The media follow this definition loosely, but they almost invariably use 'militant' as an immutable descriptive adjective, as in 'militant miners' leader Arthur Scargill' or as a noun as in 'the militants are opposed to the postal ballot', which implies that militancy is an ideological predisposition which precedes and prescribes action rather than a specific response to specific situations. Female shop stewards we interviewed, when asked to define the term militant, were unwilling to discuss it in abstract terms or make generalisations. Militancy was seen as an aspect of behaviour, but they suggested that one had to consider behaviour in its context, as a reaction to situational variables. The majority of respondents stressed the different responses required by different situations when asked whether they would describe themselves as militant, as the following quotations illustrate.

I can be militant very much at times. If I had a grievance with the foreman and he was trying to get out of it in a crafty way I would get very annoyed. Militant means strong. I can stick to my guns once I've made a decision.

I can be militant if I know I'm in the right. I wouldn't be militant for militancy's sake. Some people can be fobbed off for quite a long time by management's answers. You have to weigh up whether they intend giving you what you want or whether you're banging your head against a brick wall. Sometimes being militant is the only way to let them see if you are sincere — you've *got* to withdraw labour in some form.

The sociological literature on militancy tends to be confined largely to an examination of trade union militancy, and, with few exceptions, tends to take militancy as a self-explanatory term which does not itself require examination or explication. There are two exceptions worth noting. R.M. Blackburn[18] has said that 'militancy is basically the extent to which an organisation will go in asserting the interests of its members against employers in fulfilling a *trade union* function', but acknowledges that manifestation of militancy thus defined depends, as well as on the 'character' of the union, on 'opportunities and chances of success of such action, which in turn are governed by the work and market situations as well as by the wealth and completeness [i.e. membership density] of the union ... and by the need for militancy, since the behaviour of the employer is always an important element in the situation'. V.L. Allen[19] devotes an entire chapter to 'The Meaning of Militancy' and reinforces the relativity of the concept, which he stresses refers to methods rather than aims: 'exploiting fully whatever power or influence they possess'.[20] This does not preclude the making of militant *demands,* which he rightly sees as part of the bargaining process and as such, a means rather than an end. His final definition of militancy is action where

> the aims consist of exploiting market advantages in order to maximise wages and get the best possible working conditions and hours of work. The methods consist of negotiating with employers according to the profitability of their enterprises, using price-leadership tactics to force up wages in the least efficient enterprises and of refusing to accept any unsatisfactory price for labour. A union acting this way will provide the greatest benefits for its members within the capitalist system. It cannot do more without altering the system.[21]

The final use of militancy is that generally implied by much media comment and by the attitudes of some political activists of the left, where little action short of that designed to alter or weaken the capitalist system in the short or medium term is considered to be militant. In this sense, militant becomes synonymous with revolutionary, both as an adjective and noun.

By any of these definitions, it is not difficult to find examples of women's militancy and even of women behaving more militantly than men, both in industry and elsewhere. The Trico strike, the Fakenham Leather Factory work-in, the Leeds Clothing strike, and the strike at Salford Electrical Instruments at Heywood are all comparatively recent examples of women's militancy, in some cases without the support or with the declared opposition of their representative union and/or male fellow workers. Labour history provides numerous examples of women's strikes and women's active participation in the development of the labour movement. Feminist historians are unearthing the hidden women activists of history and it is surprising (although on reflection it should not be) how high the female attendance at Chartist and labour movement demonstrations and meetings was, and how high the female proportion was of those who were charged and imprisoned as leaders and activists.[22]

My own current research indicates that men and women in the engineering and clothing industries in Stockport join and express support for unions and engage in widespread action according to the traditions of their industry rather than according to sex. The attitudes and behaviour of men and women in engineering are more alike than those of women in engineering and women in clothing. Tom Lupton[23] came to similar conclusions in the course of his classic participant-observer study of workers in electrical engineering and rainwear, in so far as day-to-day industrial action was concerned. He found that engineering workers operated collectively whereas the rainwear factory employees were highly individualistic, regardless of gender.

Two observations need to be made to counterbalance the impression that female- and male-dominated industries and unions are radically different with respect to industrial relations conflict. First, although it can be misleading to discuss militancy in terms of recorded industrial action, as far as that aspect of militancy is concerned, it is as well to remember that strikes are not distributed evenly throughout the industries which are labelled strike-prone — such as coal-mining, docks, shipbuilding and motor vehicle manufacture. In manufacturing, 95 per cent of establishments were free of officially recorded stoppages and only 0.1 per cent of establishments had seven or more stoppages in the period 1971-73. Further analysis by industry confirms the point that stoppages are concentrated in a small minority of establishments and that these 'strike-prone' plants are 'distributed among a number of industries rather than being concentrated in a few. There are no industries in which stoppage activity is widespread'.[24] As an example of the extent to which industrial statistics can be misleading, it has been calculated that between 1962 and 1965 in the motor industry, 60 per cent of working time lost from 'within the companies' occurred in one firm alone.[25]

Second, it should be remembered that not all strikes in male-dominated industries are either exclusively or predominantly men's strikes. One of the most famous recent women's strikes was at Fords in Dagenham in 1968, about the grading of women's jobs, where a three-week strike ended in victory for the women. In other words, it is very misleading to take aggregate strike statistics and correlate these with the proportion of females in employment in the industry, as Parkinson did, and conclude that women are less militant than men. The most important correlation is with plant size, with establishments employing over one thousand people being significantly more strike-prone than smaller units.[26] This draws our attention once more to organisational factors.

The passive woman worker thesis does not merely suggest that women are unwilling to engage in industrial action on their own behalf. There is also the implication that women are positively opposed to militancy, and have a pacifying influence on the work force generally. It is possible to document examples of apparent counter-militant activity by women whose main occupation is mother and wife, a recent widely-publicised example of which was the Cowley wives demonstrating against their husbands' strike at British Leyland in 1974. It is even easier to find examples of women's acquiescence in badly-paid work under appalling working conditions, which I take to be the converse of militancy rather than that peculiarly unspecified commodity of moderation with which it is frequently juxtaposed. To say that moderate is an appropriate antonym of militant is rather like saying that medium is the opposite of large. The concept of moderation may be of heuristic value in discussing trade union politics, but acquiescence or passivity are more useful concepts in the context of this particular exercise. It is often argued that the majority of women accept pay and conditions which the majority of men would not work for. Do such examples support the passive woman worker thesis? I will argue that they do not.

The Passive Woman Worker: A Reappraisal

If we go back to the definitions of militancy given by Blackburn and Allen, which, like the definitions given by the shop stewards I interviewed, consider militancy as behaviour in specific contexts, it is possible to consider women workers' behaviour in a different light. To do this, it is also necessary to consider the tensions between the family and production and the resultant market position of the majority of women, which stems directly from the domestic sexual division of labour and the ideology that veils it.

Women's Market Position

The theory that most women's orientation to work is different from that of most men, and that their commitment to employment is lower than men's because their other role of wife and mother is considered by them to be their 'main' job, has frequently been used to account for women's apparent acquiescence at work as manifested, for example, in low involvement in trade union activities. Blackburn, for example, points out that there are clear differences in the class positions of men and women in terms of both work and market situations, since women generally do lower grade routine work for less pay and poor chances of promotion. He considers the important variable in determining militancy to be the degree of commitment to work, which he sees as partly a cause and partly a result of women's lower class position. He suggests that work may be seen as only temporary and often the work itself, with its low status and poor prospects, offers little incentive to higher commitment.

It has been observed in various contexts such as newly industrialising nations that unless commitment is sufficiently high, workers are unlikely to become involved in unions. Thus, skilled workers tend to unionise before unskilled and amongst women it appears to be in occupations offering them some prospects of a career, such as teaching, that unions are most successful in recruiting.[27]

Blackburn concludes that, from the limited evidence available, it seems that variations in union membership amongst women, as amongst men, are due to factors determining the level of their commitment to work; and he seems to be talking about factors intrinsic to the job rather than extrinsic orientations. I think that Blackburn is correct in diagnosing women's inferior class and market positions as the basis of their lower rates of union membership and activism, and wrong in setting up the intermediary of commitment to work between them. It seems to me that the crucial variable is the lack of industrial bargaining power of the majority of women, deriving from their own position in the labour market and the market position of the industries in which they are concentrated.

Unskilled labour is rarely a scarce resource and, as such, has little industrial muscle. In addition, the fact that labour is *female* labour has traditionally affected its market value and continues to do so despite the Equal Pay legislation, as the average earnings figures show. It has been illuminatingly argued[28] that women's market position is analogous to that of male semi-proletarians in the Third World, in so far as they are not presumed historically or culturally to be wholly dependent on their wages for meeting the costs of the production and reproduction of their labour power. In both cases, the employer can pay wages which are lower than the value of labour power, which might be defined as the minimum acceptable wage that can be paid to workers to maintain them as efficient elements in the reproductive process. In the case of the semi-proletarian male, his wife is engaged in subsistence production on the land in order to reproduce her own labour power and the actual and potential labour power of her children. In addition, she can thus supplement or wholly provide for the reproduction of her husband's labour power as necessary. In the case of the married woman, her husband is presumed to be partially responsible for her and her children's subsistence according to tradition and the dominant ideology of family life. A topical illustration of how such different values of labour power operate is given by Rogaly[29] when, in discussing wage levels at Grunwick, he says:

> Although a net wage of, say £25 or £30 in August 1976 was not enough to support a family and was hardly luxurious for an individual supporting himself or herself, for a young person living at home, or a student, or a woman helping with the mortgage, it might have seemed like a useful contribution to family income.

The analogy with semi-proletarian males can be taken further. Both married women and semi-proletarian males can be argued to form part of the industrial reserve armies of their specific societies: since they are not presumed – and frequently do not expect – to be wholly dependent on wage labour for survival, they can be utilised and dispensed with according to current economic needs, and it is easy to see how this happens with married women. In areas characterised by unemployment, and at times of national unemployment, female activity rates decrease and incentives to married women, and particularly mothers of dependent children, are withdrawn or unstressed, whereas the reverse operates where demand for female labour is high. The classic example is munitions and engineering during war-time, where it was found convenient to run nurseries for employees' children when demand for female labour was high. It is ironic that women are assumed to be extrinsically motivated and therefore willing to do boring, badly-designed jobs with poor working conditions but, because of their market position reflected by the established differences in the general values of male and female labour power, they are also paid low wages. In this they differ from the classic extrinsically-orientated male worker, who is assumed to *trade* good conditions of employment and job satisfaction for high earnings.[30] Superficially, women would seem to be the ideal workers, according to this analysis: only concerned with pecuniary rewards and prepared to accept low wages.

It is not within the scope of this chapter to discuss the reasons for the concentration of female employees in certain industries and occupations, but I will take the sexual division of labour in the work force as given and ask: are there any reasons why most female-dominated industries should have lower union density and be less subject to militant action, *apart* from the preponderance of women?

There are two distinct categories of female employment: white-collar service occupations and manual labour in industries characterised by unstable product market conditions. Within these large categories there are distinct sub-categories, and I would emphasise that it is possible to understand militancy only by relating specific manifestations of it directly to the pressures from which they emerge; but I will make a few generalisations which seem to me to be valid, concentrating on the manual labour sector. It has already been stated that white-collar unionisation represents the biggest growth area in trade union organis-ation generally as well as in the organisation of women, and developments in the industrial relations behaviour of white-collar em-ployees have been discussed in detail elsewhere.[31]

In most of the manufacturing industries where women workers are found in large numbers, the unstable product market conditions of the industries in question make it improbable that industrial action will be perceived as likely to be effective. Indeed, it may well be irrational, so that it is unlikely to be resorted to even where other characteristics normally correlated with militant shop floor behaviour, such as piece-work, are present. Clothing and footwear are the two most graphic examples of such industries. They have comparatively unsophisticated technology and operate in a highly competitive market where there is a high turnover of firms and low profit margins. In industrial relations at both national and local levels there tends to be a normative consensus that conflict which interferes with production is to be avoided at all costs. Referring to the footwear industry, Armstrong, Goodman and Wagner[32] comment that 'there appears to be a close and general aware-ness amongst employees of the relatively fine margin between economic survival and collapse of their employer who in many cases is not a re-mote impersonal figure but a known individual'.

In addition, many of the female-dominated occupations with low union density — catering, clothing, footwear, distributive trades and some of the service industries — also have other features which are correlated in other industries with a low level of industrial action, independently of the ratios of men and women employed. They are made up of small firms, or at least small units of production, which means that the work force is scattered and unable to express (or often perceive) common interests. The unions which represent such workers are also characterised by high membership turnover reflecting the high labour turnover of the industries and the difficulty of organis-ing such a diffuse population. This has a circular reinforcing effect: 'the basic function of trade unions is participation in job regulation'.[33] The more effectively a union is able to fulfil this function, the more successful it is in recruiting members.

The crucial fact to remember here is that women and men in such industries are similarly characterised by high job turnover and apathy towards their unions. Handing in one's notice is ultimately the only effective short-term response to a collective problem where there is no developed collective solidarity. This is the response of many unskilled workers of both sexes in exploitative work situations. Coates and Silburn,[34] discussing poverty, observe that in a slum where the roof leaks, it is a much easier, practicable and more effective solution in the short term to put out a bucket to catch the drips than to organise a petition or campaign for better housing — that is, to adopt the individual as opposed to the collective response. Women workers are often faced with a choice which is analogous to this, and a decision to choose the effective short-term solution rather than the possibly ineffective long-term solution may not be less rational — or less militant.

Women and Militancy

This may go some of the way to explaining women's lower levels of union organisation as against that of men, but it is also necessary to consider why their activism is lower when they *are* union members. There is a great deal of truth in Parkinson's reflection that trade unions have generally been and essentially are male institutions, and there are numerous documented examples of male hostility to the admission of women members and the support of what are seen as 'women's issues', such as equal pay and the provision of day nurseries. Most of this derives from the historical fact that women's labour has been used to foster competition and depress the value of labour power (in the same way as immigrant labour has), but the result has been that unions have developed as male-orientated organisations according to a pattern which has usefully been labelled homosocial.[35] Like other homosocial activities and a large proportion of male occupations, the organisation and time-tables of formal trade union activities reinforce the sexual division of labour, which implies the provision of domestic services within the family by a more socially passive partner. By this, I mean that it is difficult to be an active member of a trade union without being prepared to spend extensive periods of non-work time on union responsibilities and activities. I have discussed in a previous paper[36] the fact that married women shop stewards whom I have interviewed were generally not prepared to attend evening branch meetings and weekend conferences, but I argued that this was not because they were un-interested, or were less interested in the union than in their families, but because they were prevented from doing so *because of* their family commitments, often mentioning explicitly that husbands discouraged or forbade such activities. They accepted that they had to cook the supper and wash and iron in the evenings, not because they thought such activities right and proper for women, but because they saw no way out of it: their acceptance of the domestic role was pragmatic rather than ideological.[37] It is significant that most active female shop stewards in our sample were either unmarried or childless.

This raises the question of whether militancy and militant *trade union* action are synonymous or even necessarily related. I have avoided discussing the common confusion between militancy and activism, which are distinct though related concepts. I have concentrated on the former to the exclusion of the latter except in so far as activism is *militant* activism. In fact, there are few trade union activists amongst both the male and female working population, and whilst gender is not a dependent variable in activism, marriage or motherhood for women may be, as may the homosocial 'club' aspect of trade unionism, which is likely to inhibit women from participating. Trade union movement activists generally have ideological predispositions to behave and react in specific ways, but whereas activism can be independent of the work situation and current work experience, militancy is unlikely to be. Both the Allen and Blackburn definitions of militancy implied rational maximisation of outcomes and it is clear that joining a union or operating collectively may not be the way to do this. In many of the clothing factories where I have been interviewing men and women in Stockport, the majority of the employees decided against joining the appropriate union because they considered it ineffectual and felt that they could bargain over piecework prices individually or in groups more effectively than the union would. If we take one factory sample as a case study, only 26 per cent were union members and of the remaining 74 per cent, 72 per cent were neither anti-union nor apathetic but gave specific reasons for their non-membership relating to the reputation of, or their previous experience of, the union. Seventy-two per cent of the non-members had formerly been trade union members and 45 per cent of these were disenchanted members of the appropriate recognised union, the National Union of Tailors and Garment Workers.

The reasons given by most union members in all the industries of which I have experience, when asked why they had joined the union, were along the lines of 'it was the expected thing'. In the light of this response, *refusal* to join may be a more politically conscious decision, or it may be at least a realistic assessment of the appropriately rational behaviour for the circumstances. Research on trade union membership suggests that the majority of employees who join unions do not do so for ideological reasons, except to the extent that 'the union gets us pay rises and I wouldn't want to be a free riding passenger' is an ideological response.

From a consideration of the industries and unions, it seems to me that situational variables can be used to give plausible explanations of both women's militancy and women's acquiescence in industrial relations, which rely very little on sex or even gender *per se*. What about the examples of women's counter-militancy, such as the Cowley wives' demonstration: or even the privatised woman generally, whose main investment in the family has been accused of conflicting with class solidarity? If we make a distinction between offensive and defensive militancy, I think that even these aspects of women's behaviour can be seen as a rational type of militancy in relation to their class and market situation. I define offensive militancy as the struggle to *advance* material well-being and/or political consciousness, and defensive militancy as the struggle to *preserve* material well-being. A high proportion of action labelled by the press and participants as industrial militancy is defensive militancy: for example, the refusal to accept redundancies. For women whose sole or main occupation is mother and homemaker, anti-strike activism and home-centredness can be seen as defensive militancy and rational behaviour on a short-term basis, whether or not they are also seen as manifestations of false consciousness in relation to longer-term interests. Such a paradox is not difficult to understand if we consider contradictions between the ideological pressures upon workers of both sexes and their experience of work and family life. Marilyn Porter[38] has initiated an exploration of the complex relationships between consciousness and experience, particularly what she calls the 'second-hand experience' of industrial disputes that strikers' wives have. She concludes that people who lack direct experience of industry can only make sense of industrial disputes in terms of the effect such disputes have on their own daily lives and any additional information that gets filtered through to them by other individuals and the media. Women's militancy and acquiescence, both at work and in the home can be argued to be a function of their experience as workers rather than as women. Both men and women generally react in ways which seem to them to be rational according to the possibilities of their market situation and the market situation of their employers. Women's market situation is frequently restricted and prescribed by gender, but men similarly situated in the labour market behave in the same way.

Notes

1. C.N. Parkinson (ed), *Industrial Disruption* (London, Leviathan House, 1973), pp. 177-8.
2. J.S. King, Department of Employment, 'Women and Work: Sex Differences and Society', *Manpower Paper No. 1* (London, HMSO, 1970), p. 15.
3. C. Middleton, 'Sexual Inequality and Stratification Theory' in F. Parkin (ed), *The Social Analysis of Class Structure* (London, Tavistock, 1974).
4. Department of Employment, *Gazette*, November 1977.
5. Department of Employment, 'Women and Work: A Statistical Survey', *Manpower Paper No. 9* (London, HMSO, 1974).
6. L. Mackie and P. Pattullo, *Women at Work* (London, Tavistock, 1977).
7. DE, *Gazette*, November 1977.
8. Mackie and Pattullo, *Women at Work*, p. 52.
9. Ibid., p. 40.
10. Royal Commission on Industrial Relations (CIR), *Report No. 52 on General Accident, Fire and Life Assurance Corporation (Second Report)*, 1973, p. 23.
11. DE, *Gazette*, November 1977.
12. Mackie and Pattullo, *Women at Work*, p. 89.
13. R.D. Barron and G.M. Norris, 'Sexual Divisions and the Dual Labour Market', in D.L. Barker and S. Allen (eds), *Dependence and Exploitation in Work and Marriage* (London, Longman, 1976), p. 47.
14. R. McNabb, 'The Labour Force Participation of Married Women', *Manchester School of Economic and Social Studies*, no. 3, September 1977.
15. The Stockport research referred to throughout the text is an ongoing SSRC-sponsored project entitled 'Manual Workers and the Sexual Division of Labour', jointly directed by the author and David Bennett at Manchester Polytechnic.
16. Stockport Metropolitan Borough, *Digest for the North Area 1974*.
17. G. Spray, 'Women's Labour in an Underdeveloped Region: A Perspective on Hull', unpublished paper given at British Sociological Association Sexual Divisions and Society Study Group Seminar, Bradford University, February 1977.
18. R.M. Blackburn, *Union Character and Social Class* (London, Batsford, 1967), p. 31.
19. V.L. Allen, *Militant Trade Unionism* (London, Merlin Press, 1966).
20. Ibid., p. 19.
21. Ibid., p. 41.
22. D. Thompson, 'Women and Nineteenth Century Radical Politics: A Lost Dimension', in J. Mitchell and A. Oakley (eds), *The Rights and Wrongs of Women* (Harmondsworth, Penguin, 1976).
23. T. Lupton, *On the Shopfloor* (Oxford, Pergamon, 1963).
24. DE, *Gazette*, February 1977.
25. H.A. Turner, *Is Britain Really Strike Prone? A Review of the Incidence, Character and Cost of Industrial Conflict*, University of Cambridge Dept. of Applied Economics, Occasional Paper 20 (Cambridge, CUP, 1969), p. 46.
26. DE, *Gazette*, January 1978.

27. Blackburn, *Union Character*, p. 56.
28. V. Beechey, 'Some Notes on Female Wage Labour', *Capital and Class*, no. 3, Autumn 1977.
29. J. Rogaly, *Grunwick* (Harmondsworth, Penguin Special, 1977), p. 35.
30. J.H. Goldthorpe, D. Lockwood, F. Bechhofer and J. Platt, *The Affluent Worker: Industrial Attitudes and Behaviour* (Cambridge, CUP, 1968).
31. G. Bain, D. Coates and V. Ellis, *Social Stratification and Trade Unionism* (London, Heinemann Educational, 1973); Blackburn, *Union Character*.
32. E.G.A. Armstrong, J.F.B. Goodman and A. Wagner, 'Normative Consensus, Constitutionalism and Aspects of Ideology in Industrial Relations: The case of the Footwear Industry', *Journal of Management Studies*, vol. 15, no. 1, February 1978, p. 30.
33. Bain *et al.*, *Social Stratification*, p. 138.
34. R. Coates and R. Silburn, *Poverty: The Forgotten Englishmen* (Harmondsworth, Penguin, 1973), p. 128.
35. Jean Lipman-Blumen discusses formal and informal sexual segregation in terms of what she calls a homosocial theory of sex roles, in 'Toward a Homosocial Theory of Sex Roles: An Explanation of Social Institutions', in M. Blaxall and B. Reagan (eds), *Women and the Workplace* (Chicago, UCP, 1976).

> The basic premise . . . suggests that men are attracted to, stimulated by, and interested in other men. It is a process that is noticeable in early childhood and is channeled and encouraged by the entire range of social institutions within which males live. The stratification system, which ranks individuals and groups in terms of their value to society, systematically places males in more highly valued roles than females (p. 16).

She suggests that the result of the differential valuation and socialisation of males and females results in men preferring the company of other men.

> Contrary to the claims of some theorists, men have not turned women into sex objects. Rather, from a structural viewpoint, women have been forced to fashion themselves as sex objects to attract men and distract them away from the greater interest and prestige with which they invest interaction with other men into the comforts of heterosexual relationships (p. 17).

I find the concept of homosocial illuminating in considering the sexual division of work and leisure, particularly where gender socialisation is more distinct and prescribes different behaviour by, and treatment of, men and women. For example, in the course of my current research amongst manual workers, it is frequently argued by both managers and employees that women could not do certain jobs because of 'the language' used by the men already employed. If it is suggested that some women might be immune to corruption or embarrassment, the response is invariably that the men would not feel comfortable continuing their unmodified behaviour in the presence of women or modifying their linguistic usage. In other words, they are more relaxed in, and *prefer,* the company of other men only. An extreme example of sexual segregation in a community is given by N. Dennis, F. Henriques and C. Slaughter. Talking of the different roles of husbands and wives in the family, they commented: 'A man's centres of activity are *outside* his home; it is outside his home that there are located the criteria of success and social acceptance. He works and plays, and makes contact with other men and women, *outside* his home. The comedian who defined "home" as "the place where you fill the pools in on a Wednesday night" was something of a sociologist. With the exception of a small minority of men . . . the husbands of Ashton for preference come home for a meal after finishing work and as soon as they can feel clean and rested they look for the company of their mates, i.e. their friends of the same sex.' N. Dennis, F. Henriques and C. Slaughter, *Coal is Our Life* (London, Eyre and Spottiswood, 1956), pp. 180-1.

36. K. Purcell, 'Working Women, Women's Work and the Occupation of Being a Woman', *Women's Studies International Quarterly*, vol. 1, no. 2, Summer 1978.

37. M. Mann, 'The Social Cohesion of Liberal Democracy', *American Sociological Review*, vol. 35, no. 3, June 1970.

38. M. Porter, 'Consciousness and Secondhand Experience: Wives and Husbands in Industrial Action', *Sociological Review*, vol. 26, no. 2, 1978.

6 THE MALE APPENDAGE – LEGAL DEFINITIONS OF WOMEN

Katherine O'Donovan

Role Allocation by Law

'You ought to help her because, after all, she is your mother.'[1] 'You ought to send your child to school.' 'You ought to work hard to support your family.' 'You ought to iron his shirts because he is your husband.' As can be seen, these statements are based on expectations of behaviour from incumbents of social roles in their relations with others. A way of acting is suggested as appropriate conduct from one in a specific relationship with another. However, the ought statement, whilst founded on the fact of a social relationship, varies according to a notion of conduct appropriate to a role. In the example 'You ought to help her because, after all, she is your mother', as Dorothy Emmet makes clear, the obligation to help follows not only from the fact of parenthood but also from a social relationship in which people occupy roles *vis-à-vis* each other. The obligation is moral not legal, and if there is a sanction it will be social.

The legal obligation in the statement 'You ought to send your child to school' does not preclude a moral judgement, but here failure to fulfil the expectations of the role of parent will probably result in legal intervention, as would failure to support one's family. The legal sanction may even be deprivation of the opportunity to play that particular role in that relationship. There may be disagreement among the actors as to suitable behaviour for a role, but where the relationship of the actors has been recognised by the law there will be specified rules to which the community will expect conformity. Such rules are usually referred to as the rights and duties of parents or the obligations of spouses. They may also be termed the minimum requirements for the role, that is, the rules to which all performers of the role must conform. Non-conformity with rules that comprise the minimum role requirement will result in legal sanction. Failure to provide for one's family may lead to imprisonment. A mother who cannot conform to the legal rules of motherhood may find herself deprived of the opportunity to play this role at all, if her child is taken into care. Thus the law gives its view of parenthood and, in so doing, helps to define the parent/ child relationship and what a parent is. For a particular incumbent of a social role a personal definition will be based on norms worked out in the relationship with others, and in particular relationships the norms agreed may be unique to those involved. Nevertheless the legal definition is important because it specifies the minimum role requirement and reflects and informs expectations of how an individual incumbent of a role will behave.

The imposition of roles on the basis of anatomical and physiological differences between people is done by society, with reliance on legal institutions in many instances. Justifications for different treatment of men and women by law are various. They may rest on sex differences but usually it is gender role differences that are invoked. Yet it is the law itself which helps to construct the gender role differences, as is shown below. A distinction must be made between sex differences and gender. Sex differences are the natural anatomical and physiological differences between women and men: for instance, the ability to menstruate, gestate and breast-feed. Gender is the social classification of a person as feminine or masculine. Gender role is the social role allocated on the basis of gender, but which extends much further than mere biological disparity.[2] Legal institutions support the ordering of society on a gender role basis. That an individual has no choice of sex is clear, but society is free to choose the social consequences, if any, to be attached to sex – that is, the gender role to which the individual must conform. At present the law defines and reinforces gender roles for individuals which do not necessarily have an inevitable connection with sex differences. In so doing the law is inhibiting change and causing hardship to those who do not adjust their personal lives to the gender stereotyped expectations of legal institutions.

Relationships recognised by law are structured and defined by that recognition. Legal rules may constitute the relationship by defining its creation, its consequences and its termination. Other rules may specify behaviour, through the allocation of rights and duties according to role. In marriage the rules, both constitutive and behavioural, are based on gender and their sum constitutes the role of husband or wife.

Having espoused a role, the performers may hope to modify it in practice, but legal rules cannot be changed by personal redefinition. So the legal minimum role requirement will remain. Since marriage is central to the experience of most women, I propose to explore gender role allocation by law in marriage. In 1973, 88.4 per cent of women in the age group 34-44 were married, a further 3.1 per cent were divorced and 1.7 per cent were widowed: a total of 93.2 per cent with marriage experience. Of the age group 25-34, 89.1 per cent had experience of marriage.[3] Despite the fact that 49 per cent of married women were economically active in 1976,[4] married women are not treated as autonomous individuals by law and social policy. Instead, they are defined in terms of marriage, a unit headed by the husband with the wife as dependant.

The Traditional Legal View of the Married Woman

The traditional view of the legal status of married women is to be found in the *Commentaries* of William Blackstone published in 1765. The *Commentaries*, considered today as 'an excellent primer of English law',[5] were one of the first compilations of the laws of England, both written and unwritten. In a legal system which looked to court precedent — earlier cases decided in court — for guidance in dispute resolution, Blackstone's writing was enormously influential because for many decades it was considered the most reliable statement of what the law then was. Blackstone laid down the effect of marriage on a woman as follows:

> By marriage, the husband and wife are one person in law: that is, the very being or legal existence of the woman is suspended during the marriage, or at least is incorporated and consolidated into that of the husband: under whose wing, protection, and cover, she performs everything.[6]

The legal consequences of the absorption of the wife's legal person into that of her husband have been documented elsewhere;[7] the principal effect was to deny the married woman access to property, to the courts, or to any form of legal action, without the concurrence of her husband.

Legislation has been passed, from the Married Women's Property Acts, 1870-82, to the Guardianship of Minors Act, 1971, in attempts to undo the state of the law as described by Blackstone. This process is usually described as putting 'a married woman in the same legal position as her unmarried sister'[8] and has not been altogether successful in changing the law, since it has not been formulated in terms of putting the married woman on the same footing as the married man. Consequently, for many legal and administrative purposes, husband and wife continue to be treated as a unit headed by the husband. This will be discussed in detail later; but here I wish to raise the question — less irrelevant than it at first appears to be for our understanding of modern marriage laws — of whether Blackstone was correct in his description, which he ended as follows: 'We may observe, that even the disabilities, which the wife lies under, are for the most part intended for her protection and benefit. So great a favourite is the female sex of the laws of England.'[9] No explanation was given by Blackstone for the principle that husband and wife are one person in law, yet his statement was highly influential on subsequent generations of judges and legislators, who used it as a justification for refusing to consider women as persons in their own right.[10] But there is evidence to suggest that, whatever the practice of the courts prior to Blackstone's publication of his *Commentaries,* married women in the seventeenth century were able to take an active part in the economic life of the community. Alice Clark gives details of married women who were accepted members of the business community and of guilds, able to trade as single women and be sued for their debts.[11] Similar evidence was found by Mary Beard, who said of Blackstone's principle of the unity of husband and wife that it 'contains a great deal of misleading verbalism, and . . . in upshot it is false'.[12] She accused Blackstone of being a rhetorician who mislead subsequent generations into citing his statement as evidence of women's subjection.

If the statement of the law in the *Commentaries* is correct, it is indeed surprising to find married women in the seventeenth century – who in legal theory were unable to contract or sue – engaging in commerce, and acting independently of their husbands. Their activities cannot be explained by a subsequent change in the law. The common law then and when Blackstone was writing was, so far as we know, based on the same principles. Indeed the earliest English legal textbook devoted exclusively to women's legal position confirms Blackstone's words. *The Lawes Resolution of Womens Rights,* printed in London in 1632[13] but which seems to have been written in the last years of Elizabeth I by an unknown lawyer, is addressed to women. The work is largely concerned with property rights and rules relating to dower, wife's estates, marriage and widowhood. Many examples are given of the principle that husband and wife are one person:

a women is Covert Baron as soone as she is overshadowed with her husbands protection and supereminency (Book 3; Sec. I).

When a small brooke or little river incorporateth with Rhodanus, Humber or the Thames, the poore Rivolet loseth her name, it is carried and recarried with the main associate, it beareth no sway, it possesseth nothing during coverture (Sec. III).

The Wife must take the name of her Husband (Sec. V); That which the Wife hath is the Husbands (Sec. IX); her husband is her sterne, her primus motor, without whom she cannot doe much at home and lesse abroad (Sec. XLII).

The text makes clear that 'here wanteth equality in the law, women goe downe stile, and many graines allowance will not make the ballance hang even'. The sympathetic author advises: 'Have patience (my Schollars) take not your opportunities of revenge, rather move for redresse by Parliament . . .' (Sec. XIV).

So although it may be considered that Blackstone was complacent and condescending about the legal status of married women, we cannot say he was wrong, since the earlier book of 1632 confirms his pronouncement. Yet there does seem to have been a dichotomy between legal theory and the lives led by some married women. One explanation for this may be drawn from the use of the world 'Schollars' in addressing readers of the *Lawes Resolution of Womens Rights*. The book was intended for literate women of the propertied classes, just as the *Commentaries* were intended for lawyers. That is why both works are so concerned with property rights on, during and after marriage. English family law draws its character from laws concerned with the concentration and transmission of wealth in the families of the landed classes.

The married women in the seventeenth century found by Clark and Beard to be active in business and in guilds were, in some cases, treated as single women. Borough customs and the special laws of the City of London enabled married women to trade as single women.[14] There seen s to have been a divergence between the common law – the law administered in the Royal courts – and 'the law of the smaller folk' which 'lives on only in some of the borough customs'.[15] The latter courts appear to have been more willing to indulge in legal fictions to circumvent the legal consequences of marriage. We may surmise that the classification of a woman as married or single was all-important to the Royal courts because on such matters of status depended the legitimacy of children and, therefore, inheritance, the right of a widow to dower, and questions of property generally. For those with little or no property, there are indications that the legal formalities of marriage may have been less material. Lord Hardwicke's Act, requiring solemnisation of marriage in the Church of England, was passed in 1753 and was the first serious attempt by English law to regulate marriage. Until then formal proof of marriage may sometimes have been difficult. Until 1753 there were three forms of marriage, the most lax of which required the parties merely to declare that they took each other as husband and wife (*per verba de praesenti* or *per verba de futuro* followed by consummation).[16] Marriage records will certainly have been kept in the Church of England from 1753 because the Act required marriage in church and registration of marriage, and indeed parish records were kept prior to then, but in order to be married it was not necessary to go to church until 1753, and it was only in 1836 that the present system of registration was introduced.[17]

Proof of marriage is important today in law, as a comparison of the rights of co-habitees with those of the married will show. Its importance lies partly in the fact that 'upon it may depend rights and obligations owed by or to the State in relation, for example, to tax, social security, and allegiance'.[18] And in establishing claims to children and property on the ending of a marital or quasi-marital relationship, the first legal question is whether the couple were married. However, as has been suggested above, current notions of state-regulated marriage are fairly recent. As Laslett said of the pre-1753 relationships: 'Neighbours decided whether any particular association could be called a marriage'.[19] The modern state, in eliminating local court autonomy, eliminated recognised legal fictions which allowed exceptions to the legal concept of unity of husband and wife. This concept was also taken over in the state's regulation of the citizen through administrative machinery, yet originally the unity of husband and wife served quite different purposes and may have applied only to a small number of relationships in the past.

The Treatment of the Married Couple as a Single Unit

For certain purposes – for instance, the administration of Supplementary Benefit – the household is the unit taken into account, and if there is a man present in a marital or cohabitation relationship he is assumed to be the head and it is he who gets the benefit, if any. There is a scale for householders which is considerably higher than that for dependants. The woman in the relationship will always be classified as a dependant, even if she is working and the man is not. Similarly, for National Insurance purposes, if the husband is present, he is assumed to be the head of the nuclear family – the relevant unit for this purpose – and a woman is expected to look to him for support of their children and, usually, of herself.

Hilary Land has explained the assumptions underpinning the treatment of married women as their husbands' dependants in the social security system. Beveridge's belief that 'during marriage most women will not be gainfully employed' determined the structure of the system.[20]

Despite participation of married women in work outside the home, they cannot provide benefits for their husbands and children unless the husband is incapable of work; they are treated as single persons, which is an improvement of their position at the time when Land was writing, but continues the stereotype that a married woman does not support a family. Demands have been made in the United States for the benefits a wife receives as a single person to be added to those she receives as a dependent spouse. The argument is that the family is making double contributions for little gain.[21] However, it is unlikely that such a demand would have support in Britain, since recent developments in social security law have been away from the treatment of the wage-earning married woman as her husband's dependant. This trend has been, in part, a response to legal requirements of the European Economic Community. But the proposed *Directive* on equality of treatment in social security does not envisage provision of equal benefits for spouses and for parents regardless of sex.[22]

Symbolic of the man's headship of the household is the surname. English law does not require a woman to take her husband's name on marriage; but the ability to do so is seen as a 'right' in family law text-books,[23] possibly a survival from the time when the wife — being unable to contract or own property — had the power to pledge her husband's credit for the necessities of life. The question of name is an emotive one, as evidenced by a number of court cases questioning a mother's right to change her children's surname to that which she has assumed. The courts have ruled that a change of name requires the consent of both parents.[24] This seems reasonable; but the judiciary bring to this issue the assumption that the child's (first) surname will be that of the father. So, in 1977, where a mother changed her name when pregnant and gave that surname to her child on its subsequent birth, she was considered to have changed the child's name without the father's consent. The court ruled that: 'The child's name is that of his father'.[25]

The Board of Inland Revenue persists in treating the married couple as a unit, and in assuming that the husband is head and breadwinner. From 1799, when income tax was introduced, husband and wife have been taxed as a unit represented by the husband. The husband was and is responsible for the payment of tax for the couple and therefore all correspondence and rebates are addressed to him. Since 1972, it has been possible for the wife, with her husband's agreement, to elect to be separately taxed on her earned income. She is then dealt with as a single person, but only as regards her earned income.[26]

The Obligation to Maintain

As a result of the doctrine of unity of the married couple, the traditional rule required the husband to maintain his wife and children, since the law did not recognise any capacity in the wife to maintain herself. The wife's obligation to support her husband and children arose only when the husband was incapable of work. The refusal of National Insurance benefits for her husband and children to a wife whose husband is considered capable of work is officially explained on these grounds. A wife is classified as a dependant, even if she is a wage-earner. The rule that the husband must always support the family is based on a legal rather than a social role,[27] but it inhibits choice of activity within the family. The maintenance obligation of the husband is used to justify other legal rules defining wives as dependants, particularly in social security law. The denial of the invalid care allowance to married women is an example of this: unlike the husband, she is not considered to work outside the home (even if she in fact does) and therefore is held not to require a paid assistant to care for the invalid. However, the Domestic Proceedings and Magistrates Courts Act, 1978,[28] will impose equal maintenance obligations on spouses, thus removing a major rationale for institutional arrangements that treat spouses according to ascribed gender roles.

The husband's maintenance obligation is the explanation offered for refusal of financial benefits to the wife in a number of situations, yet in legal practice that obligation means very little. During marriage it is virtually impossible for a wife living with her husband to enforce maintenance. This is because the courts are traditionally unwilling to interfere in a marital relationship as just an 'ordinary domestic arrangement'. Behind this lurks the idea that, since husband and wife are a unit, their domestic life is a private world in which the law must not intervene. This was explained by a former Master of the Rolls, Lord Evershed as follows:

> It was in the year 1604, not far removed from the date when Shakèspeare wrote the lines from The Taming of the Shrew
> [She is my goods, my chattels; she is my house
> My household stuff, my field, my barn
> My horse, my ox, my ass, my anything.]
> . . . that, according to Coke's report of the judgement in Semayne's Case, it was judicially laid down that the house of everyone is to him as his castle and fortress. More than three centuries later Atkin L.J., in a famous judgement, said: 'The parties themselves are advocates,

judges, courts, sheriff's officer and reporter. In respect of these promises (of maintenance in marriage) each house is a domain into which the King's writ does not seek to run, and to which its officers do not seek to be admitted.'[29]

An indication of the law's traditional reluctance to enter this private domain was that little legal remedy was provided for domestic violence until the passing of the Domestic Violence and Matrimonial Proceedings Act, 1976.[30]

Although legal provisions contain a view of marriage in which the husband is breadwinner and the wife dependant, the law does little to protect the dependant-wife during marriage. The conditions of domestic production are unregulated and, as we have seen, there is no enforcement of payment for it. The only legal provision on housekeeping is the Married Women's Property Act of 1964, which provides that where savings are made 'from any allowance made by the husband for the expenses of the matrimonial home or for similar purposes ... the money ... shall ... be treated as belonging to the husband and wife in equal shares'. The gender role assumptions here are obvious, but even more interesting is the fact that the law does not intervene to enforce payment, but only to ensure that the husband retains a half interest in any savings made by a prudent wife.

Family lawyers explain this as an indication that the law is only directed to pathological situations, to family breakdown.

The normal behaviour of husband and wife or parents and children towards each other is beyond the law – as long as the family is 'healthy'. The law comes in when things go wrong. More than that, the mere hint of anyone concerned that the law may come in is the surest sign that things are or will soon be going wrong.[31]

However, should the family breakdown be indicated by the wife deserting or committing adultery, the courts have ruled that she cannot look to her husband for support while they remain married.[32]

On divorce a husband's responsibility for maintenance continues, especially where there are children, and a wife too acquires the duty of supporting the children. Thus the sexes would appear to have identical legal roles. However, the judicial attitude becomes apparent from the leading case on the subject, where the provision of future maintenance, known as periodical payments, was the justification for cutting the wife's share of property acquired during marriage from a half to a third.

> If we were only concerned with the capital assets of the family, and
> particularly with the matrimonial home, it would be tempting to
> divide them half and half . . . That would be fair enough if the wife
> afterwards went her own way, making no further demands on her
> husband . . . Most wives want their former husbands to make period-
> ical payments as well to support them; because after the divorce he
> will be earning far more than she; and she can only keep up her
> standard of living with his help. He also has to make payments for
> the children out of his earnings, even if they are with her.[33]

So because of her calls on her husband's future income, a wife does not
get an equal share of family assets. But the wife's future dependence, if
it exists, is because of her child-care responsibilities; and one of the
reasons why she will probably be a low-wage earner after divorce may
be because she has foregone training and experience because of marriage.
  Judicial imperviousness to women's lot was further evidenced by the
following explanation for the award of the lion's share to husbands.

> When a marriage breaks up, there will thenceforth be two house-
> holds instead of one. The husband will have to go out to work all
> day and must get some woman to look after the house — either a
> wife if he remarries or a housekeeper if he does not. He will also
> have to provide maintenance for the children. The wife will not
> usually have so much expense. She may go out to work herself,
> but she will not usually employ a housekeeper. She will do most
> of the housework herself, perhaps with some help. Or she may
> marry, in which case her new husband will provide for her.[34]

Clearly the assumptions behind this statement are based on beliefs
about the sexes and their roles. One method of testing the neutrality
of the judiciary in the interpretation of legal provisions is to try to
imagine how the above paragraph would sound if the gender roles were
reversed. In the case quoted above, Lord Denning was interpreting the
gender neutral language of the current divorce law. That gender neutral
provisions can be interpreted in a biased manner is clear from Albie
Sachs's work on the male monopoly cases from 1869 to 1929, where
the neutral word 'person' was interpreted by the judiciary to mean men
only.[35]
  Another example of gender bias can be found in a recent study of

divorce court registrars whose function it is to deal with issues of maintenance, property, and custody of and access to children. Registrars have wide discretion in the exercise of their powers and, consciously or unconsciously, they use it to favour the party in a conflict with whom they identify, or of whom they approve.

> My own view is that I think some weight should go in favour of the good wife and I would be likely to order a bad wife less. The local community, which still retains strong traces of its religious up-bringing, would respect this view.[36]

> Must one treat all wives in the same way unless they are nympho-maniac or of the worst order – are they to be treated like a faithful wife of 20 years standing who has been nastily and shabbily treated by her husband?[37]

Although guidance from the higher courts indicates that the wife should be awarded (at least) one third of matrimonial assets, the report suggests that many registrars do not give her even this.

It might be argued that, in order to avoid the stigma of dependence, a wife should forego any claim to future maintenance. But this over-looks two points. First, the courts take the view that a man ought to support his dependants, especially if they are otherwise likely to be supported by the state, and this view is shared by the Supplementary Benefits Commission. Second, domestic production, although unpaid, is treated as being of value by legal institutions where an accident has eliminated the producer of it, or increased the labour involved. This is not the place to go into the details of the domestic labour debate (see Mackintosh in this volume). It suffices to point out that within the terms of legal analysis the courts currently value housework and child care at about thirty pounds a week in actions relating to a wife's desertion or death.[38] So, for a woman to be paid by her ex-husband for such services would appear to be merely just.

Recently judges have adopted the attitude that marriage is not a 'bread ticket for life',[39] recognising that a woman without children may be able to support herself. But the woman with small children has little alternative to accepting maintenance from her former spouse or from the state. If maintenance is ordered by a court, current statistics show that it will be regularly complied with in only 45 per cent of cases[40] and that enforcement is difficult. Beveridge proposed that a wife should be paid an 'end of marriage benefit' which would consist of a temporary separation benefit, similar to widow's benefit, and guardian and training benefit where appropriate. This would have enabled the divorced woman to undertake training for employment, but the idea was rejected by the government in 1944.[41] Of course, in an ideal world where roles were chosen, a woman would not automatically take on the caring role in relation to the children on breakdown of marriage; but, as we shall see, women and men tend to specialise in activities considered appropriate to their gender roles.

Activity Specialisation

There is no direct legal obligation on the wife to specialise in household matters, although by family law and policy it is assumed that she will – as Mary McIntosh has shown in this volume. The most sensible arrangement in a marriage would be for the low-wage partner to specialise in household production, while the high-wage partner specialises in the market. In addition to the disincentive to wives joining a market which pays low wages for many types of 'women's work', families choosing to maximise their income in response to market forces will find that although there are no legal rules requiring the wife to undertake housework and child care, a myriad of structures with legal bases provide disincentives for the husband to do so. These disincentives reflect and reinforce assumptions about women's social role in contexts in which the assumptions may no longer be valid, or at least might not be valid if the legal structures were neutral. That the great majority of married women accept the tasks of housework and child care is undeniable, but so is women's increasing participation in the work force. If legal structures were neutral in role allocation, issues relating to the imposition of domestic production on women might be clarified. It is not intended here to suggest that legal changes would bring about material changes in society, but at least some of the complexities surrounding the question of sex roles and gender roles would be dissipated.

The assumption that a wife or 'some female person' should care for a man's children and do his housework underlies income tax and social security provisions. In the tax system this takes the form of giving additional personal allowances to married men with incapacitated wives and to single parents, but denying it to married women with incapacitated husbands. The allowance reflects the assumption that it is a married woman's unpaid job to care for children and that if she cannot do so, her husband is entitled to financial assistance for someone else to perform the job. In contrast, a woman on her own, even if working, is not considered by the courts as in need of an allowance for a substitute child-minder. Similarly, other financial provisions are so constructed that they provide incentives for women, where available, rather than men, to undertake a domestic role. The housekeeper tax allowance is paid only where a woman is employed, so a male housekeeper is not recognised for tax purposes. And the daughter's service allowance cannot be claimed for sons.[42] In social security legal provisions there are a number of examples of gender bias. The invalid care allowance is not paid to married women – presumably because they are expected to do such work unpaid. Where additions for adult dependants are given to those who get the allowance, these are limited to a wife or to 'some female person ... who ... has the care of a child or children of the beneficiary's family'[43] – so a male dependant with care of children is excluded. The disabled married woman is ineligible for the non-contributory invalidity pension 'except where she is incapable of performing normal household duties'.[44] The additions for dependants are as shown above.

The award of custody of children in divorce and other matrimonial cases reflects the allocation of the role of child-caretaker to women. A recent study showed that in 81 per cent of divorce court cases and 94 per cent of magistrates' cases custody was given to the mother. Where there was a contest by the father, however, the outcome was not so predictable.[45] It is clear that women demand custody and men expect them to have it, accepting, not challenging, traditional assumptions.[46] While this is a fairly recent development in legal administration – until 1886 the law did not recognise any custody or guardianship rights of the mother – since it is combined with other assumptions in the law, it leaves the wife at a financial disadvantage. In order to perform child-care tasks, the divorced woman may need economic support. As has already been stated, she is at a disadvantage in the job market and the maintenance she needs will be used as an argument against her when divorce financial arrangements are made. Yet the maintenance is necessary for child care. Recently, a man forced to care for his two children (because of his wife's desertion after an accident befell him), was awarded twenty pounds a week to hire a substitute – this being the court's estimate of the value of his wife's services less her consumption.[47] This case indicates that maintenance of a child-caring wife is not full recompense for her work.

In drawing up the pleadings for divorce, the legal profession uses clichés such as that the wife was a 'loyal, faithful and good wife',[48] or that she did not fulfil her 'wifely duties'. The 'loving and unselfish wife' is entitled to recognition of her good behaviour by the court in awarding maintenance.[49]

These phrases and the legal provisions discussed above suggest that, despite the judicial view that the law should not interfere in the marriage relationship, there is a definite legal notion of how a woman should act and what being a 'good wife' entails. In other words, the law does not intervene in the unequal economic relationship found in marriage, but maintains – through its provisions, assumptions, judicial and other official attitudes – an ideology of gender roles which ensures that individuals who deviate from these roles are penalised.

Neutralising Sex-based Legal Roles

Differentiation between men and women by law and custom appears to be a feature of all known societies and figures even in Engels's theory of the family, although not as sexual stratification in the early stages of his assumed pattern of evolution.[50] A society in which there was no official recognition of physiological sex differences between persons would be new to us and we cannot say what it would look like. Sexual integrationists have argued that an individual's sex is an entirely physiological characteristic and is no barrier to sexual integration. This is not to ignore the current form of reproduction which temporarily incapacitates mothers, although some feminists consider this an obstacle to be overcome by extra-uterine reproduction.[51] Any special provision for maternity can be justified as necessary to the infant's well-being rather than being seen as a peculiar right based on gender.[52]

There seems to be no reason why the law, which has espoused an ideology of equality as evidenced in recent legislation, should continue to reinforce roles by gender-based legal rules and incentives. It would be a fairly simple matter to phrase legislation in gender-neutral terms, thus denying legal recognition to gender roles. The roles of breadwinner, homemaker, and child-caretaker would not necessarily subsequently disappear. It is arguable that social roles are part of the institutions of society. However, these social roles should be based on choice, not on sex. Gender roles are not chosen but imposed on individuals, and that such major social consequences should follow on the slight physiological differences between women and men is increasingly a surprise to scholars.[53] The abolition of legal allocation of roles based on gender would increase the areas of autonomy and freedom for people. This argument is not an objection to role-based law but to gender-based law. Indeed, it is clear that a person who provides unpaid services in the home and foregoes a cash income needs the protection and recognition of the law, and that such a person should receive direct any income, allowances and benefits (such as child benefit) that are intended for the support of domestic production. No doubt there would be problems of proof between couples as to who was performing the home role in the relationship. But these are not insuperable if the emphasis is placed on social function rather than on gender.

To accomplish such a change in legal institutions would require study of those different types of laws. In the area of law relating to current roles in marriage or quasi-marriage, whilst the roles of bread-winner and homemaker might be retained for administrative purposes, these would not be gender-based. Neutral words such as spouse or part-ner could be substituted for wife and husband. It would be a matter of personal choice for a family to decide its arrangements (although job market constraints would, of course, continue to limit choice). This would not resolve the complex problems of whether the family or the individual should be treated as the unit of account for matters of taxation and welfare, but it would help to expose issues masked by current sexual ideologies. The Supplementary Benefits Commission is actively considering adopting a neutral social security system 'leaving people as free as possible to make their own arrangements in whatever way suits them best'.[54]

Where laws are based on physiological differences between the sexes, I suggest that examination would reveal that the necessity for these laws is more apparent than real. The criminal law protects persons from rape and sexual assault but there is no reason why this should be linked to sex. The South Australian legislature has amended its legislation on sexual offences to encompass male and female aggressors and victims. This has been done by the use of the words 'person' and 'his or her'. Where the criminal law has given special recognition to post-natal depression, this can be subsumed under general rules relating to diminished responsibility.

Legislation that protects women at work from adverse conditions considered suitable for men has been justified by both gender-role differences and physiological differences. Its retention is supported by feminists as part of a general strategy for improving working conditions. Research would indicate whether the rationale for protective legislation was based on role or on physiology. If it is role-based, then it would seem logical that all those persons assuming a particular role in society — for instance, the care of small children — should benefit from protective legislation. If the rationale is physiological, then all persons with similar physiological needs must also be protected.

The third category is gender-neutral or androgynous laws. Where such laws already exist, study would reveal the extent to which, in the course of interpretation, judges and officials bring to their work conventional ideas and assumptions concerning women. As we have seen in the administration of the divorce laws, neutral wording of legal language is not good enough; it may mask deeply ingrained attitudes and prejudices on the part of the interpreter. It is debatable whether the veil of impartiality is more easily pierced when it covers blatantly discriminatory legislation or when legal provisions are ostensibly neutral. In my opinion, non-gender-specific legislation would clarify issues which at present are so often explained as 'that's the law'.

This plea for an end to official ascription of role based on sex is not intended to suggest that legal changes would bring about social revolution or even true economic equality between the sexes. Far more fundamental measures are required for that. However, gender-neutral legislation is a necessary, if far from sufficient, condition for justice to individuals in society.

Notes

1. D. Emmet, *Rules, Roles and Relations* (London, Macmillan, 1966), p. 37.
2. A. Oakley, *Sex, Gender and Society* (London, Temple Smith, 1972), p. 158.
3. Central Statistical Office, *Social Trends No. 6* (London, HMSO, 1975), Table 1.12.
4. Central Statistical Office, *Social Trends No. 7* (London, HMSO, 1976), Table 5.3.
5. G. Jones, 'Introduction: The Sovereignty of the Law', *Selections from Blackstone's Commentaries on the Laws of England* (London, Macmillan, 1973), p. xlvii.
6. W. Blackstone, *Commentaries on the Laws of England*, 7th ed. (Oxford, Clarendon Press, 1775), Bk. 1, p. 442.
7. M. Finer and O.R. McGregor, 'The History of the Obligation to Maintain' in *Report of the Committee on One-parent Families* (Finer Report), Cmnd. 5629, vol. 2 (London, HMSO, 1974).
8. P.M. Bromley, *Family Law*, 5th ed. (London, Butterworths, 1976), p. 108.
9. Blackstone, *Commentaries*, Bk. 1, p. 445.
10. A. Sachs, 'The Myth of Judicial Neutrality: The Male Monopoly Cases', in P. Carlen (ed), *The Sociology of Law*, Sociological Review Monograph 23 (University of Keele, Wood and Mitchell, 1976).
11. A. Clark, *Working Life of Women in the Seventeenth Century* (London, Routledge, 1919).
12. M. Beard, *Women as Force in History* (New York, Macmillan, 1946), p. 82.
13. This book, of which there are two copies in the British Museum, was printed in 1632. The preface is initialled by I.L. and there is a section entitled 'To The Reader' by T.E. T.E. did not know by whom the discourse had been

composed, but implied that the author was already dead in 1632. From T.E.'s description of his decision to have the work printed, we can conclude that he (T.E.) was a lawyer, because he mentioned the Lent Vacation as the time when he added 'many reasons, opinions, Cases and resolutions of Cases to the Authors store'.

14. M. Bateson, 'Introduction', *Borough Customs*, vol. II (London, Selden Society, vol. XXI, 1906), p. cxiii.

15. W.S. Holdsworth, *A History of English Law* (London, Methuen, 1923), vol. 3, p. 535.

16. Bromley, *Family Law,* p. 33.

17. For advice on this matter, I am grateful to Belinda Meteyard, whose M.Phil. dissertation entitled 'Legal and Administrative Provisions as a Factor in the Maintenance of the Marriage Rate' deals with Lord Hardwicke's Act of 1753.

18. Law Commission, *Report on Solemnisation of Marriage in England and Wales,* no. 53, 1973, para. 104.

19. P. Laslett, *Family Life and Illicit Love in Earlier Generations* (Cambridge, CUP, 1977), p. 108.

20. H. Land, 'Women: Supporters or Supported?', in D.L. Barker and S. Allen (eds), *Sexual Divisions and Society: Process and Change* (London, Tavistock, 1976), p. 110.

21. 'The social security system also places a double burden on the married woman who works outside the home. She is forced to pay a full social security tax, but the benefits she receives as an independent worker are not added to those she would be entitled to as a spouse. The family thus pays a double tax when she works, but she collects for only a single worker'. L.J. Weitzman, 'Legal Regulation of Marriage: Tradition and Change', 62 *Calif. L. Rev.,* vol. 62, 1974, p. 1191. In 1973 a bill was introduced in Congress (H.R. 11999, 93rd Cong., 1st Sess.) to enable working women to collect their own pension plus any pension as husband's dependant.

22. *Official Journal of the European Communities,* 11.2.77, No. C34/4, 'Proposal for a directive concerning the progressive implementation of the principle of equality of treatment for men and women in matters of social security'.

23. Bromley, *Family Law,* p. 112.

24. See *R (BM)* v. *R (DN) (child: surname)* [1978] 2 All E.R. 33; *Practice Direction* 24 May 1976 [1978] 3 All E.R. 451; *Re W.G.* (1976) 6 Fam. Law 210.

25. In *D* v. *B (otherwise D) (child: surname),* [1977] 3 All E.R. 751, the mother had left the father of the child she was expecting, and to whom she was married, before the birth. She registered the child's name as that which she had assumed by deed poll before the birth, and which was the surname of the man with whom she went to live. In the Family Division of the High Court, Lane J. considered the law on the matter and stated: 'Applying those authorities to this case, I hold that the mother was incompetent to change the child's surname, by deed poll or by registration of birth, without either the father's consent or an order of the court. The child's surname is that of his father'. The judge did not say what would happen in the case of a married couple with different surnames who had maintained these throughout marriage. The judge, in discussing the issue, used language like 'he should bear his father's name' – a phrase redolent of property rights. Since this paper was written the Court of Appeal has reversed the decision of Lane J. and held that a mother is competent to give her surname to her child. See *Times Law Report,* May 25 1978. It is noticeable that *The Times* published this under the heading 'Child permitted to take name of mother's lover', suggesting that a woman does not have a surname of her own; it is either her husband's or her lover's.

26. Equal Opportunities Commission, *Income Tax and Sex Discrimination*

(Manchester, EOC Pamphlet, 1977), p. 11. Since this paper was written the Finance Act 1978, S. 22 has been passed to enable a wife who is paying taxes on a pay-as-you-earn basis to receive her own rebates.

27. R. Lister and L. Wilson, *The Unequal Breadwinner* (London, National Council for Civil Liberties pamphlet, 1976).

28. This Act, which has just received the Royal Assent, provides: 'Either party to a marriage may apply to a magistrates' court for an order under section 2 of this Act on the ground that the other party to the marriage — (a) has failed to provide reasonable maintenance for the applicant; or (b) has failed to provide or make a proper contribution towards reasonable maintenance for any child of the family.' The Act also proposes that similar provisions apply in applications to the higher courts.

29. Lord Evershed, 'Foreword' to R.H. Graveson and F.R. Crane, *A Century of Family Law* (London, Sweet and Maxwell, 1957), p. xv.

30. Select Committee on Violence in Marriage, *Report*, House of Commons, Session 1974-75, vol. 1, paras. 42-53.

31. O. Kahn-Freund and K.W. Wedderburn, 'Editorial Foreword' to J. Eekelaar, *Family Security and Family Breakdown* (Harmondsworth, Penguin, 1971), p. 7.

32. *Gray* v. *Gray* [1976] Fam. 324.

33. *Watchel* v. *Watchel* [1973] Fam. 72 at 94, per Lord Denning.

34. Idem, at 95.

35. Sachs, 'Myth of Judicial Neutrality'; A. Sachs, 'The Myth of Male Protectiveness and the Legal Subordination of Women' in C. Smart and B. Smart (eds), *Women, Sexuality and Social Control* (London, Routledge and Kegan Paul, 1978).

36. W. Barrington Baker, J. Eekelaar, C. Gibson and S. Raikes, *The Matrimonial Jurisdiction of Registrars* (Oxford, Centre for Socio-Legal Studies, 1977), para. 2.21, quoting an anonymous registrar.

37. Ibid., para. 2.23.

38. In *Regan* v. *Williamson* [1976] 2 All E.R. 241, where the High Court considered compensation for the loss of a 'good wife and mother' in an accident, £21.50 per week was awarded after £10 had been deducted for the cost of previously keeping the deceased.

39. In *Brady* v. *Brady* [1973] 3 Fam. Law 78, Sir George Baker reduced an order for £3 a week to 10p where the marriage lasted only five months, saying: 'In these days of "woman's lib" there is no reason why a wife whose marriage has not lasted long, and who has no child, should have a bread ticket for life.'

40. Finer, *Report*, vol. 1, p. 100.

41. Ibid., p. 147.

42. Equal Opportunities Commission, *Income Tax and Sex Discrimination*, p. 15. The Finance Act, 1978, S. 19 has removed the gentler distinctions in the housekeeper allowance and has also amended the daughter's service allowance to cover 'son or daughter'.

43. Social Security Act, 1975, S. 37 (3) and Statutory Instruments 1976/409, S. 13 (1).

44. Social Security Act, 1975, S. 36 (2).

45. S. Maidment, 'A Study in Child Custody', *Family Law*, vol. 6, no. 7, 1976, pp. 195-200; vol. 6, no. 8, 1976, pp. 236-41.

46. J. Eekelaar, E. Clive, K. Clarke and S. Raikes, *Custody After Divorce* (Oxford, Centre for Socio-Legal Studies, 1977). The authors found that in 73.3 per cent of their cases of breakdown of marriage the children were living with the wife; in the great majority of cases the court confirmed the status quo. The study indicates that 'wives are more tenacious than husbands in their attempts to obtain possession of the children' (p. 9); that husbands in most

cases are content to leave to the wife the task of raising the children; but that where the children were already with the husband the court was unlikely to move them. This suggests that the courts do not necessarily assume that a father is unfit for child rearing.

47. In *Oakley* v. *Walker* [1977] 121 Sol. Jo. 619, where, because of his accident, a wife deserted her husband, leaving him with two small children to care for, he received compensation of £20 a week to enable him to employ a substitute.

48. 'The wife put in an answer, some part of which is in what has become the standard form of cliché in these cases, alleging that she was a "loyal, faithful and good wife". Just why these three adjectives have crept into the standard form of pleading, I do not know'. Ormrod L.J. in *Le Marchant* v. *Le Marchant* [1977] 3 All E.R. 610 at 612.

49. *Duchesne* v. *Duchesne* [1950] 2 All E.R. 784 at 791 (Pearce J.).

50. F. Engels, *The Origins of the Family, Private Property and the State* (London, Lawrence and Wishart, 1972).

51. S. Firestone, *The Dialectic of Sex* (London, Jonathan Cape, 1971), p. 233.

52. A. Jaggar, 'On Sexual Equality', *Ethics*, vol. 84, July 1974, p. 285.

53. E. Goffman, 'The Arrangement between the Sexes', *Theory and Society*, vol. 4, no. 3, Fall 1977, p. 302.

54. Supplementary Benefits Commission, *Annual Report 1976*, Cmnd. 6910 (London, HMSO, 1977), 1.7.

7 THE WELFARE STATE AND THE NEEDS OF THE DEPENDENT FAMILY

Mary McIntosh

This chapter takes up an issue that has been raised many times in feminist discussions, but attempts to cast it in a new light. The issue is that of the division of labour of women and men in the reproduction of the population. It will examine, in relation to contemporary capitalism, some of the analytical problems posed by the fact that the 'dependent family' supported by a male breadwinner who earns a 'family wage' is the primary institutional form for the reproduction of the working class.

It is important to note here that, from a social point of view, the reproduction of the population involves far more than what zoologists mean by the reproduction of the members of an animal species. It means not merely the biological production of infants who will form the next generation but all of the other processes whereby people are replaced, repaired and replenished from day to day as well as from generation to generation. From day to day, it requires not only biological necessities such as food, shelter, sleep and exercise, but also those social conditions that will preserve people's personality structure and outlook on life. From generation to generation, it requires socialisation, education and training. In each society it involves the maintenance of a certain range of the old and the disabled as well as of those who can fend for themselves.

From the Marxist perspective of this chapter, the reproduction of the population is only a part of the reproduction of the conditions of capitalism as a whole. All the elements of the productive system and the legal, political and cultural superstructure are reproduced and developed as well. From the point of view of the capitalist system, the section of the population that must be reproduced is the working class, in the very broad sense of all those who depend upon wages or salaries for their support and do not own productive or finance capital. The reproduction of the capitalist class is not of great significance, since it is the reproduction and expansion of capital itself (rather than of the people who happen to own it) that matters as far as the system is concerned. But the working class occupies a quite different place as the supplier of the transforming element of labour power that is essential

154 *The Welfare State and the Needs of the Dependent Family*

for the accumulation of capital.

To speak of the division of labour between men and women in the reproduction of the working class thus takes us far beyond the division between those who provide sperm and those who bear and suckle babies in the sexual reproduction of members of the species. The significance of the sexual division of labour in the production of infants and the question as to how inevitable it is have long, and rightly, been a focus of feminist debate. This chapter is concerned with issues that are not so fundamental in a trans-historical sense but are specific to contemporary capitalism, where the reproduction of the working class is primarily achieved through the institution of households based on the nuclear family: the family household system.

The chapter falls into three sections, each taking up a major problem, which can be summarily presented as follows:

1. The first arises from the fact that this institutional form of household, if based on kinship, cannot be universal and even if it were, cannot be adequate to the reproduction of a working class dependent upon wage labour. This makes it necessary to question how far we can explain the form of the family and women's oppression within it in terms of a functional relation between the family form and capitalist wage labour or other requirements of capital. It will be argued that the family system is 'inadequate' to its supposed functions of reproduction.

2. The second problem is that of defining 'needs', which must be done if we are to speak of the adequacy or inadequacy of a system for reproduction. Needs must be seen as historically determined by class struggles and struggles between women and other groups to define their needs and rights.

3. The third problem is to identify the part played by the state both in these struggles over the definition of need and also in bolstering the family household system so that it can function as effectively as possible in relation to capitalist production.

All of this may seem rather tangential to the problems of women; so it may be as well to state that I see the key to the understanding of women's oppression as lying in the understanding of the nature of the family. Women are oppressed elsewhere — in paid work and in many political, legal and cultural spheres — and there are many important non-familial mechanisms that need to be studied. But ultimately the very construction of men and women as separate and opposed categories takes place within, and in terms of, the family.

Furthermore, neither the oppression of women nor the family is eternal and unchanging. Though there are important and challenging elements of continuity — such as have been explored in psychoanalytic work — the family and women's oppression also have a specific character in each different epoch. This paper is part of the contemporary attempt to identify women's position in the dependent, privatised family of late capitalism and to understand its relation to the organisation of production in the public sphere in the capitalist mode that dominates in our time.

Dependence and the Capitalist Wage System

The Reproduction of the Conditions of Capitalism

The way in which contemporary Marxist analysis approaches the problem of the relation between the institution of the family and capitalist production is through the idea of *reproduction*. The family is not seen as a part of capitalist production but as the locus (among other things) of activities that are essential to the reproduction of the conditions of capitalism. Most notably, perhaps, as the place where children are brought up and where intimate pressures are brought to bear on adults, it plays an essential part in the reproduction of ideology, including those elements of ideology that directly sustain the relations of production. But there are two distinct and sometimes contradictory ways in which the family system operates for the reproduction of capitalism that are of particular importance in relation to women.

On the one hand, it serves for the reproduction of labour power (though variably and inadequately, as we shall see). There is a family household system in which a number of people are expected to be dependent on the wages of a few adult members, primarily of the husband and father who is a 'breadwinner', and in which they are all dependent for cleaning, food preparation and so forth on unpaid work chiefly done by the wife and mother. This system serves for the reproduction of the working class by distributing the wage around for the support of a larger number of people than are actually in paid work at any given time: children, retired people, the sick and disabled, those who do domestic work, the unemployed. It also provides the setting for the unpaid domestic work and caring of women, which keeps the cost of servicing today's and tomorrow's workers low.

On the other hand, as a system in which married women *can* be dependent on their husbands (though in fact many are not), it enables them to serve as a reserve army of labour; they can be drawn into wage work when they are needed, but 'disappear almost without trace into the family'[1] when they are redundant to paid employment.

This double linking of women's domestic dependence and wage work means that there is no simple functional relation between the family and capitalist production. Each of the links has developed historically in a very uneven way, each necessarily in relation to the other, but frequently in a contradictory relationship. Though the analysis to be presented in this paper has an appearance of timelessness, there is in fact no reason to suppose that the present period represents any kind of mature system. It may well be a period of transition; and one of the uses of analysis may be to help us understand what directions of change are possible.

The Family Household and the Reproduction of Labour Power

In Volume I of *Capital*, Marx wrote: 'The maintenance and reproduction of the working-class is, and must ever be, a necessary condition to the reproduction of capital. But the capitalist may safely leave its fulfilment to the labourer's instincts of self-preservation and of propagation.'[2] The point that he wished to emphasise was that this reproduction, unlike for instance the reproduction of capital itself, is not the task of any department of capitalist production. It takes place outside of capitalist production proper. Nevertheless, though Marx may be right in saying that the individual capitalist does not concern himself with the reproduction of the labour power of his own employees, capitalists as a class have done much to sustain the appropriate household institutions, through state policies concerned with marriage, the family and income maintenance. This is a topic to which I shall return in more detail at the end of this chapter.

The concern here is whether the institution of the family household (be it a product of 'the labourer's instincts' or of state policies) can be adequate to the reproduction of a working class dependent upon wages. The central problem is that only certain members of the class, the workers themselves, earn a wage. The rest of the working class subsist upon state support, or upon private pensions and savings, or by dependence upon their relatives. The first two I shall return to later; the third is organised largely through the family household.

The family household is usually seen in social science as a group in which the members share their income and their consumption. Indeed, in many studies of standards of living, including those conducted by official bodies (see the various reports of the Royal Commission on the Distribution of Income and Wealth, from 1975 onwards, and the evidence to this Commission by the Women's Liberation Campaign for Financial and Legal Independence), the basic unit of account is the family or the married couple rather than the individual. The family is the 'income unit' and also the 'consumption unit'; consumption is seen as being one of the chief remaining 'functions' of the modern family. For this reason it is impossible to get any large-scale evidence about how well the dependants of wage-earners live. There is plenty of small-scale evidence, however, to indicate that most wives (as well as children) do much less well than their wage-earning husbands[3] and other dependants probably fare even worse.

More important, however, is the fact that households can vary a great deal in size and many of them do not have a male breadwinner. This is inevitable as long as households are formed almost exclusively on the basis of close kinship ties. Eleanor Rathbone, the great campaigner for family allowances in the inter-war period, expressed most strikingly the inadequacy of the existing theories of wages that related the minimum wage to what was necessary for the upkeep of an average or normal family. She wrote, in 1924:

> But there is no general rule as to the size of dependent families. The number of dependants on a labourer's wages varies from zero to ten or eleven. Even if it were possible to fix on a family of a particular size as necessary to keep up the population to an actual or desired figure and to treat that as the normal for which wages do or should provide, families would still pass through various stages of dependency in arriving at the normal and receding from it as the children grow up. . . . Nowhere in these classic authorities do I find any recognition of the waste of resources at the one end and the human suffering at the other involved in a system which stretches families of all sizes and stages of development to fit the Procrustean bed of a uniform wage.[4]

In presenting her case, Rathbone's concern seems to have been as much about the waste as about the human suffering. She paints a picture of bachelors and childless men spending freely on drink and gambling the money intended for wives and children they do not have. Though she is arguing for a system of family allowances to supplement the income of large families, she suggests that, unless the national product were to increase, this would have to be financed from the wages of others: 'If the allowance were the result of the redistribution of the existing wage-bill — the bachelor's surplus would be cut for the benefit of his

comrade's family.'[5] What is most impressive about her book, whatever
we may think about its political assumptions, is the clarity with which
she demonstrates the inadequacy of the wage as a system for the
support of people living in families of vastly different sizes and stages
of their cycle. Since her day, the cycle has shortened and the proportion
of families with more than one wage-earner has probably increased,
while the amount of variation in family size has decreased a good deal.
But the principle still remains: despite the advent of the so-called
'family wage' and the assumption that wages should be at a level high
enough to support the average family, there is a sense in which *the
needs of wage-earners' dependants are unrecognised and unrecognisable
in the capitalist wage system.*[6]

Furthermore, there are many who live in households with no wage
earner: the retired, the disabled, the separated, the widowed, the single
parent, the unemployed, are often among these. These are the people
whose needs were already in Rathbone's day more or less recognised by
the state, in the Poor Law system and its successors. In respect of them,
the inadequacy of the wage system had by that time been established.
There were many problems about which of these people could be
pushed into self-support, by such devices as the 'workhouse test' and
about whether the support of some of them condoned immorality and
undermined the family. But the principle that there were some at
least who needed state support was accepted. The emerging area of
struggle related to the needs of wage-earners' dependants: to what
degree would their needs be recognised by the state?

Rathbone saw the situation in which wage earners have a variable
number of dependants as one that had developed historically. In the
first chapter of her book, called 'The Growth of the Dependent Family',
she described how in the mid-nineteenth century 'the labours of the
children and their mothers, both in production for use and in production
for exchange, must have reduced the financial burden of fatherhood
to a modest level'.[7] The gradual enforcement of the dependence of
children came about through their exclusion first from factory work
and then from other employment and through the extension of
compulsory education. This in turn, together with protective legislation
on women's factory employment, made their mothers more dependent.
At the same time, urbanisation and advances in productive techniques
reduced the possibilities of domestic production of things for family
consumption and increased the amount of commodities a family
needed to buy, so that wives who did not go out to work were more of
a financial burden.

During this period, Rathbone suggests, men's real wages did rise to adjust to some extent to their new situation, though she says that 'they would probably have risen in any case, as the period was one of great wealth and increasing assertiveness on the part of wage-earners'.[8] Her argument is that the new dependent family presents new problems which cannot be solved simply by higher wages: 'whereas the labour of wives and children, whatever its evils, did at least help to proportion the income of the family to its numbers and needs, the rise in wages was spread out thin over the general body of men wage-earners, without regard to family responsibilities'.[9]

The question of the dependent family has recently been raised again, in Marxist terms, by Jane Humphries.[10] She argues that recent Marxist analysis of the family has been mistaken in concentrating on the part played by domestic labour in the reproduction of the labour power of male workers. The tendency, she says, has been to see the proletarian family only from the viewpoint of capital, as an institution on which capitalism has come to depend. She, on the other hand, wishes to see it from the point of view of the working class, as an important mutual support system that has been successfully defended against expansionary capitalism. She asks us to compare two extreme forms of household, (1) one in which a single wage earner receives a family wage and the activities of the other members are outside capitalist jurisdiction, so that they can produce things for home consumption and raise the family's standard of living; (2) the other in which all the able-bodied members, including the children, are in wage work, so that the family wage is received piecemeal. She says: 'Under the assumption that the same family wage is received in both situations, the standard of living of the working class must be higher in (1) and the surplus value creation (per family) greater in (2).'[11] This is an interesting passage in two respects. First, it ignores the point made by Rathbone that families vary in size. It thus ignores the fact that in practice, though the household may remain outside the jurisdiction of the capitalist, it is more and more subject to the jurisdiction of the state, as a result of working-class pressure for the recognition of the needs of those in large families and in households with no wage earner or a low wage. Second, it represents a refusal to analyse separately the position of women, men and children within the working class. Indeed, Humphries's political message is that women should abandon the bourgeois feminist struggle to transform the family and should throw in their lot with the rest of the working class in support of a male wage adequate to sustain a family. She argues for 'a materialist analysis based on a non-individualistic theory of needs'.

From her perspective it is individualistic and divisive to raise questions, as I have done, about the distribution of goods and services within the household. Yet, from the evidence touched on above, it may be argued that this view of the family is over-rosy, presupposing as it does that the family, as an institution under capitalism, provides support adequate to meet the needs of *all* its members.

Theories of Needs

We have now reached a point where it is necessary to break off and examine more rigorously what can be meant by the statement that 'the needs of wage-earners' dependants are unrecognised and unrecognisable in the capitalist wage system'. What sense can we give to the notion of 'unrecognised needs'?

Neo-classical economics is not a great deal of help here since, although needs are very important in explaining economic behaviour, they can only be discovered through their appearance as effective demand. Unsatisfied needs do indeed exist, but in so far as they can be satisfied it is through the market. The needs of children and housewives, who are not economic agents, are thus subsumed under those of the household; the needs that are met by women's domestic work are not counted by these theorists as needs in the economic sense.

There is a long tradition in Britain of empirical study and policy analysis of the problem of poverty and the definition of subsistence. To a large extent this has been couched in the same terms as neo-classical economics. The problem has been to define the money income that is required by a household. There has been dispute about whether an absolute or a relative definition of poverty is appropriate, but all writers have had to accept that there is at least some historically variable element in subsistence. Even Rowntree's attempts in 1899[12] to estimate the minimum weekly expenditure necessary for subsistence accepted that there was a cultural element, especially in the clothing items of the budget where allowance had to be made for Sunday best as well as for workday clothes. Nowadays it is commonly agreed that the experience of poverty includes a sense of relative deprivation, so that a particular real level of subsistence becomes less acceptable the further it is below the average or common level in the society at the time.

One of the difficulties of using these kinds of discussion for analytical purposes is that both absolute and relative definitions of poverty have been directly political in context, in the sense that they have been used to evaluate social policies. It is interesting therefore to look at the stance that Marx took on this problem, for he argued that the analysis must start by looking at production and reproduction and not at distribution and consumption. So Marx did not start from the point of view of the consumers and the problem of whether they are getting enough. He even went so far as to draw an analogy between the worker and the work animal: 'The consumption of food by a beast of burden is none the less a necessary factor in the process of production because the beast enjoys what it eats.'[13] He analysed the individual consumption of the labourer (and of the working class as a whole) as productive consumption:

> The capital given in exchange for labour-power is converted into necessaries, by the consumption of which the muscles, nerves, bones and brains of existing labourers are reproduced and new labourers arc begotten. . . . It is the production and reproduction of that means of production so indispensible to the capitalist: the labourer himself. . . . The fact that the labourer consumes his means of subsistence for his own purposes, and not to please the capitalist, has no bearing on the matter.[14]

So, for Marx, the question of 'wants' or 'needs' enters the analysis in relation to capitalist production – in relation, that is, to the reproduction of the labour power necessary to capitalist production. He deals with 'wants' or 'needs' most explicitly when he discusses the problem of assessing the value of labour power. According to the 'labour theory of value', the value of any commodity is determined by the amount of socially necessary labour-time required to produce it. So, in turn, the value of the commodity labour power 'is determined by the value of the necessaries of life habitually required by the average labourer'.[15]

As the phrase 'habitually required' suggests, he saw this value as one that varied historically, holding to the relative rather than the absolute definition of subsistence. The labourer's absolute wants he termed 'natural wants', but he wrote:

> On the other hand, the number and extent of his so-called necessary wants, as also the modes of satisfying them, are themselves the product of historical development, and depend therefore to a great extent on the degree of civilisation of a country, more particularly on the conditions under which, and consequently on the habits and degree of comfort in which, the class of free labourers has been formed. In contradistinction therefore to the case of other commodities, there enters into the determination of the value of

labour power a historical and moral element. Nevertheless in a given country, at a given period, the average quantity of the means of subsistence necessary for the labourer is practically known.[16]

There are three factors that contribute to the determination of the value of the necessary means of subsistence. First, the value of the commodities needed varies with technical change, as some commodities become more and others less efficiently produced; second, special skills require special training and the expenses of this enter into the value of labour power;[17] and third, 'the fixation of its actual degree is only settled by the continuous struggle between capital and labour',[18] the settlement often involving the state, as in the economically similar case of the length of the working day, which 'has never been settled except by legislative interference'.[19]

From a feminist perspective, the way in which Marx conceived each of these factors is in some respects unsatisfactory, though I would argue that fundamentally his approach was the right one.

(1) One of the important elements in determining the value of commodities needed, which Marx does not discuss or see as variable, is the amount of domestic labour used to convert commodities into consumables or to substitute for commodities. The role of women's domestic labour and the fact that the male wage worker gets his wife's domestic services free has been the basis of the so-called 'domestic labour debate'.[20]

(2) Marx does not make it clear whether the special training that is required for special skills (or all the other extra expenses of their reproduction) is to be understood as a technical given or as determined by custom and the outcome of struggles. The working class is highly differentiated in terms of its socially recognised needs, with skilled and white-collar workers requiring more training, leisure and general income. So what is considered necessary for the reproduction of unskilled labourers or housewives is much less than for more specialised workers. To take an extreme contrast: in 1936 B.S. Rowntree[21] estimated that a family of five needed £137 16s 0d a year to keep above the poverty line; seven years earlier Virginia Woolf[22] had said that a woman writer needed 'a room of her own and five hundred a year'. The costs of reproduction of different kinds of labour power are evidently very different. In general, however, it is women's occupations, and especially housework, that are thought to require no special facilities and little training beyond what a mother can provide, while men's

paid work of comparable complexity and range would involve formal qualification or apprenticeship.

(3) In seeing the wage level as the outcome of the struggle between capital and labour, Marx was happy, for analytical purposes, with the 'average labourer' and his average family; he assumed that the wage was used equitably for the maintenance of the whole family. He was aware that women and children were often employed and that they had 'different sorts of labour power'; but this complicated the analysis of the value of the labour power of the adult man, so for the sake of simplicity he ignored it.[23] But from a feminist perspective this simplification is one that blinds us to the fact that the 'family wage' and its crystallisation in legislation and welfare state practices are also a product of a struggle in which the interests of women and men were opposed.

For the purposes of the argument of this chapter, one important fact about Marx is that although he saw needs as socially produced and often − like the needs for education, health care, housing and transport − as only satisfiable through the creation of corresponding institutions,[24] he nevertheless saw them as needs of individuals, not as the needs of some abstracted social system and not as the needs of groups, such as classes or households. He also rejected one conception of 'unrecognised needs', but this referred to needs that the individual is unaware of[25] and not to the needs that are conscious, historically determined, and yet unsatisfiable through the existing institutions.

It is now possible to clarify what 'needs unrecognised by the wage system' refers to. It refers to the needs of unwaged individuals of the working class. The level and nature of these needs has become socially defined in a history of struggle. To some extent this has been class struggle between capital and labour, which has defined the level of these needs as referred needs of the wage-worker (the family wage of the average family) and which has defined some needs as needs for state support or state provision. Other struggles also play a part, but it is most unlikely that any *wage* system could provide adequately for the needs of all unwaged individuals of the working class. The main interest here is in the fact that there is a variety of types of state provision by which needs unrecognisable in the wage system could be recognised.

The State and the Pattern of Dependency and Work within the Family

If we ask, 'how are women's needs determined historically?' the answer is: not directly through the struggle over wages but indirectly through struggles over the customary, statutory and administrative definitions of family responsibilities, and privately within each family unit. To say this is, at the same time, to indicate that men's needs are not determined only in struggles over wages, since the question of how many people the wage must support and how much domestic labour is provided free are determined in the indirect struggles.

The reproduction of the working class is not a straightforward matter, since what constitutes adequate reproduction for the various categories within the class is a subject of constant struggle. In Britain at present, state policy seeks to bolster the system of the family household, so that needs for income and for care are met within this household as far as possible. Even where it recognises needs for collective consumption, such as the needs of the sick and the senile, it frequently does so through an ideology that retains a definition of these needs as properly belonging in the family.

Thanks, particularly, to the work done by Hilary Land[26] there is now an immense amount of evidence on the important part that the state in Britain plays in preserving the dependent family system and the wife's responsibility for housework and caring for people. Katherine O'Donovan (in her chapter in this volume) discusses the ways in which the legal system assumes and enforces women's dependence upon their husbands and, as she mentions, Hilary Land has argued that the same is true of the social security system of income maintenance and of the taxation system.

While state policies presume dependence, however, they do not provide adequate financial assistance when the wife is not able to obtain support from her husband. There are many cases where women are not and cannot be dependent upon husbands. In Britain in 1974 there were over half a million married couples where the wife was the sole or primary earner.[27] When the wife is sick or unemployed she is ineligible for many benefits that the husband would receive. She cannot claim Supplementary Benefit at all. She can only claim Unemployment or Sickness Benefit if she has paid full contributions and not taken the 'married woman's option' to pay a smaller contribution. (This option is now being phased out, but was formerly frequently taken.) Even if she has paid the full contributions, her benefit covers only herself and not her husband or children, as his would. Family income supplement for low wage-earners is available only to families where it is the husband, not the wife, who is in full-time low-paid work. State policies like this make it unwise for a couple to rely too heavily on the wife's income.[28] They do not eliminate such cases entirely, but they must surely help to diminish the number. And provisions like widows' pensions and the custom of men taking out life insurance make it less necessary for a wife to be able to support herself alone.

Land and Parker[29] argue that state policies are premised on assumptions about 'the needs and obligations which are presumed to arise from marriage' as distinct from, and in addition to, those presumed to arise from parenthood. The dependant-breadwinner form of marriage is supported whether there are dependent children in the family or not. From the day of his marriage, for instance, a man can claim a 'married man's tax allowance' regardless of whether his wife works or of whether there are any children or adults in need of care in the household. The same principle of married women's dependence runs right through the social security system and, again, is not related to motherhood.

The social security system also assumes that women are responsible for housework. Non-contributory disablement benefits, for instance, for which men incapable of paid work are eligible, are only available to a married woman if she is 'incapable of normal household duties'. This indicates very clearly the assumption that her dependence is related to housework: if she can do the housework her husband should support her, and if she cannot then he need not give support. So too in the tax system, a married father can only claim an allowance for employing a resident housekeeper if his wife is permanently incapacitated; the wife of an incapacitated husband cannot claim such an allowance, it being assumed that even if she has to go out to full-time work she will still carry on her 'normal responsibilities' in the home.[30]

The assumption that the wage system together with the 'normal' dependent family is adequate to the needs of the working class meets one of its greatest challenges in the claims on behalf of the needs of one-parent families. During the 1970s, those families have figured as one of the major emergent problems in welfare discussions; the Finer Report[31] crystallised a growing awareness of the extent of the problems. Estimates made for the Finer Committee by the Department of Health and Social Security showed that in 1971 there were 620,000 one-parent families, of which about 400,000 were families where the father was absent, a further 120,000 were widows' families, and the remaining 100,000 were motherless families. There were some 1,130,000 children in these families. These figures represent about one in ten of all families and one in twelve of all children.

Not surprisingly, many of these families live on the edge of poverty at the official Supplementary Benefit rates. In 1975, for instance, about 260,000 lone parents were in full-time employment and about 80,000 in part-time, while a further 40,000 were self-employed. Yet 74,000 had incomes below the tax threshold and about 10,000 full-time and an equal number of lone-parent part-time employees had incomes below the Supplementary Benefit level. In 1977 about 36,000 of these families received Family Income Supplement. A large proportion (about 60 per cent) of families living on Supplementary Benefit are one-parent families and they tend to remain on Supplementary Benefit for longer periods than others.[32]

The solutions proposed for these problems all involve trying to help this odd family to approximate to the 'normal' one in its effectiveness. Financial and practical assistance would help the lone parent to play the part of two. Yet it is thought that this must be done in a way that will not encourage the breaking up of two-parent families or unmarried motherhood. This is an old concern, which was well expressed when mothers' pensions were discussed in the House of Commons in 1923 and Viscountess Astor said that the women's organisations

> do not ask for the inclusion of unmarried mothers because in their cases there is someone who ought to shoulder the responsibility. We do not ask for relief for deserted wives because of the danger of collusion.[33]

On the whole, then, policy seeks to give more generous support to the one-parent family that did not choose this 'abnormal' arrangement, and it offers only minimal support, for the sake of the children, to any who may have chosen to reject the normal pattern. Places in local authority nurseries are more readily available to children of lone parents than to other children; but this is to enable the parent to go out and earn an income for their support, rather than because there is any recognition of public responsibility for their care.

During the twentieth century there has been a convergence in state policy on the family towards a consistent set of assumptions about family dependence. Increasingly, the small nuclear family is defined as the sole unit of mutual support. Thus, social security has expanded to recognise the dependence of wife and children on a male breadwinner, so that whereas the National Insurance Act of 1911 provided sickness and unemployment benefit only for the insured person and not for any dependants, the present benefits, apart from the earnings-related ones, make allowance for a man's - though not a married woman's - dependants. Meanwhile, the range of 'liable relatives' to be turned to before non-contributory benefits can be claimed has contracted; whereas the Poor Law Act of 1927 stated that

> it shall be the duty of the father, grandfather, mother, grandmother, husband or child of the poor, old, blind, lame or impotent person, or other person not able to work, if possessed of sufficient means, to relieve and maintain such a person,[34]

since the National Assistance Act of 1948, financial dependence has been assumed only between husband and wife (and, by analogy, heterosexual co-habitees) and between parents and children. Children are not expected to support their parents, nor parents their children once their education is completed.

In the course of this convergence, with the break-up of the Poor Law system, the state came to recognise the needs of the old and of disabled men and unmarried women as unmet by the wage system, and allowed the principle of individual dependence on the state, regardless of household circumstances. Their relatives may be expected to house and care for them, but not to support them. Disabled, sick and unemployed married women, as we have seen, are still expected to depend in the first place upon their husbands.

Thus, although the assumptions underlying state policy have been modified through time, they serve to support a dependant-breadwinner form of family household as the primary means by which the wages of workers are distributed for the financial maintenance of the working class as a whole. The other way in which the family serves for the reproduction of the working class, by being the basis of women's housework and domestic servicing, is also underpinned by state policies — though, again, there have been modifications in the way this operates.

It has already been argued that the wife's dependence is seen as being directly related to her performance of household duties for her husband. But women are also expected to provide care for other categories of people: their children and other relatives incapable of caring for themselves, especially their own and their husband's parents.

Women's responsibility for children and its implications for the position, opportunities and outlook of women are so well known that they scarcely need labouring here. It is worthwhile pointing out, however, that children's dependence on care by their own mothers is far greater and more prolonged than it was in the nineteenth century. Nowadays, children cannot easily be sent to live in another household. They are not company or help to the elderly; they do not care for younger children; they do not work in the home or in anything productive; they cannot be apprenticed or go into service until they are sixteen. The most usual ways for them to live apart from their parents are where they are formally fostered or adopted by a pair of substitute 'parents'.

By contrast, in the middle of the nineteenth century a large proportion of urban households contained children who were living with relatives other than their own parents. When a mother died, or was unmarried or had remarried, children were often sent to live with other relatives.[35] There were also many more children in orphanages, whereas policy at present is that children should, wherever possible, be kept with their parents or else fostered or adopted, and only short-stay or difficult cases taken into children's homes. The ideology that small children suffer irreparable damage to their personality if they are deprived of full-time and continuous maternal care is now so widely accepted that we sometimes forget how recent it is. Yet working-class Victorian mothers would have been almost as puzzled as Asian immigrants (accustomed to an extended family household) are today if they were told by social workers that they should devote themselves full-time to the care of their young children. A major reason why single motherhood is such a burden is the total dependence of children in the present period. Their financial needs may be to some degree recognised by the state, but their need for care is ascribed firmly to their mother.

In terms of state policy, one of the effects of the idea of 'maternal deprivation', in the period since the publication of John Bowlby's famous report in 1951,[36] has been a reaction against placing children from broken or incompetent homes in institutions. Immense efforts have been made by social caseworkers to persuade and help mothers to take responsibility for their children in the officially approved manner.[37] There has been much discussion of the concept of 'shared care', in which social agencies and the family would together undertake the care of children and other incapable people. But, as Land and Parker[38] put it: 'The state (both centrally and locally) has hitherto tended *either* to assume responsibility for child care *or* to leave the family to cope as best it can until crisis or tragedy occur [italics in original].'

In the past few years, the key area of uncertainty has been about children's need for protection from parental violence. On several recent occasions, social services departments have been accused of negligence when a child on their books has died from battering by its parents. Yet the policy that defines child care as a family responsibility cannot readily condone 'interference' by social workers in such cases. To do so would be to undermine one of the major reproductive roles of the family household and an important part of women's work within it.

The care of other incapable people within the household is also placed firmly in the hands of women and is more widespread than is often realised. Whereas child care takes up fewer years of women's lives than it used to, because families are smaller and more closely spaced, caring for the old and infirm probably takes up more time, since such people live longer now. According to Audrey Hunt,[39] about a half of those housewives between 35 and 64 can expect to give some help to elderly or infirm relatives at some time or another, and at any one time about one in five of them have a disabled person or someone over 65 living in their household.

It is state policy to encourage such people to be cared for within family households. If they are invalids, allowances are available to women who give up work to look after them. Less than one in four of the most incapacitated old people are living in institutions. Significantly, those who do are more likely to be the ones without a daughter or daughter-in-law who could care for them. Ethel Shanas[40] noted 'a marked inverse correlation between the numbers of close relatives and the likelihood of institutionalisation in old age' and also that 'more people in institutions than outside who have children have sons only'. She found that three times as many old people lived with married daughters as with married sons, and that when they lived separately it was primarily the daughters to whom they turned for help with their housework and shopping.

The care, as well as the financial support, of those who are not capable of wage work is an important element in the reproduction of the working class as a whole. At present it is largely carried out by abler women within the household and through the kinship network. State policy assumes and encourages this form of provision, and when it offers alternatives it does so as a 'last resort' rather than as a matter of course.

In contrast, the need for medical care is more fully recognised by the state. Indeed, many tasks once performed at home by women have been replaced by professional services in clinics and hospitals – so much so that women's organisations complain about the medical profession's dominant control over contraception, abortion and childbirth. State responsibility for health care begins at an early age with ante-natal and post-natal care and school medical inspections. Many old people are treated as senile or geriatric patients in mental hospitals rather than cared for in old people's homes. Yet it is interesting that this extensive state involvement is somewhat provisional in nature. There is a sense in which the needs are socially defined as 'properly' falling to the family household to satisfy, so that when public spending is restricted, for instance, many fringe forms of medical care 'revert' to female relatives. When hospital places for the senile, homes for the handicapped, nursing homes for post-operative patients and so on are not available, these people are sent 'home' if there is a woman there to care for them.

The Mental Health Act of 1959 is an interesting illustration of a longer-term change of this sort. It introduced a policy of 'community care' for the mentally ill. To combat the degrading effects of institutionalisation and to spare public expenditure, it was proposed to keep hospital stays as short as possible and to offer social-work support so that patients could be cared for at home. A need that had previously been recognised by the state retained its medical definition, but was referred 'back' to the family household to be satisfied. Again, of course, it was mainly women who took on the burden of caring for these people.

Given the ideology that such forms of care properly belong to the family, there remains the ultimate possibility of these aspects of reproduction being organised through the family household and carried out by women.

It has been possible here to touch on only a few of the ways in which the state has been involved in struggles over the definition of the needs of various sectors of the working class whose members do not themselves earn wages. Some of these needs, both financial and practical, have been recognised directly by the state. For the rest, they have either remained as yet unmet or else have been met through a state-supported family household system of a male breadwinner, dependent children and a potentially dependent wife responsible for domestic work and caring for children and other incapable relatives.

The analysis presented here is intended to show some of the ways in which women's dependence is related to the capitalist wage system, coupled with the family household, and also to suggest that gains can be made by women demanding the recognition and fulfilment of more of their needs and those of the people they take care of. The link between dependence and the capitalist system is not immutable, fixed by its functional place in the reproduction of capitalism, since what constitutes adequate reproduction of the working class as a whole depends upon the definition of 'needs' as defined in struggle. Furthermore, the wage system is not unique to capitalism but operates in much the same way for the reproduction of labour power in present-day socialist societies. What is called for − in both cases − is political struggle for state recognition of the needs of both sexes and all unwaged

individuals, combined with a transformation of the dependent household
so that women can participate in production on the same basis as men.

Notes

I should like to thank the members of the Women's Liberation Campaign for
Legal and Financial Independence for their encouragement in my work on which
this paper is based.
1. Veronica Beechey, 'Women and Production' in A. Kuhn and A.M.
Wolpe (eds), *Feminism and Materialism* (London, Routledge and Kegan Paul,
1978).
2. Karl Marx, *Capital*, vol. 1 (London, Lawrence and Wishart, 1970), p. 572.
3. Eleanor Rathbone, *Family Allowances: A New Edition of 'The
Disinherited Family'* (London, George Allen and Unwin, 1949), p. 41 f; Michael
Young, 'The Distribution of Income Within the Family', *British Journal of
Sociology*, vol. III, no. 4 (December, 1952); M. Young (ed), *The Poverty Report,
1974* (London, Maurice Temple Smith, 1974); M. Young (ed), *The Poverty
Report, 1975* (London, Maurice Temple Smith, 1975); Christine Delphy, 'La
fonction de consommation et la famille', *Cahiers Internationaux de Sociologie*
(1974) pp. 23-41; L. Oren, 'The Welfare of Women in Labouring Families,
1860-1950' in M. Hartman and L.W. Banner (eds), *Clio's Consciousness Raised*
(London, Harper, 1974); E. Wilson, *Women and the Welfare State* (London,
Tavistock, 1977), pp. 79f.
4. Rathbone, *Family Allowances*, p. 9.
5. Ibid., p. 36.
6. I owe the idea of 'unrecognised needs' to Patrice Grevet, *Besoins Populaires
et Financement Public* (Paris, Editions Sociales, 1976).
7. Rathbone, *Family Allowances*, p. 5.
8. Ibid., p. 6.
9. Ibid.
10. J. Humphries, 'Class Struggle and the Persistence of the Working Class
Family', *Cambridge Journal of Economics*, vol. 2, no. 3, 1977, pp. 241-58.
11. Ibid., p. 251.
12. B. Seebohm Rowntree, *Poverty: A Study of Town Life* (London,
Macmillan, 1901).
13. Marx, *Capital*, p. 572.
14. Ibid.
15. Ibid., p. 519.
16. Ibid., p. 171.
17. Ibid., p. 172.
18. Karl Marx, 'Wages, Price and Profit' in *Marx and Engels: Selected Works
in One Volume* (London, Lawrence and Wishart, 1968), p. 226.
19. Ibid., p. 226.
20. T.D. Fee, 'Domestic Labour', *Review of Radical Political Economy*,
vol. 8, no. 1, 1976; S. Himmelweit and S. Mohun, 'Domestic Labour and Capital',
Cambridge Journal of Economics, vol. 1, no. 1, 1977, pp. 15-31.
21. B. Seebohm Rowntree, *Poverty and Progress: A Second Social Survey of
York* (London, Longmans, Green & Co (Ltd), 1941).
22. V. Woolf, *A Room of One's Own* (Harmondsworth, Penguin, 1945), p. 78.
23. Marx, *Capital*, p. 519.
24. Agnes Heller, *The Theory of Need in Marx* (London, Alison and Busby,
1976), Chapter 3.

25. Ibid., p. 73.

26. Hilary Land, 'Women: Supporters or Supported' in D.L. Barker and S. Allen (eds), *Sexual Divisions in Society: Process and Change* (London, Tavistock, 1976); H. Land, 'Social Security and the Division of Unpaid Work in the Home and the Paid Employment in the Labour Market' in Department of Health and Social Security, *Social Security Research Seminar* (London, HMSO, 1977); H. Land, 'Who Cares for the Family?', *Journal of Social Policy*, July 1978; H, Land and Roy Parker, 'Family Policies in Britain: The Hidden Dimension' in A.J. Kahn and S.B. Kammerman (eds), *Family Policy* (New York, Columbia University Press, 1978).

27. L. Hamill, 'Wives as Sole and Joint Breadwinners', paper presented to SSRC Social Sciences Research Workshop, London, 1976.

28. Ruth Lister and Leo Wilson, *The Unequal Breadwinner* (London, NCCL pamphlet, 1976).

29. Land and Parker, 'Family Policies in Britain'.

30. Land, 'Who Cares for the Family?'.

31. Finer Report, *Report of the Committee on One-parent Families* (London, HMSO, 1974), 2 vols.

32. National Council for One-parent Families, *Information*, no. 5 (rev.), November 1977.

33. House of Commons Official Report, Fifth Series, vol. 161, col. 392; quoted in Finer, *Report*, vol. II, p. 133.

34. Poor Law Act, Section 41 (1).

35. Michael Anderson, 'Family, Household and the Industrial Revolution' in Anderson (ed), *Sociology of the Family* (Harmondsworth, Penguin, 1971), pp. 34 ff.

36. J. Bowlby, *Maternal Care and Mental Health*, Geneva World Health Organisation, Monograph Series, no. 2, 1951.

37. Wilson, *Women and the Welfare State*, pp. 84 ff.

38. Land and Parker, 'Family Policies in Britain'.

39. Audrey Hunt, *The Home Help Service in England and Wales* (London, Government Social Surveys, 1970), p. 424.

40. E. Shanas, P. Townsend, D. Wedderburn, H. Friis, P. Milhøj and M. Stehouwer, *Old People in Three Industrial Societies* (London, Routledge and Kegan Paul, 1968), p. 112.

8 DOMESTIC LABOUR AND THE HOUSEHOLD

Maureen M. Mackintosh

A central theoretical concern of the Women's Movement in Britain and elsewhere in the capitalist West has always been the analysis of the relation of the family to capitalism, or, more precisely, the relation of women's struggles within and concerning the family to her struggles in the sphere of wage work and other aspects of more public life. The debate over the theoretical analysis of domestic labour[1] was just one of many attempts to address this concern. Starting from the Marxist analysis of the capitalist mode of production, the contributors to the debate set out to analyse the nature of housework and its relation to work done under conditions of wage labour.

This debate, it is widely agreed, argued itself into a cul-de-sac from which it was very difficult for it to get any further in its own terms. I shall argue in this chapter that one reason for the creation of this impasse was the lack of a wider perspective, historical or cross-cultural, on the question of the content, the use value nature, of the work involved. In order to present this case, I shall examine the performance of tasks typical of domestic labour within capitalism — child care, cooking, cleaning — in a society which is as yet incompletely dominated by the law of value and where therefore a great deal of other production — agriculture, fishing, craft work — is still household-based. The society in question is part of the rural economy in Senegal in West Africa, where I lived from May 1975 to August 1976.

I shall then use the results of this examination to reflect upon the domestic labour debate in Britain, and to suggest one possible direction of future work. I should be clear from the beginning as to what I see as the purpose of this kind of 'comparative' analysis. I am not in any sense suggesting that the situation which I describe in Senegal is identical to the situation in pre-capitalist Britain. Only historical research can analyse the evolution of the household in Britain. Instead, I am using international comparison between Britain and a society subject to imperialism but incompletely penetrated by the law of value, to illuminate the nature of the assumptions on the basis of which we — those of us with a training in economics in particular — have analysed capitalist society.

Domestic Labour and Capitalist Production

The central theoretical issue on which the domestic labour debate
turned was the value analysis of domestic labour within capitalism: is
domestic labour value-creating, and if not, what is its relation to the
creation of value? Another way of posing precisely the same question
would be: how does the production of goods and services within the
home relate to the accumulation of capital? This debate was of course
not resolved to everyone's satisfaction, and among those still interested
there are conflicting views. I do not propose to summarise these
positions, since the subject of this paper is the limits rather than the
details of the debate. I begin, however, by describing briefly the position
which I find the most satisfactory, since this position informs a great
deal of what is to follow.

Housework in the capitalist West, as I and others have argued in more
detail elsewhere,[2] is production within the home of use values (goods
and services such as cooked meals and washing) for immediate consumption. The products of housework do not pass through the market.
Housework is therefore not value production, the goods and services
produced are not produced for exchange, and the conditions of their
production are not directly subject to the law of value. Domestic labour
is private labour, not socialised labour. Since it is labour which is not
brought into relation, through the buying and selling of commodities,
to labour performed in the production of commodities, it does not
enter into the formation of abstract labour, which is the basis of value.
It is therefore not subject to the same pressures for increased productivity
as is labour subject to the wage relation. Labour within the household
cannot be directly compared to wage labour, for theoretical purposes,
because it is not commensurate with it through the market.

This does not mean however that domestic labour within capitalism
is unaffected by the operation of the law of value. On the contrary,
pressures from the sphere of wage labour have had an impact on the
content of housework in ways that a number of writers have documented.[3] Some goods and services which used to be produced within
the home are now bought and sold as commodities, certain kinds of
household equipment have reduced the time necessary to produce an
adequate standard of cooked meals and cleanliness. But it does mean
that domestic labour is performed under relations of production which
are not those of value production and wage labour.

It is here that we reach one of the limits of the domestic labour
debate as it has so far been conducted. None of the writers on the
subject, myself included, have been able to specify in a satisfactory way

the social relations under which domestic production is conducted. Discussions of the subject have been descriptive rather than analytical: the description of ideal-typical relations between men and women within the home. The sexual division of labour within the home – that is, the fact that it is women who perform most of the domestic labour – had within the terms of the debate to be taken for granted. Once it was taken for granted that it is women who do the housework, then the analysis of domestic labour could be used to examine the question of how women's work within the home is related to her subordination both within the home and outside it.[4] But the original begging of the enormous question of the nature of the sexual division of labour within the home has meant that the nature of the social relations of domestic production have remained unspecifiable, and therefore the potential contribution of the theoretical work on domestic labour to our understanding of the family under capitalism has been extremely limited. Hence the marked loss of interest within the Women's Movement in the domestic labour debate.

Why was the domestic labour debate set up in terms which led it into this cul-de-sac? One answer to this question is that our perspective, limited to the experience of housework within the capitalist West, and lacking an historical or international perspective on the phenomenon we were analysing, led us to equate or conflate certain phenomena which are in fact distinct. One example of this is that we held our concept 'domestic' to be unproblematic, whereas in fact we were using the word in two analytically distinct senses: domestic work as work done within the home, and domestic work as a particular kind of work, such as child care, cooking and cleaning, servicing the members of a household. In our society, work which is domestic in the first sense is also generally domestic in the second sense, but this fact is specific to our society (that is, not universal) and it requires explanation.

Once the debate was set up in these terms it was inevitable that the question of the sexual division of labour within the home should be begged. We took domestic labour as an unproblematic unity, the relation of which to value production was the subject of analysis: the result was that we could analyse neither the use value nature of the work nor the nature of the home in which the work was done. There has been, of course, a good deal of description of the content of domestic work, and a frequent reiteration that the work was in some sense reproductive work, work to do with the reproduction of labour. But this perception could not be integrated into an analysis which did not question the relation between the nature of the domestic work and the form taken by the household.

We need therefore to deconstruct the concept of domestic work and examine its components. The next section seeks to do this through the examination of the sexual division of labour, and the distinction between types of work, in a society where many kinds of work (including agricultural production) are household-based.

Domestic Labour in the Household-based Economy: The Theoretical Problem

If Marxist economists studying domestic labour under capitalism have tended to take the work done within the household as an unproblematic whole, Marxist anthropologists have tended to do the same thing when studying societies where a wide range of production is household-based and not produced for the purpose of exchange. A number of economic anthropologists have variously tried to define a mode of production whose defining characteristic is that production is carried out within the household. Universally, these attempts, while admitting the existence of a sexual division of labour in production within the household, do not integrate this division of labour into the analysis of the mode of production as a whole, but merely comment upon it in a descriptive way. This is true of anthropologists working with a wide range of ideological perspective.

Thus Sahlins's 'domestic mode of production'[5] refers to 'economies organised by domestic groups and kinship relations', where the 'household is as such charged with production, with the deployment and use of labour power, with the determination of the economic objective'. 'Domestic' in Sahlins is used to mean internal to the household; non-domestic work would involve co-operation between households. Sahlins's discussion of relations between members of the household in production is purely on the descriptive level. Thus: 'Division of labour by sex is not the only economic specialisation known to primitive societies. But it is the dominant form, transcending all other specialisation in this sense: that the normal activities of any adult man, taken in conjunction with the normal activities of an adult woman, practically exhaust the customary works of society.' There is no further discussion of the content of, or the explanation for, this division of labour.

Besides the lack of reference to the concrete nature of the work of men and women within the household, there is also in Sahlins an assumption that there is no important division of labour either among men or among women. In the work on domestic labour under capitalism also, the lack of a division of labour in the domestic sphere is another aspect of domestic labour which is taken for granted, since it cannot be explained independently of an explanation of the structure of the household. This assumption is, however, much less factually plausible for the household-based economy.

In the work of Meillassoux[6] one can trace the same absence of investigation of the division of work within the household. This is even more striking because Meillassoux's work is much more carefully theorised than that of Sahlins, and because his concern to explain the reproduction of the 'domestic community' leads him to examine in some detail the relations between the sexes. Production, for Meillassoux, is agricultural production, and the relations of production are the relations of production in agriculture. The relations of reproduction on the other hand are purely relations of marriage and kinship, the relations of men to their progeny. The work of caring for children, washing, cooking, cleaning — the work which feminists see as fundamental to an understanding of the whole sexual division of labour in capitalist society — has vanished. Extraordinarily, this work, in the rare references to it in Meillassoux's most recent work, is casually referred to as 'domestic work' in spite of the fact that the whole household community is called the 'domestic community'. The confusion of definition is apparently unrecognised, presumably because the importance of the work is totally discounted. The dependence of men upon women for food, because of the sheer incapacity of men to produce cooked food, is recognised at one point, but no conclusions are drawn beyond the need (which is a *non sequitur* except on specified assumptions) of a man for a wife.

One could multiply examples of the absence of analysis of the sexual division of labour in production from contributors to this literature. Two such examples would be the work of Terray[7] and that of Hindess and Hirst[8] on primitive communism. These writers tend simply to omit the typically female tasks of cooking, cleaning and child care from their catalogue of production: they fall down the divide between agricultural work on the one hand, and the relations of kinship and filiation on the other, between production and 'reproduction'.

To some extent, Marxists who ignore the importance of cooking, cleaning and so on are simply reflecting the prejudices of orthodox development economists. Typically, at least until very recently, these economists have transferred the prejudices of their own society against the classifying of cooking or child care as work at all directly to the household-based village economy. Thus one writer of Marxist politics but orthodox economics could list for India, under the heading of 'non-work and leisure' in the village economy, the following 'domestic duties': cooking, collecting firewood and water, mending the roof, and child-bearing.[9] However even within this tradition, evidence is gradually accumulating concerning the hours of work involved in these tasks, and the importance of their performance to the standard of living of the household in the village economy. Those of us attempting to examine these economies from a Marxist-feminist perspective have to take this evidence into account, not simply in order to add it into the total quantity of work which has to be done to maintain the household, but in order to develop an understanding of the way in which this work differs from other types of work in society, even when the society is one where agriculture too is in a different sense also a domestic task.

Domestic Labour in a Senegalese Village Economy

The Senegalese village which I shall now discuss is one where, until the very recent arrival on part of its land of a foreign-owned plantation, all the production done within the village boundaries was household-based. That is to say, for the agricultural production which produced both the main subsistence (non-marketed) crop and the cash crops which were the main source of money income in the village, the household was the unit of decision-making and of effective land appropriation. A large majority of the agricultural labour time spent on the fields of a household was drawn from within that household. Besides agriculture and tasks of cooking, cleaning and child care, the only activities productive of goods and services within the village were cattle herding, charcoal-making, one or two artisan activities such as the making of clothes, and retail selling of some goods from outside the village such as fresh fish and rice. Since 1973, the plantation had been providing the first ever local source of large-scale agricultural wage work.

Leaving aside the cattle herding, artisan work and retail selling, I shall examine the agricultural and non-agricultural work for similarities and differences in its organisation. The non-agricultural activities then include the following: food preparation, cleaning, washing, care of children, wood and other gathering activities, care of the sick, physical maintenance of the house and its fencing.

Men and women engage in both agricultural and non-agricultural activities in this village. Men do the bulk of the agricultural labour but some women have fields of their own and there are some agricultural tasks on the men's fields which are typically done by women. In the non-agricultural sphere, men do the repair, building and maintenance of the house; women do all the other tasks.

The division of labour between the sexes is, however, much more rigid in the non-agricultural sphere. There are tasks where men and women work side by side in agriculture; there are none in the non-agricultural sphere. Technical change in agriculture — the introduction of donkey- or horse-drawn equipment — has eroded the women's role in agricultural production since the women do not use the equipment. Men have taken over tasks that used to be done by both men and women, and even sometimes tasks that were generally done by women alone. An example of the latter is the winnowing of the peanuts, previously done by women pouring from a bowl, now sometimes done by men with the newly-introduced forks. Furthermore, in agriculture, young male labour is quite frequently used to replace female labour, winnowing again being an example or the dehusking of peanuts, without there being a stigma attached to a young man who does this. The rigidity of the sexual division of labour in agriculture is most marked in the subsistence crop (millet) and it is least marked in the newest cash crop (wet season vegetables) where there is considerable fluidity of definition of the sexual division of tasks.

No such fluidity exists in the non-agricultural sphere. Men construct and maintain the physical buildings and walls. All other tasks of caring for and maintenance of the people in the household are done by the women of that household. There are no tasks done by both men and women. Men provide the subsistence food, millet, either by growing it or occasionally buying it for cash when the crop is finished. Once provided, it is under the control of a woman in the household. Otherwise, the provision of food is the sphere of the women. They may gather or cultivate plants to eat with the millet; if additions to the millet — oil or tomato, for example — are bought, the women will do the buying, even if the men have sometimes provided the cash. Food preparation is done by the women exclusively, and all members of a household eat from a common pot. The physical caring for other human beings is entirely a woman's task, including washing clothes and caring for the sick. This division of labour according to gender is not undergoing any process of change. Whereas as children, girls and boys, may both be taken to work in the fields on tasks which, while generally divided on lines of gender, are not rigidly so, in the non-agricultural sphere there is strong hostility from both men and women towards the use of boys to assist in women's tasks.[10]

The non-agricultural tasks are extremely time-consuming. The following is a description of a day's work of a young woman who does all the tasks for the household in which she lives. She get up at around (we decided) 5 a.m.: that is, well before it is light. She pounds millet for perhaps one hour. Then she goes to the well for water (which may mean a long wait) and prepares breakfast, which consists of millet couscous largely prepared the day before. The next stage is preparing the ingredients for lunch, which may be millet porridge or rice, and may involve gathering or going to the village shop. They eat at midday or 1 p.m. The couscous for supper and the next day's breakfast is prepared during the afternoon, to be eaten about 7.30 p.m. If her mother-in-law is working at the plantation she takes food to her. In the evening she pounds millet again. She goes to bed at around 9 p.m. During the day, usually in the morning, she does the washing as necessary for six adults and a child, and she has a one-year-old child constantly with her. She herself is sixteen years old.

There is one time-consuming activity which is not in this list: the gathering of wood. The women do this intensively at certain periods of the year, of which this (the description was taken in March) was not one. The heaviest work is the pounding of the millet and the fetching of water, especially for washing clothes.

A young woman doing all the non-agricultural labour for a household therefore spends her whole working day upon it. She does not have a field of her own, and does little agricultural work, though in the rainy season she takes food to the people in the fields. Later, as she becomes older and has daughters to help her with the cooking and washing and child care, she may take on more agricultural labour.

The rigidity of the sexual division of non-agricultural work has become even more evident since the arrival of the plantation, offering wage work during six months of the year to both men and women. The participation rate of the women as well as the men in the plantation labour force is extremely high, there being no feeling among the men that the women should not do this work. The working day on the plantation is normally from 7.30 in the morning to mid- to late afternoon, though packers often work more irregular hours in shifts. For the men, this plantation work is an alternative to other activities during the plantation season, which is the dry season in Senegal when they do not work on their own crops. From this village some younger men used to go away to work for the dry season; older men stayed in the village, doing various tasks of maintenance of fields and houses and tending a longer-duration cash crop which has now largely been abandoned. The men who remained did not work long hours in this season, so the plantation has not meant an intolerably long working day. The women on the other hand, inevitably, have simply added their plantation work to their non-agricultural tasks which they undertake all the year round, thereby stretching their physical endurance almost to breaking point.

This, for example, is a working day of a woman, doing the non-agricultural work for a household all on her own, and also working at the plantation. She gets up at least an hour earlier than the young woman just described, to pound her millet, fetch water and make breakfast for the household. She prepares and leaves something for lunch, perhaps couscous to be heated, for the children, which has been partly prepared the night before. She leaves the children with an old woman in the compound and goes to work at about 7 a.m. She returns from work around 4 or 5 p.m., and goes to the well or the plantation tap for water on her way home. Once home, she prepares the couscous for supper and for the next day, and pounds the millet again. When there is washing to be done she does it at night. She always goes to bed later than when she is not working at the plantation, and when she is washing perhaps as late as 11 p.m. or midnight. She is up again the next day at 4 a.m.

With the women under this kind of pressure, there has nevertheless been no breaking down at all of the division of labour by sex in non-agricultural tasks. Not only do men never do any of this work, but young boys also do none, despite the fact that they are in the household, and do not begin to work on the plantation at as young an age as the girls. As the woman just described explained, 'I have only sons, so there is no one to help me'.

There are a number of ways in which women try to cushion the appalling strain of this double day. One is by simply not working as regularly as the men. As one woman said: 'I work until I see that all my clothes are dirty, then I take a day off, do all my washing, and start all over again.' To the extent that it is possible, women shift the way in which their work is spread over the year — for example, they all make sure that they have collected their firewood before the start of the plantation season — but the very nature of their work, daily maintenance of a household, means that there is very little they can do in this respect. Therefore they inevitably need days off when their household work piles up or a child is ill. The result of this constraint on women's work outside the household is the start of a process with which we are also extremely familiar in Europe. Employers take advantage of these constraints on women to treat their female employees differently from the men they employ. The men's jobs tend to be stabilised, to last all season, and they are paid at least the minimum wage. The women's jobs tend to pay less, the women are treated as an interchangeable mass of workers, frequently hired at the gate each day, and the management make far less effort to stabilise the work force. Within a year of the plantation's establishment, a familiar pattern of sex-based hierarchy of pay and conditions in the labour force had been set up. The women, trapped by their home obligations, can do nothing about this inequality of conditions. Thus the rigidity of the sexual division of labour in domestic tasks is visibly the source of women's greater oppression within the sphere of wage work.

The other way in which women cushion the strain of doing two days' work in one is through the use of an already existing division of labour among women in the household. Not all women do non-agricultural household labour. There are only a few exceptions to the generalisation that women only do this work if their status in the household is that of wife or daughter. Nor do all wives do this work. This village is virilocal, wives moving soon after marriage to join their husband's household; it is also polygamous. Furthermore, in general as a man gets older, he will retain a married son in his household. The result of this is that 60 per cent of households in this village contain more than one married woman.

A girl starts to help her mother with her household work when she is quite young; by ten she is doing quite a lot of cooking and fetching water, but is not yet strong enough, for example, to get the washing clean. By thirteen, two years before she is likely to marry, a girl may be doing virtually all her mother's work in the home. Once she marries and leaves her parental home, a young woman works for her mother no more. Instead, if she is the first wife of a young man, she is likely to take on all her husband's mother's household work. This is the main way in which an older woman is finally relieved of the burden of housework. In principle the mother-in-law does no more work, and she will say that she does none. In practice she may help, but it will be her own decision to do so. This means that an older, active woman with a daughter-in-law at home can go to work on the plantation without exhausting herself in the way that the younger women do. The young woman whose working day was described earlier agreed that the division of labour was always organised in this way and that her mother-in-law 'would never agree to stay in the house while I went out to work'.

If a woman is the second wife of her husband, the situation is different. In this case the first wife will already be doing the work in the household, and the second wife will share the work, turn about, so many days (the number varies) each. The only break in this will be if

Domestic Labour and the Household

a woman has just had a child, when she will have a break from the work.

There are also in households a number of women who are neither wives nor daughters of the household head (the household head being almost always male in this village). The most common case is the divorced sister of the head of the household, and in general this sister will do no work in the household, except as an irregular favour to one of the other women. Adult female kin of the household head do not do the work in the household: the rules that determine who does the housework depend on the marriage relation and kin ties between men. Thus, by extension, a woman marrying a younger brother of the head of the household had replaced in the housework the oldest wife of that older brother of her husband. Furthermore, a woman whose bride-price was not fully paid, though she was living in her husband's household, was doing no housework.

All that has been said above about the division of non-agricultural household work between women refers chiefly to cooking and does not extend to child care. Child care is the individual mother's responsibility, and any sharing of this by other women is done as a favour. Only older daughters can be relied upon to look after younger children when necessary. Child care therefore obeys somewhat different rules from other non-agricultural tasks, and, as in our society, very young children are the strongest constraint preventing women from going out to work for a wage. A woman, if she is prepared to work very long hours indeed, can reorganise cooking, cook in the morning for lunch time and do her washing at night; but if she has no one to look after a young child she is tied. Sometimes sisters married into different households help each other with child care in these circumstances, something which never seems to happen for other household tasks. The extent to which co-wives help each other with child care seems to vary greatly from household to household, and to depend a lot on individual personalities.

Thus there exists a division of labour among women in the performance of non-agricultural household tasks. I return below to the rules by which this work is allocated and their implications. Before this I want to discuss one more piece of evidence concerning the strength of the social boundary cutting off these household tasks from the rest of the productive work of this society. This evidence concerns what happens to this non-agricultural work when the economy becomes much more monetised than the village economy I was describing above. This evidence comes from the village in which I actually lived in Senegal, which is closer to Dakar, the capital city, than the above village, and as a result much more penetrated by monetary exchange relations.

In this situation there comes to exist what is almost a separate sphere of exchange in the village: that of petty selling between women. This selling is either of vegetables and fish bought in small-quantity lots and broken down for retail resale, or partially prepared food (couscous only needing final steaming), or small cooked foods (fried doughnuts for example, or grilled peanuts). There is an enormous amount of this petty selling, which I only slowly became aware of through living in a household, and it is very important to the way in which women succeed in providing for their families. Its proceeds supply the small sums of money of which women are in constant need, in order to buy small quantities of relish to add to the staple foods, or to take a child to the dispensary. Women may even sell some of their crops from their fields in this small-scale way, though if they have many crops they will sell them wholesale.

Men never go in for this small-scale petty selling. They sell their crops wholesale, they buy millet when they have to do so (and in the village now in question they frequently have to, millet growing having declined) in as large lots as possible and leave it to the women to break it down. If they pay money for minor ingredients to the meals they give the cash to the women to shop, but they would never have a woman buy a sack of grain for them.

It is the sexual division of the non-agricultural tasks in the household which creates these two separate types of exchange and the sex-typing of the petty selling. Women also grow crops, but men do not cook food or care for children, and so they also do not become involved in this petty exchange economy.

I have established therefore that in this Senegalese village economy, where there is agricultural as well as non-agricultural labour which is non-value-producing, and where the production unit for the cash crop is also the household, one can nevertheless make distinctions between the women's non-agricultural labour (which I shall henceforth refer to as 'domestic labour' for the purpose of theoretical discussion) and the other household-based labour, largely in agriculture. In particular, the sexual division of labour, the allocation of certain tasks exclusively to women, is much more rigid in domestic labour than in agricultural labour (or, though I have not discussed this in detail, in other tasks). One can justifiably refer to a sphere of domestic labour which requires separate analysis in this society, as in societies where the domestic labour, also done largely by women, is the only non-value-producing labour.

What kind of separate analysis, then, is required? The final section of this chapter can only begin to attempt an answer to this question. I examine the relation of the sphere of domestic labour to the constitution of the household and to various concepts of reproduction, first for the Senegalese case, and then for our own society.

The Household and Reproduction

'The household' is a very different kind of concept from such concepts as 'kinship' or 'the family'. It is a much more concrete category than these, and it is firmly rooted in certain kinds of economic activity: that is, the production and consumption of the products of domestic labour.

In the Senegalese case, the forms of co-operation of women in domestic work were firmly enclosed by the household walls; there was no cross-household co-operation except of an extremely sporadic and exceptional sort. By 'co-operation' I do not mean the harmonious sharing of tasks, but rather the creation of the complex unit within which division of labour for these domestic tasks occurs. This unit consists of the women in one household, household membership being determined by birth, or possibly co-optation and assimilation (nieces brought in to help), for unmarried girls, and by marriage for women, except that divorced or widowed women may temporarily or permanently join male kin. But the latter, as we have seen, are not part of the domestic labour unit. It is as daughters or wives that women work in the household, and they aid and replace each other within the household as a single unit. There is only one cooking pot on the fire for any household at any moment.

In fact, for there to be more than one cooking pot at any moment would be contradictory, because the household in this village is virtually defined in terms of the sharing of a common pot. However this does not mean that the household is a redundant concept, another word for the domestic unit of work. No doubt it is true that a concept of the household and its boundaries has sometimes been imposed by researchers on a reality in fact far more complex; nevertheless, in the village I am describing the unit which I am calling the household is a category that the villagers use to organise their descriptions of their society. It has a physical existence — boundary walls within the larger compound — and the implications of membership of the household go beyond the fact of the common cooking pot which it contains. To say that the household contains those who eat from a common pot, that is those who consume the product of a single unit of domestic labour, is not a tautological statement at all.

There is an institution in this village society which reinforces this conception of the household, which I am suggesting is one based in the economic relations of domestic labour, and that is the formation of joint households at the time of the heaviest village agricultural labour. At this time, brothers who have separated to form households of their own will re-group into a single household, the women forming a single unit of domestic labour and taking it in turns to cook. This larger unit is referred to by the same word as the smaller units from which it is constituted: it is a household in the full sense of the word. It is easy to suppose that this serves to capture any available economies in the performance of domestic work at a period when women, more in the past than at present, were also performing agricultural labour. In pursuit of this hypothesis, it would be interesting to compare the organisation of domestic labour, and its technical conditions, in similar villages where this joint household system is nevertheless lacking. This is, however, impossible from existing data, since research into the organisation of domestic labour in Senegal − indeed in Africa − is virtually non-existent.[11]

I am suggesting, therefore, that the social institution of the household should be seen not as defined in terms of the unit of domestic labour, but as derived from it. The relations which constitute the domestic labour unit also constitute the household, though the household has, in this society, many facets other than simply that of the production of the products of domestic labour. I am proposing this derivation of the household as one which has greater generality. The household, defined as the smallest co-residential unit in a society, is constituted on the basis of the relations under which women perform domestic labour for the feeding and care of all household members, including men and children. Its size and organisation will be partly determined by the technical conditions under which the domestic labour is performed in the society in question. Membership of this household may also be the basis for the performance of a great deal of other labour in the society, or it may not. The former is true in the Senegalese village; the latter is true in most social classes in Britain.

I should add a comment on the technical conditions of domestic production. Although the content of the work that I am calling domestic labour is the same in the Senegalese example and in Britain (cooking, cleaning, child care), the technical production processes involved are of course very different. The time taken for each task, and the heaviness of the labour involved, are much greater in the Senegalese village, and the products of this labour cannot be replaced by products bought on the market. The result is that a household without a woman in good health and strength cannot survive. There are a number of ways in which a man unable to take on the full burden of the agricultural labour for the support of his household can be assisted in this society, but assistance with domestic work for a woman who is chronically ill or weak is much more problematic, unless she has in the same household co-wives or daughters or a daughter-in-law. A really viable household in this village society requires more than one woman able to take on the full burden of the domestic tasks. This is not so in Britain today. I find it curious how much of the debate about the changing nature of the household has centred on the direct demands of work outside the home[12] and how little on the mediating effects of the changing technical demands of the domestic labour within the home.

What then are the relations under which domestic labour is performed, the relations which constitute the unit of domestic production? This is the question which raises the issue of reproduction, in the various senses in which that word is used in the literature, since the feature of domestic labour from which we began and to which we have returned is that it is all, or almost all, done by women, and it consists of the production of essentially identical types of use values in two very different societies. The interest of feminists in the concept of reproduction has always — all confusions of definition apart — been because of our desire to understand the link between the inferior position of women in society and the fact that it is women who bear and rear children. This is still clearly the question that we should be asking.

The confusions of definition have, however, been dreadful, in the feminist as in the non-feminist Marxist writing. I shall consider the theories of the household-based economy first. In an earlier commentary on Meillassoux's work I argued[13] that Meillassoux, in common with other writers who have tried to formulate modes of production for this type of society, detached the relations governing the production of people and their distribution through the society — the relations of kinship, marriage and filiation — from all basis in social production and thereby emptied them of content. The effects of this show up at their worst in Hindess and Hirst,[14] where no content for kin relations is specified at all: 'All that is required for the economic level is some system of social relations where children are reared by adults.' Meillassoux admits the subordination of women as part of the content of the kin relations that he describes, but he sees the maintenance of this subordination as unproblematic. I went on to argue that we need to distinguish the social relations of human reproduction from the ways in which the reproduction of the mode of production as a whole is ensured or enforced. I now think, looking back on this formulation, that it offers no way out of the problem just stated. No amount of reformulation of definitions will help, in the absence of a theory of how women's subordination is reproduced through her participation (or absence of participation) in social production.

It is this theory which an analysis of domestic labour should help us to work towards. The institution of the household is a mediating link in societies. It mediates two sets of social relations, both of which have economic content in the sense that they are based in production activities, and is itself an economic institution. The first set of relations is those which reproduce the subordination of women and the alienation from her of the control of her body, her progeny and the products of her domestic work. The second set of relations is those governing the performance of social labour other than domestic labour, relations which may be more or less oppressive or exploitative.

In the household-based economy, the household is the institution which contains within itself both of these sets of relations. But, and this is the force of the analysis of the Senegalese case above, even in this case one can see that there are two mutually imbricated sets of social relations present, the division between them coming to the surface in the differences between domestic labour and other labour. On the one hand one has the set of relations which involves the marriage, filiation and residence rules, the performance and control of domestic labour, and the resultant exclusion of women from certain roles in the rest of social production. These relations are those that constitute the household and control its membership. On the other hand, one has the relations involved in the performance and control of agricultural labour. This second set of relations is the one that has been the subject of the debate concerning the lineage mode of production,[15] and the debate has centred on the control by the older men of the younger. These two sets of social relations are mutually determining, and one set cannot continue to exist without the other. In a household-based system, the control by male elders of the whole system involves the maintenance of the subordination both of women to men and of younger men to male elders. To threaten the subordination of women would be to threaten the stability of the household and therefore of the system as a whole. The specific way in which in a household-based society these two sets of power relations are mutually dependent for their reproduction has yet to be the subject of detailed research. There will be forms of these mutual determinations which are specific to the household-based economy. But the existence of the two sets of relations and the existence of some forms of mutual dependence between them is something one should look for in all societies.

Which brings us back to domestic labour in capitalist society. The domestic labour debate established one point quite clearly: that domestic labour is production, it produces goods and services which contribute to the standard of living in our society. It embodied one particular confusion which concerns us here: the tendency to see the nature of these goods and services, for the purpose of our analysis, as use values like any others, which happened to be produced within the home.[16] This confusion was precisely that also perpetuated by the theorists discussed above, who, in their analyses of household-based economies, failed to distinguish domestic from other labour.

The interpretation of domestic labour within capitalism which I am now proposing does not, in a sense, contain anything which we did not already know about domestic labour. What I am trying to do is to reassemble what we know, the results of the domestic labour debate, and all that has been said in the Women's Movement about the way in which women's work in the home constrains and constructs her position in the rest of society, in such a way that it makes sense as theory and in particular in such a way that we can begin to answer the question: what are the social relations of domestic production?

First I am arguing that we must stop sliding between 'the household' and 'the family' in our discussions of domestic labour in capitalist society. The household is an institution which we must examine for itself, without taking it for granted that we know what we mean by the term. I am proposing that the household, in capitalist society as in other societies, is an economic institution, because it is rooted in the production of the products of domestic labour: use values such as cooking or child care, and especially child care. The theoretical issue which then has to be examined is how the marriage relation operates to constitute the household in our society. Clearly most households in this society are still constituted on the basis of marriage, and the performance of domestic labour is still closely linked to the status of being a wife. Equally clearly, however, the marriage relation does not have the same force as in a society where the household is the basis for all social production, nor does the control of progeny have the same importance as in a society where filiation is the basis for the control and allocation of labour. Yet the marriage bond is still a subordinating one for women, and domestic labour is the economic content of that subordination. A woman is not in control of her work within the home —

the upbringing of children for example – since she does that work within an institution in which she is subordinated. And the fact that she does that work operates to maintain that subordination by excluding her from certain other forms of participation in social production.

For the set of social relations that constitutes the household, and which creates and maintains women's subordination, is mutually interwoven – and therefore to some extent mutually determining – with the set of social relations that governs other social production, in this case the relations of capitalist value production and wage labour. The household, the location of women's domestic labour, is the mediating institution for these two sets of relations: women's position and work within the household traps her and forces her into a subordinate position also within the wider society.

If one sorts out two sets of social relations in this way, then one can to some extent sort out the confusion of meanings of 'reproduction' in both the societies I am discussing. Since I have not been attempting to construct a complete theory of either society (a construction which would obviously have involved many issues outside the scope of this chapter) I can only sketch this. However, if one refers to the first set of social relations, those through which women are subordinated and the household constituted, as 'relations of reproduction', then one is doing so in recognition of the fact that oppressive societies seek to subordinate women in order to control the process and results of human reproduction. That is one meaning of the word. The other sense in which one might wish to use 'reproduction' is quite different: one wishes to investigate, for any society, how the two kinds of oppressive or exploitative social relations manage to be maintained against the opposition of the oppressed or exploited.

Notes

1. See especially J. Gardiner, 'Women's Domestic Labour', *New Left Review*, no. 89, 1975; J. Gardiner, 'The Political Economy of Domestic Labour in Capitalist Society', in D.L. Barker and S. Allen (eds), *Dependence and Exploitation in Work and Marriage* (London, Longman, 1976); J. Gardiner, S. Himmelweit and M. Mackintosh, 'Women's Domestic Labour', *Bulletin of the Conference of Socialist Economists*, vol. 4, no. 2, 1975; S. Himmelweit and S. Mohun, 'Domestic Labour and Capital', *Cambridge Journal of Economics*, no. 1, 1977; J. Harrison, 'Political Economy of Housework', *Bulletin of the Conference of Socialists Economists*, vol. 4, no. 1, 1973; W. Seccombe, 'The Housewife and Her Labour under Capitalism', *New Left Review*, no. 83, 1974; W. Seccombe, 'Domestic Labour – Reply to Critics', *New Left Review*, no. 94, 1975; M. Coulson, B. Magas and W. Wainwright, 'The Housewife and her Labour

under Capitalism – A Critique', *New Left Review*, no. 89, 1975.

2. Especially Gardiner, Himmelweit and Mackintosh, 'Women's Domestic Labour', Himmelweit and Mohun, 'Domestic Labour and Capital', is a survey of the debate written from the same theoretical point of view.

3. Through transferring some use values to the commodity sphere, and the use of domestic equipment.

4. Thus there has been a discussion of the way in which women's work in the home constrains her participation in the wage labour force.

5. M. Sahlins, *Stone Age Economics* (London, Tavistock, 1974).

6. Especially C. Meillassoux, *Femmes, Greniers et Capitaux* (Paris, Maspero, 1975).

7. E. Terray, *Le Marxisme devant Les Société's 'Primitives'* (Paris, Maspero, 1972). For a critique of Terray, see especially M. Molyneux, 'Androcentrism in Marxist Anthropology', *Critique of Anthropology*, vol. 3, nos. 9 and 10, 1977.

8. B. Hindess and P.Q. Hirst, *Precapitalist Modes of Production* (London, Routledge and Kegan Paul, 1975).

9. B. Dasgupta, 'New Technology and Agricultural Labourers in India', in S. Hirashima (ed), *Hired Labour in Rural Asia* (Tokyo, Institute of Developing Economies, 1977). 'Childbearing' may (?) be a misprint for 'childrearing'.

10. One manifestation of this hostility is the attribution of male homosexuality to the performance as a young boy of women's household tasks (an explanation I heard several times, but in the city, not the village).

11. Thus an elaborate discussion of the organisation of agricultural production of a village whose population is drawn from the same ethnic group as the village I am describing, in J.M. Gastellu, B. Delpech, M. Diouf and Y. Diouf, *Maintenance Sociale et Changement Economique au Sénégal, II Pratique du Travail et Reéquilibres Sociaux en Milieu Serer* (Paris, Travaux et Documents de l'ORSOM, 1974) contains no detailed discussion of domestic labour.

12. In particular, the need of capital for a mobile population.

13. M. Mackintosh, 'Reproduction and Patriarchy: A Critique of Claude Meillassoux, *Femmes Greniers et Capitaux*', *Capital and Class*, no. 2, 1977.

14. Hindess and Hirst, *Precapitalist Modes of Production*.

15. C. Meillassoux, *Anthropologie Economique des Gouro de Côté d'Ivoire* (Paris, Mouton, 1964); C. Meillassoux, 'From Reproduction to Production', *Economy and Society*, vol. 1, no. 1, 1972; Terray, *Le Marxisme*; P.-P. Rey, *Les Alliances de Classes* (Paris, Maspero, 1973).

16. In case this seems very unfair to the contributors to the debate, I should repeat what I said earlier: I mean by this that the description of these use values was not integrated into the economic analysis.

NAME INDEX

Compiled by Carol Bundy

Italicised numbers refer to full citations of sources.

Aldersley, M. 108, 109
Alexander, S. *32 n. 32*
Allen, V.L. 122, 124, 129, *131 nn.
 19, 20, 21*
Anderson, M. 82, 86, *93 n. 8*,
 94 n. 11, 95 n. 62, 96 nn. 85, 87,
 91, *172 n. 35*
Annan, N. *31. n. 1*
Ardener, S.G. 7
Armstrong, A. *94 n. 12*. 95 n. 59,
 96 n. 87
Armstrong, E.G.A., Goodman, J.F.B.
 and Wagner, A. 127, *132 n. 32*
Astor, Lady N. 166
Atkin, L.J. 141

Babington, T. 26
Bain, G., Costes, D. and Ellis, V.
 132 nn. 31, 33
Baker, Sir G. 151 n. 39
Barnardo, Dr T.J. 74
Barrett, R.M. *62 n. 22*, 63, n. 63
Barrington, B.W., Eekelaar, J.,
 Gibson, C. and Raikes, S.
 151 nn. 36, 37
Barron, R.D. and Norris, G.M.
 94 n. 16, 118, 131 n. 13
Bateson, M. *150 n. 14*
Beard, M. 137, 138, *149 n. 12*
Becker, L. 100, 102
Bedford, 9th Duke of, 73
Beechey, V. *132 n. 28*, 171 n. 1
Bennet, A. 87
Bennet, D. 131 n. 15
Berkner, L. *96 nn. 80, 92*
Beveridge, Sir W. 139, 144-5
Blackburn, R.M. 121, 124-5, 129,
 131 n. 18, 132 nn. 27, 31
Blackstone, W. 136-8, *149 nn. 6, 9*
Blaxall, M. and Regan, B. *94 n. 15*
Booth, B. *95 n. 51*
Booth, C. 70, 75, 86, *94 n. 33*
Bosanquet, C.P. 43, 48, 54, 55,
 62 nn. 25, 34, 63 n. 48
Boucherett, L. 49

Bowlby, J. *172 n. 36*
Bradley, I. *63 n. 60*
Breines, W., Cerullo, W. and
 Stacey, J. *93 n. 10*
Brewer, Rev.J.S. 40-1, 44-5, 55,
 62 nn. 21, 28
Bromley, P.M. *149 n. 8*, 150 nn. 16,
 23
Brontë, the sisters 106
Brown, F.K. *32 nn. 10, 28*
Burdett-Coutts, A. 34, *61 n. 1*
Burnett, J. *96 nn. 75, 95*, 97 n. 10
Butler, S. 17

Chalkin, C.W. *96 n. 83*
Charles, Mrs 49
Chew, A.N. 108-9, 109-10, 111 n. 19
Clark, A. 137, 138, *149 n. 11*
Clegg, H.A., Fox, A. and
 Thompson, A.F. *111 n. 4*
Cleveland, Duke of 72-3
Coates, R. and Silburn, R. 129,
 132 n. 34
Cobbett, W. 23, *31 n. 2*
Cooper, M. 104-5, 106
Cooper, S. 100, 101, 102, 103, 104,
 106, 107, 108, 109, 110,
 111 nn. 9, 24
Coulson, M., Magas, B. and
 Wainwright, W. *190 n. 1*
Cowper, W. 22, 23, 25, *32 nn. 14,
 18*
Craik, C. 70, *94 n. 32*
Crow, D. *93 n. 2*

D'Aeth, F.G. *63 n. 58*
Dasgupta, B. *191 n. 9*
Davidoff, L. 8, *95 n. 48*, 96 n. 94
Davidoff, L., L'Esperance, J. and
 Newby, H. *94 n. 29*
Davin, A. *63 n. 57*
Davis, D.B. *31 n. 7*, 32 n. 16
Delphy, C. *171 n. 3*
Denning, Lord 143
Dennis, N., Henriques, F. and

Slaughter, C. *132 n. 35*
Derbyshire, E. 99, 100, 101, 105-6, 107
Dickens, C. 17
Dickenson, S. 104, 108
Duchesne v. *Duchesne 152 n. 49*
Dyos, H.J. and Baker, A. *95 n. 60*
Dyos, H.J. and Reeder, O. *94 n. 27*, 95 n. 38

Earle, F. 97 n. 110
Eekelaar, J., Clive, E., Clarke, K. and Raikes, S. *151 n. 46*
Emmet, D. 134, *149 n. 1*
Engels, F. *97 n. 117*, 147, 152 n. 50
Evershed, Lord *151 n. 29*

Fawcette, M.G. 98, 108, 109
Fee, T.D. *171 n. 20*
Finer, M. and McGregor, O.R. *95 n. 58*, 149 n. 7
Firestone, S. *152 n. 51*
Fletcher, Rev.J.M.J. *61 n. 14*, 62 nn. 22, 23, 63 n. 61
Forster, E.M. 74
Franklyn, J. *97 n. 113*
Fraser, D. *62 n. 32*
Fry, E. 62 n. 30

Gardiner, J. *190 n. 1*
Gardiner, J., Himmelweit, S. and Mackintosh, M. *94 n. 13*, 190 n. 1, 191 n. 2
Gaskell, Mrs E.C. 87
Gastellu, J.M., Delpech, B., Diouf, M. and Diouf, Y. *191 n. 11*
Gauldie, E. *95 n. 47*
George, M.D. *94 nn. 23, 28*
Gillis, J. *96 n. 69*
Gisborne, T. 16, 23, 24, 27, 30, *32 nn. 26, 27*
Gissing, G. 68, *94 n. 25*
Goffman, E. *152 n. 53*
Goldthorpe, J.H., Lockwood, D., Bechhofer, F. and Platt, J. *132 n. 30*
Gore-Booth, E. 104
Gray v. *Gray* 151 n. 32
Greg, W. *97 n. 101*
Grevet, P. *171 n. 6*

Halévy, E. 27, *32 nn. 16, 25*
Hall, C. 8, 10, 13, *32 n. 16*, 38, 94 n. 30

Hamill, L. *172 n. 27*
Haraven, T. and Modell, J. 66, *93 nn. 6, 9*, 95 n. 37, 96 n. 91
Hardie, K. 99-100, 103
Harris, W. *95 n. 41*
Harrison, B. *62 n. 19*, 96 n. 78
Harrison, J. *190 n. 1*
Hay, Capt. 72
Heasman, K. *61 n. 7*
Heaton, A. 102, 103, 111 n. 11
Hecht, J.J. *61 n. 18*
Heller, A. *171 n. 24*, 172 n. 25
Hill, F.D. 50-1, *62 n. 38*
Hill, F.D. and Fowke, F. *62 nn. 40, 43*
Hill, O. 49, 53, 54, 55, 56-7, 60, 61 n. 16, *62 n. 35, 63 nn. 47, 51, 52, 53, 54, 55, 64*
Himmelweit, S. and Mohun, S. *171 n. 20*, 190 n. 1, 191 n. 2
Hindess, B. *94 n. 21*
Hindess, B. and Hirst, P.Q. 177, 187 *191 nn. 8, 14*
Hirschon, R. and Humphrey, C. 14
Holdsworth, W.S. *150 n. 15*
Holroyd, M. *96 n. 82*
Hopkins, E. 42, 59-60
Howkins, A. 96 n. 77
Howse, E.M. *31 n. 2*
Hubbard, L.M. 34
Humphries, J. *94 n. 11*, 159-60, 171 nn. 10, 11
Hunt, A. 169, *172 n. 39*

Irvine, H.C. *61 n. 2*

Jacobus, M. 7
Jaggar, A. *152 n. 51*
Jamieson, Mrs 26
Jones, G. *149 n. 5*
'Juloc' *97 n. 104*

Kahn-Freund, O. and Wedderburn, K.W. *141 n. 31*
Katz, M. *93 n. 8*, 96 nn. 68, 72, 97 n. 114
Kelly, E.H. *63 n. 58*
King, J.S. 113-14, *131 n. 2*
Kingsley, C. 38, 42, 43, 55, *61 n. 16*, 62 nn. 22, 24, 25, 26
Kipling, R. 88
Kitson Clark, G. *61 n. 10*
Knutsford, Viscountess *32 n. 22*

Land, H. 139, 140, *150 n. 20*,

164-5, 172 nn. 26, 30
Land, H. and Parker, R. 165, 168, *172 nn. 26, 29, 38*
Lane, J. 150 n. 25
Laslett, B. *93 n. 7*
Laslett, P. *97 n. 116*, 139, *150 n. 19*
Lee, J. *93 n. 7*
Leslie, M. *63 n. 57*
Liddington, J. 8, 9, 11
Liddington, J. and Morris, J. *111 n. 1*
Lipman-Bluemann, J. *132 n. 35*
Lister, R. and Wilson, L. *151 n. 27*, 172 n. 28
'Lois' *62 n. 27*
Lupton, T. 123, *131 n. 23*

Macaulay, Z. 16, 20, 26
McIntosh, M. 8, 11, 12, 13, 145
McKendrick, N. *32 n. 31*
McKenna, F. *96 n. 73*
Mackie, L. and Pattullo, P. *131 nn. 6, 8, 9, 12*
Mackintosh, M. 8, 12-13, *191 n. 13*
McNabb, R. *131 n. 14*
Maidment, S. *151 n. 45*
Mann, M. *133 n. 37*
Marlborough, Duchess of 75
Marle, J. 78
Marsh, C. 35, 43
Marshall, D. *62 n. 18*
Marx, K. 156, 160-3, *171 nn. 2, 13, 14, 15, 16, 17, 18, 19, 23*
Mason, M.H. 50
Maurice, F.D. 61 n. 16
Meillasoux, C. 177, 187, *191 nn. 6, 15*
Meteyard, B. 150 n. 17
Middleton, C. *131 n. 3*
Mill, J.S. 100
Molyneux, M. *191 n. 7*
More, H. 16, 17, 22-3, 24, 25, 27, 28, 29, 30, *31 nn. 5*, 10 *32 nn. 12, 19, 20, 23, 24, 29, 30*
Morton, T. 34
Mowat, C.L. *63 n. 45*
Munby, A.J. *95 nn. 56, 61*, 96 n. 84, 97 n. 103
Munby, H. 76-7

'New England Man, A' *96 n. 96*
Nightingale, F. 58

Oakley, A. *149 n. 2*

Oakley v. *Walker 152 n. 47*
O'Donovan, K. 8, 12, 13, 164
Oren, L. *171 n. 3*
Ormrod, L.J. *152 n. 48*
O'Rorke, L.E. *61 n. 8*, 62 n. 26
Orwell, G. 74
Owen, D. *63 n. 45*

Paine, R. 22
Pankhurst, C. 98, 111 n. 19
Pankhurst, E. 98, 104, 108
Park, R., Burgess, E.W. and McKenzie, R. *93 n. 5*
Parker, R. 172 n. 26
Parkinson, C.N. 112, 128, *131 n. 1*
Partridge, E. *95 n. 55*
Pinchbeck, I. 23, *32 n. 13*
Pitt, W. 20
Porter, M. 130, *133 n. 38*
Power, S. 111 n. 24
Pringle, J.C. *61 nn. 4, 6*, 62 n. 44, 63 nn. 46, 59
Prochaska, F.R. *32 n. 28*, 61 n. 18, 62 n. 20, 63 n. 60
Purcell, K. 8, 9, 11, *133 n. 36*
Purcell, K. and Bennett, D. 131 n. 15

Quelch, H. 107-8
Quinlan, M. *31 n. 3*

Ranyard, Mrs 35, 45, *61 n. 7*, 62 n. 29, 63 n. 62
Rathbone, E.F. *61 n. 12*, 157-9, 171 nn. 3, 4, 5, 7, 8, 9
Reddish, S. 103, 104, 108
Remusat, Count C. de *95 n. 53*
Rex, J. and Moore, R. *93 n. 5*
Reynolds, S. 74
Richardson, D. *97 n. 105*
Rickman, Mrs 77
Roberts, R. 90, *97 n. 109*
Roberts, W. *31 n. 10*, 32 n. 20
Rogaly, J. 126, *132 n. 29*
Roper, E. 102, 103, 104
Ross, E.M. *62 nn. 36, 39, 42*, 63 n. 56
Rover, C. *111 n. 8*
Rowntree, B.S. 160, 162, *171 nn. 12, 21*
Ruskin, J. 61 n. 16

Sachs, A. 143, *149 n. 10*, *151 n. 35*
Sahlins, M. 176-7, *191 n. 5*

Samuels, R. *94 n. 34, 96 nn. 74, 76*
Schneider, D. *93 n. 3*
Scott, A.M. *94 n. 17*
Seccombe, W. *97 n. 117, 190 n. 1*
Seymour, C. *95 n. 67*, 97 n. 111
Shairp, L.V. *63 n. 57*
Shanas, E., Townsend, P., Wedderburn, D., Friis, H., Milhøj, P. and Stehouwer, M. 169, *172 n. 40*
Shelley, Lady 18
Sheppard, G.W. 49, 55, *62 n. 37*
Sherwell, A. *95 n. 45*
Sherwood, Mrs 23
Silcock, H. 103
Simeon, C. 16
Simey, M. *61 n. 17*
Simey, T.S. and Simey, M.B. *95 n. 54*
Smith, A. 68
Spray, G. *131 n. 17*
Spufford, M. *94 n. 22*
Stephen, J. 16, 23-4, 27, *32 n. 15*
Stone, L. *94 n. 24*
Strachey, L. 81
Summers, A. 10

Taylor, B. *93 n. 1*
Taylor, S. 95 n. 49
Teignmouth, Lord 16
Terray, E. 177, *191 nn. 7, 15*
Thackeray, W.M. 17
Thomas, D. 90, *97 n. 106*
Thompson, D. *131 n. 22*
Thompson, E.P. 18, *31 n. 6*
Thompson, P. 96 n. 77
Thornton, H. 16, 20, 30
Thornton, J. 16, 20, 30
Tressell, R. *96 n. 88*

Trevelyan, G.O. *31 n. 2*
Trimmer, S. 37, *61 n. 15*, 62 n. 30
Trudgill, E. *31 n. 9*
Turner, H.A. *131 n. 25*
Twining, E. 47, 49, *62 n. 31*
Twining, L. 36, 47, 48, 49, *61 nn. 13*, 16, *62 nn. 31*, 33, 37
Twining, R. 62 n. 37

Venn, J. 16
Vigne, T. 96 n. 77

Walkowitz, J. *96 n. 79*
Walters, M. *32 n. 11*
Ward, W.R. *61 nn. 9, 11*
Watchel v. *Watchel* 151 nn. 33, 34
Weitzman, L.J. *150 n. 21*
Wesley, J. 15, 18
West 23
Wightman, 37, 42-3
Wilberforce, R.I. and Wilberforce, S. *31 n. 8*, 32 n. 17
Wilberforce, W. 16, 17, 20, 21, 23-4, 25-6, 27, *31 n. 4*, 32 n. 21
Willes, J. 78
Willis, F. 84, *96 n. 93*
Wilmott, P. and Young, M. *97 n. 115*
Wilson, A. *97 n. 102*
Wilson, E. *171 n. 3*, 172 n. 37
Winbolt, Mrs 102, 103
Winstanley, M. *97 n. 100*
Wohl, A. *95 n. 40*
Wollstonecraft, M. 22, 32 n. 11
Woolf, V. 162, *171 n. 22*
Wright, T. 90, *97 n. 108*
Young, A.F. and Ashton, E.T. *61 n. 3*, 62 n. 41, 63 n. 46
Young, M. *171 n. 3*

SUBJECT INDEX

Acts of Parliament:
  Common Lodging Houses Act
    71-2
  Domestic Proceedings and
    Magistrates Courts Act (1978)
    141
  Domestic Violence and Matri-
    monial Proceedings Act
    (1976) 142
  Equal Pay Act (1970) 117-18, 125
  Finance Act (1978) 150 n. 26,
    151 n. 42
  Guardianship of Minors Act
    (1971) 136
  Labouring Classes Lodging Houses
    Act (1851) 73
  Landlord and Tenant Act (1954)
    86
  Lord Hardwicke's Act (1753)
    138, 150 n. 17
  Married Women's Property Acts
    (1870-82) 136; (1964) 142
  Mental Health Act (1959) 170
  Metropolitan Poor Amendment
    Act (1870) 51
  National Assistance Act (1948)
    167
  National Insurance Act (1911)
    166
  Poor Law Act (1927) 167
  Poor Law Amendment Act
    (1834) (The New Poor Law)
    46-51, 62 n. 32, 64
  Reform Acts (1832, 1867, 1884)
    52, 100; woman's suffrage
    amendment to 1867 Reform
    Bill 100
  Rent Act (1977) 86
  Sex Discrimination Act (1975)
    118
  Social Security Act (1975)
    151 nn. 43, 44
  Trade Union Act (1871) 52
  Women's Enfranchisement Bill
    (1905) 107-8
agricultural labour 35-6, 39, 173,
  176, 177
  See also Senegal

anti-slavery 15, 16, 19, 20, 21, 30,
  31 n. 7

Baa Baa Black Sheep (Kipling, R.)
  88
Benthamism 46, 53-4
'Biblewomen' 35, 45, 54, 59
boarders/boarding 65, 68, 76, 77, 79,
  81, 86, 88, 89, 90
boarding houses 78, 85-6, 89
boarding-out 49-51, 92
bourgeoisie see middle class
Blackburn Weavers' Association 99
Building Societies 92
Burnley Weavers' Association 100
Burnley Women Winders 111 n. 11

capitalism:
  and domestic labour debate 12,
    13, 66, 173-6, 189
  'needs' and wage system 160-3
  reproduction of the population
    153, 155, 156, 158, 159, 160
  rise of industrial capital 10,
    18-19, 23, 30
  wage system 13, 122, 170
census 67, 69, 74, 76, 77, 78, 81, 86,
  93 n. 4, 94 nn. 18, 19, 20, 96 n. 71,
  97 n. 101, 111 n. 3, 115, 116, 119
charitable organisations:
  Benevolent Institute for
    Reclaiming Women and Girls
    39
  Birmingham Society for the
    Befriending of Pauper
    Children 50
  Charity Organisation Society 34,
    53-7
  Christian Instruction Society 53
  Congregationalist Christian
    Institution Society 34
  'Ladies Charity' 39
  Manchester District Provident
    Society 34
  Metropolitan Visiting and Relief
    Association 34, 52, 53
  School Care Committee for LCC
    34

charitable organisations—*cont.*
　Society for the Promotion of the
　　Return of Women as Poor Law
　　Guardians 47
　Society for the Relief of Distress
　　53
　Workers' Department of the Girls'
　　Friendly Societies 50
　Workhouse Visiting Society 47
charity 28, 33, 37, 44, 46, 52, 53,
　58, 73, 75
　See also philanthropy, visiting
children:
　and divorce 142-6 *passim*, 151
　　n. 28, 152 n. 47
　father's name 140, 150 n. 25
　fostered/in lodging 88, 89
　and labour 158
　as orphans 46, 49-51
　state policy 167-9
　of Suffragists 105, 109
Christian Observer (ed Macaulay, Z.)
　16
Church of England 15-21 *passim*, 36,
　38, 39
Clapham Sect:
　and class 19-21, 30
　domestic ideal 24-7, 28
　origins and activities 15, 16
　See also Evangelicals, manners
　　and morals
Clarion 100
class:
　relations 39-46 *passim*, 52, 55-6,
　　75, 97 n. 112
　struggle 48-9, 154, 163
　women's attitude to 112
　See also landed class, middle
　　class, working class
Coelebs (More, H.) 24, 27, 28
Commentaries (Blackstone, W.) 136,
　137, 138

deaconesses 58-9
*Defining Females: The Nature of
　Women in Society* (Ardener, S.)
　7, 9, 13, 14
divorce 142-7, 151 n. 39
domestic ideal/ideology:
　and landladies 10-11
　social work 56-9
　trade union activity 128-9
　Victorian 15-31
　　definition 15

domestic ideal/ideology—*cont.*
　formation 21-9, 30, 31
　See also Evangelicals, gender
　　roles, visiting
domestic labour 173-90
　census definition 67
　debate 9-14, 66, 94 n. 13, 144,
　　162, 173-6, 183-90
　in household economy 176-8
　reproduction of household
　　187-90
　reproduction of population
　　155-6, 159
　See also oppression, Senegal,
　　sexual division of labour,
　　voluntary/unpaid work
domestic servants *see* servants

education of women 22, 23, 25,
　28-9, 87-8
emancipation 33, 57-61
employment *see* women's work;
　see also under specific
　　occupations
Englishwomen's Review, The 49, 102
Equal Opportunities Commission
　150 n. 26, 151 n. 42
Evangelicals 15-31
　domestic ideology 10, 15, 21-31
　and French Revolution 20-1
　marriage 26-8
　morality 15-18, 20-1, 30
　social class 15-20, 30
　visiting 35, 40
　See also Church of England,
　　manners and morals,
　　Methodists

family:
　census definition 77-8
　dependent family 12, 159-60
　domestic labour debate 66, 189
　Engels on 147
　and industrialisation 65-6
　needs 162-3
　nuclear 64, 66, 68, 71, 84, 91, 92,
　　154, 166
　one-parent 165-6
　privatisation 69-70
　reproduction of population
　　153-8, 167
　and social security system 140,
　　148, 163-71
　and wage system 155-9

family—*cont.*
  and working women 67-8, 115,
    118
  See also divorce, domestic
    ideology, Evangelicals,
    marriage
family household 154-6
femininity 22, 25, 64, 71, 113-14
feminist perspectives 22, 26, 147,
  148, 153-4, 162, 163, 173, 175,
  187
  See also women's studies
*Few Words to Volunteer Visitors
  among the Poor* (Hill, O.) 55
French Revolution, response to
  18-21, 37, 39

gender roles 9-10, 60, 65, 134-5,
  142-5, 147-9
  employment 11-12, 113, 124,
    129, 130-1
  and financial provisions 145-6,
    162
  in lodgings 67, 76, 86
  in Senegal 179
  See also legal system
Growth of the Dependent Family
  (Rathbone, E.) 158
Guardians of the Poor 48-51, 104,
  147

*Handy-book for the Visitors of the
  Poor in London* (Bosanquet, C.P.)
  48, 54, 55
home(s):
  'ideal home' 92
  lodgings and 92
  as sacrosanct 56-7, 72
  separation of work and 10, 29,
    35-7, 64, 66
  work claims 58-9
  for 'Working Girls' 74
  See also domestic ideal,
    Evangelicals, family, visiting
homosocial concept 128, 132 n. 35
household:
  dependent family 159-60
  domestic labour debate 173,
    176-8, 188-90
  Evangelicals and 21-31 *passim*
  organisation 66-7
  private 78
  reproduction of 187-90
  See also family, home, Senegal

housekeeper allowance 143, 146,
  151 n. 42, 165
housework 14, 145, 162
  domestic labour debate 173-6
  legal value of 144
  social security system 165, 167
  See also domestic labour
housing 52, 72-3, 92
  municipal 73, 74, 92
  programmes 73, 81
  Report (1931) 86, 87

Independent Labour Party 99-100,
  103, 105, 107

Labour Party 11, 103, 106-10
  passim
Labour Representative Committee
  103, 104, 108
Lancashire and Cheshire Women
  Textile and Other Workers'
  Representative Committee 104
landed classes 15, 18-20, 30, 33, 35-7
  and lodging 72
  transmission of wealth 138
landladies 10-11, 76-93 *passim*
  See also lodging
landlords 72, 76, 78, 83
*The Lawes Resolution of Womens
  Rights* (1632) 137-8
*Lectures of Ladies in Practical
  Subjects* (Brewer, J.S.) 40-1, 55
legal system:
  and Evangelicals 16-17
  free female labour 13
  gender roles specialisation 12,
    134-5, 141-9
  maintenance obligations 141-7,
    151 nn. 28, 39
  married women 135-40
legislation affecting women *see*
  Acts of Parliament
leisure 23, 33, 38, 81, 82, 132 n. 35,
  162, 177
lodgers/lodging 64-91
  class interaction 75-6
  decline of 91-3
  definition 74-8
  demand 78-81
  domestic ideal 68-74
  landlady/lodger relations 76,
    89-91, 97 n. 110
  role expectations 76, 91
  services provided 82-3

lodgers/lodging—*cont.*
  social attitudes 68-74
  source of income 85-9
  study of 65-7
  supply of 83-6
  travel 81, 91

maintenance *see* marriage
Manchester and Salford Women's
  Trade Council 104
Manchester Suffrage Society 102-3
manners and morals 15-30
  See also Evangelicals
marriage:
  and domestic labour debate 13,
    189
  Evangelical view of 26-8
  law 135-9, 141-3, 147-8
  maintenance 141-5, 151 n. 39
married women:
  active in seventeenth century
    137-8
  in employment 31, 98-9
  names 150 n. 25
  percentage of women 135-6
  as reserve labour force 155-6
  and social security 139-40, 145-6,
    150 n. 21, 164-7
  and tax 140
Marxist analysis 66, 107, 153-63,
  173, 176-8, 187
masculinity 64, 70, 71, 91
Methodism 15, 19, 36
middle classes:
  attitude to lodging 68-74, 81, 82,
    84-5
  domestic ideal 31
  industrial bourgeoisie, rise of 10,
    15, 18-19, 64
  separation of work and home 10,
    29, 35-6, 51-2, 64, 66
  sources of income 65, 87-8
  suffrage 100, 107-10
  and working class 42, 64, 71, 75,
    92
  See also Clapham Sect, class,
    Evangelicals, visiting
militancy (in labour relations) 112-33
  composition of female work force
    115-19
  gender of militancy 128-31
  market position of women 112-15
  militancy defined 121-4

militancy—*cont.*
  women in trade unions 119-20
missionary activities 16, 24, 35, 41,
  45, 54

National Union of Tailors and
  Garment Workers 129
National Union of Women's Suffrage
  Society 98, 108, 109
needs/unrecognised needs 160-3
Non-conformists 38-9

Old Wives' Tale, The (Bennet, A.) 87
oppression of women 13, 154-5, 182,
  190
oral history 11, 20-3, 105-6
outdoor relief/out relief 46-9, 51, 54,
  76

paternalism 24, 30, 72-3
Perceiving Women (Ardener, S.)
  7
philanthropy:
  defined 33
  'suitable' for women 10, 24, 28
  See also visiting
Poor Laws 46-51
  Board 48, 50, 51
  rates 46
  reform 48
  system 158
  Unions 46-52 *passim*, 76
  visiting 54
  See also Acts of Parliament
'poverty question' 35, 51-3, 55-6,
  128, 160
  See also visiting
Practical Christianity (Wilberforce,
  W.) 17, 21, 25
proletariat *see* working class
prostitutes 65, 80-1
Puritans 29, 30

Radicals 15, 18, 22
ratepayers 46, 48
religion:
  and women 34-8, 42
  See also manners and morals,
    missionary activities, visiting,
    and entries for separate
    denominations
reports:
  Finer Report (on one-parent

reports—*cont.*
    families) 149, 165, 172 n. 31
    Housing Report (1931) 86-7
reproduction of population 13,
    153-60
    and household 187-90
    See also Senegal
Senegal 173, 177-91
    agricultural labour in 178-88,
    191 n. 11
    child care in 178, 182-3
    domestic labour in 178-85
    household and reproduction
    185-7
    labour debate 12-13, 173
    marriage in 182-3
    sexual division of labour in
    178-84
servants 28, 38-43, 66-9, 75, 76, 77,
    82, 87, 90, 92
    ex-servants 84-5
sexual differences 112, 113-14, 131,
    135, 147-8
    in Senegal 178-84
sexual division of labour 22, 70, 76,
    86, 114-15, 124, 126, 128,
    132 n. 35, 154, 175-8
    See also division of labour,
    Senegal
sexual roles 91, 145
    See also gender roles, homosocial
    concept
skills and training 162-3
    levels in women's work 117-19
    skilled workers and unionisation
    125
    in weaving 99
social security system 139-41
    Department of Health and Social
    Security 95 n. 57, 165
    disablement benefit 165
    Family Allowance campaign 157
    Family Income Supplement 165-6
    legal assumptions 146, 148,
    150 n. 21, 165
    Local Government Board
    Inspector 50, 51
    National Insurance 139, 141
    Supplementary Benefit 139, 164-
    164-6
    Supplementary Benefit
    Commission 144, 148
    unemployment/sickness benefit
    164, 166

social security system—*cont.*
    welfare services 33, 52, 57
    women's dependence in 163-71
social workers 56-61
suburbs
    lodgings in 74
    move to 58, 51, 58
suffrage campaign 98-110
suffragettes 61, 98, 103, 104, 108
suffragists 98, 102-10, 111 n. 19
    radical
        and domestic ideal 11
        and elections 106-7
        and Labour Party 103, 106-10
        programme 98, 102-4
        regional strength 110
Sunday schools 16, 21, 31 n. 10, 34,
    100
Sunshine in the Workhouse
    (Sheppard, Mrs) 55

taxation:
    family dependence 164-5
    and gender role assumptions 145,
    148
    and social security 150 nn. 21, 26
textile workers 98-9, 103-6, 110
Tourist Handbook to the British Isles
    (1880) 82
trade organisation 80
trade unions 52, 80, 93, 112-13
    suffragists and 98-108 *passim*
    women in 119-31
Trades Council 107-8
Trade Union Council 103, 119

unemployment 37, 39, 46, 119, 126,
    158
Utilitarianism 30, 32 n. 16

Vindication of the Rights of Women
    (Wollstonecraft, M.) 22
visiting (of the poor) 33-61 *passim*
    and domestic ideal 56-7
    and emancipation of women 33-4,
    57-61
    functions of 34-5
    historical significance of 33
    numbers involved 34
    origins 35-41
    and Poor Law reform 46-51
    and the state 51-7
    as work 33
    See also charitable organisations

voluntary/unpaid work 10, 12-13,
  28, 56-7, 67
  and domestic role 145-8, 151
    n. 38, 155
  See also domestic labour,
    philanthropy, visiting

wage system 46, 122, 155-6, 157-9,
  165, 167, 170, 173-4
Weavers Amalgamated Association
  103
welfare state *see* social security
  system
Wigan Weavers' Association 103
Women's Co-operative Guild 101,
  103, 108
Women's Mission (Burdett-Coutts, A.)
  34
Women's Social and Political Union
  98, 104, 108
Women's Studies 7, 10, 11, 33, 94
  n. 14, 122, 173
Women's Trade Union League 103-4,
  108, 109
Women's University Settlements 59
women's wages:
  depressed 114, 117-19, 124-6
  after divorce 143
  and domestic ideology 9-13
  in Senegal 180-4
  and suffrage 103-6
  in textile trade 98-9, 103-6, 110
  in visiting 76-7
  See also domestic labour debate

women's work:
  distribution of 116
  domestic 39-41
  female work force 115-19, 127
  legislation 148
  market position 124-8
  part-time 117-18
  sources of income 64-5, 83-9
    passim, 93
  unskilled 117-19, 125-6
  See also domestic ideology,
    domestic labour, landladies,
    visiting, voluntary/unpaid
    work, and entries for specific
    occupations
Women Writing about Women
  (Jacobus, M.) 7
workhourses 40, 44, 46-7, 49, 51,
  54, 62 n. 30, 73, 75
'workhouse test' 158
Workhouse Visiting Society 47
working class:
  campaign for vote 11
  emergence of 64
  industrial proletariat 30
  living arrangements 71, 75
  needs 161, 162
  reproduction of population 164,
    167
  services to middle class 74-5
  See also class relations, lodging,
    Poor Law, suffragists, visiting